THE POLITICS AND IDEOLOGY OF PLANNING

Tim Marshall

First published in Great Britain in 2021 by

Policy Press, an imprint of
Bristol University Press
University of Bristol
1-9 Old Park Hill
Bristol
BS2 8BB
UK
t: +44 (0)117 954 5940
e: bup-info@bristol.ac.uk

Details of international sales and distribution partners are available at
policy.bristoluniversitypress.co.uk

© Policy Press 2021

British Library Cataloguing in Publication Data
A catalogue record for this book is available from the British Library

ISBN 978-1-4473-3721-8 paperback
ISBN 978-1-4473-3720-1 hardcover
ISBN 978-1-4473-3723-2 ePub
ISBN 978-1-4473-3722-5 ePdf

The right of Tim Marshall to be identified as author of this work has been asserted by him in accordance with the Copyright, Designs and Patents Act 1988.

All rights reserved: no part of this publication may be reproduced, stored in a retrieval system, or transmitted in any form or by any means, electronic, mechanical, photocopying, recording, or otherwise without the prior permission of Policy Press.

Every reasonable effort has been made to obtain permission to reproduce copyrighted material. If, however, anyone knows of an oversight, please contact the publisher.

The statements and opinions contained within this publication are solely those of the author and not of the University of Bristol or Policy Press. The University of Bristol and Policy Press disclaim responsibility for any injury to persons or property resulting from any material published in this publication

Policy Press work to counter discrimination on grounds of gender, race, disability, age and sexuality.

Cover design by Liam Roberts
Front cover image: Alamy/Adrian Sherratt

Contents

List of figures and tables		iv
List of abbreviations		v
Acknowledgements		vi
1	Introducing planning, politics and ideology	1
2	Writing on politics and ideology in planning	25
3	Ideologies in Britain, with initial linking to planning	39
4	Planning history, planning reform and politics and ideology	63
5	Planning expertise and planning law: autonomy from politics and ideology?	81
6	Ideology and politics in government, central and local	101
7	Ideology and politics in professions, lobbying, consultancies and pressure groups	131
8	Communication, the media and deliberation	159
9	Facets of planning action: heritage, local environment and design	181
10	Fields of planning action: housing, economy and infrastructure	195
11	Paths to improving the ideological and political dimensions of planning	225
References		249
Index		269

List of figures and tables

Figures

6.1	Oxfordshire showing district council areas	114
6.2	Grenoble Road area in wider Oxfordshire context	116

Tables

1.1	Political and ideological dimensions of planning	20
1.2	Schematic range of ideological and political situations	22
4.1	Key ideological and political drives in the planning sphere in the 2010–15 UK government	73
7.1	Leading political consultants, December 2016–February 2017	143
8.1	*Oxford Times* planning and related fields coverage, 2018–19	171
9.1	Impinging of ideology and politics on different fields, facets or forms of planning	183
10.1	Impinging of ideology and politics on three planning fields, distinguishing national and local processes	196
11.1	The recommendations of the Raynsford Review	240

List of abbreviations

AONB	Area of Outstanding Natural Beauty
CPRE	Campaign to Protect Rural England
DCLG	Department for Communities and Local Government
DfT	Department for Transport
DM	development management
GLC	Greater London Council
HBF	Home Builders Federation
HS2	High Speed 2
IPPR	Institute for Public Policy Research
LEP	Local Enterprise Partnership
MHCLG	Ministry of Housing, Communities and Local Government
NGO	non-governmental organisation
NIC	National Infrastructure Commission
NP	Neighbourhood Plan
NPPF	National Planning Policy Framework
NSIP	Nationally Significant Infrastructure Project
PFI	Private Finance Initiative
PINS	Planning Inspectorate
PR	public relations
RICS	Royal Institute of Chartered Surveyors
RTPI	Royal Town Planning Institute
TCPA	Town and Country Planning Association

Acknowledgements

This book draws on thinking and working over very many years, so a complete list of indirect contributions could go back a long time. So, thanks should really be expressed to numerous friends, neighbours, ex-students and colleagues. This would be above all, in this book, to those in England; but, given my habit of continuous international comparison, this also applies to many years of exchanges with academic and non-academic friends in Spain, Germany and France.

Nevertheless I must start by expressing my thanks to my very good colleagues (or ex-colleagues) at Oxford Brookes University, in the School of Planning, now School of the Built Environment. It is invidious to select names, but Elizabeth Wilson, Steve Ward, and Peter Headicar are probably those with whom I have enjoyed most discussion over many years, although hardly at all directly related to this book, whilst Sue Brownill and Dave Valler are two more colleagues who have always been good to work with. Bob Colenutt, a recent associate of the School, has also always been worth talking with, especially for his positive and broad perspectives.

Less close to home, I am very grateful to Andy Inch for reading an early draft and making most helpful comments – even if I was unable to respond fully to some of these. Huw Thomas has been supportive over very many years, and certainly influenced my thinking in this area – although the usual disclaimers must apply. Also I am grateful to Michael Edwards and Cliff Hague for sharing their experiences of the press and planning in London and Edinburgh. The referees of the original proposal made some valuable contributions to some change in the shape of the book at that stage, as did a reviewer at a much later stage. I am also grateful for the valuable help given at Policy Press at each stage of the process.

1

Introducing planning, politics and ideology

In this book, planning refers primarily to the system called town and country planning in the UK. Planning is about guiding the futures of places, deciding the changes affecting these places through development. Some people, including some planners, have thought that this was something which could be done in a broadly technical manner, as a doctor might diagnose and then treat an illness. Many planning students still may hope that this is the case, that they are joining a technically oriented profession. Their training certainly has a partly technical character. But most people will appreciate that planning is about values, which are the subject of eternal disagreement, and that therefore politics comes into the process, from the first moment. This book responds to this tension.

This is a tension which is not limited to planning. Other professions aspire to a non-political and non-ideological role, but, as in planning, those working in, say, schools or universities or the health service know (in varying degrees) that the context of their work is fully political (and they might say ideological), and they are no doubt more aware of this now than in previous eras. It is possible to bury this reality, or at least take as little notice of it as possible. But I think this is increasingly counterproductive, given the ever-sharpening circumstances facing the UK in the 2020s. The main aim here, therefore, is to open out the nature of planning's implication in ideological and political forces in a new way, so that planners and those associated with planning can be aware of how these forces work. This can help to ensure that planners, while learning and practising, have increased awareness of their situations when dealing with the challenges in which they find themselves. This introductory chapter lays out the problems that planning has with political and ideological questions, and discusses the ways that thinking about politics and ideology may help.

The relationship of planning and politics

Planning and politics have never been easy bedfellows. Planning has always had problems with thinking about its insertion in ideological forces and in both long-term and everyday politics. Most planning writers do not engage with politics to a strong and explicit degree. This has been very much the case for the most important British planning authors since the middle of the 20th century – classic writers like Barry Cullingworth, Peter Hall and Patsy Healey, for example.

In some ways this non-engagement with politics is odd, given planning's clear source in most countries in a reformist and, in a general sense, left-wing political agenda. Naturally this took many forms, sometimes visionary and utopian, sometimes directly concerned with better urban management. At periods there were also other strands, such as Conservative municipalism or rural protectionism – in any case, all these were clearly related to political agendas of the early and mid-20th century. But, because planning had to serve whatever political regimes were in power nationally and locally, there was always an urge to play down political facets and stress apparently non-political phrasing – the public interest and amenity, most commonly, at least in Britain. Equally there was the interest that many practising planners had in bolstering professional prestige, often done most safely with rather non-political language. This has been generally (but by no means invariably) reinforced by the dominant registers of the most prominent academic planners. Naturally, such planning academics have had political aims in some sense, but rarely expressed these in explicitly political language. Planning teachers are aware of the consistent difficulty students have in adjusting to planning's dual demands – learning professionalism and technical skills, and working in a thoroughly politicised everyday context.

All this applies just as much when referring to ideological agendas as to more workaday political pressures. Many planners would say that this discomfort or blind spot does not matter in practice, as practising planners learn how to muddle through the tensions. This is no doubt true, or at least has been in much of British planning history. However, it can be argued that changes in the last decade have accentuated the discomfort for many at the sharp end of planning practice – that is, generally in local authority planning or, increasingly, working in government planning roles, whether in the Planning Inspectorate, ministry, Environment Agency and so on. Pressures to follow centrally set directions are much stronger than in the 1970s, and resourcing in public sector planning is much reduced, and both pressures are worsened by the tendency of governments to hyperactive reforming of the planning system.

Approaches to the subject

How far has this topic been approached before within UK planning, and if so, how? If one searches for the last surveys of planning and politics in Britain, one has to go back to the book by Gordon Cherry in 1982. Even this though was focused more on the normal dynamics of politics, particularly in local government, rather than on underlying processes and ideological currents, as would typically be exposed by political scientists analysing a particular field of societal action (say on schools or health or foreign policy). A literature review follows in Chapter 2, for those interested in seeing the relevant work, and the gaps.

The book deliberately addresses both ideological and political dimensions of planning. These could be tackled separately, as both have been under-analysed, especially ideology, certainly in recent years. There is a difference between the two: politics is (more or less) understood as being important, while ideology remains behind a curtain, with people much less aware of it. It is argued that there is gain in looking at the two together, in part because they are so closely linked. It is probably this intertwining of the underlying and fundamental structuring of planning with more 'everyday' operations of planning politics that makes analysis of these dimensions difficult, encouraging actors of all kinds to leave well alone and focus on the substantive and processual aspects of planning, as less risky and more manageable.

The book will argue that the ideological dimension of planning has been too long buried under various forms of timidity or caution or professional defensiveness. This has made the successive reforming pressures, especially since 1979, much more difficult to respond to and engage with. Professional planners in particular have been very guarded in their response, leaving much of the defence or development of planning to other urban or environmentalist actors. Especially since 2010 this has left planning in the UK highly exposed to forces largely wishing to cut back the effectiveness of planning in promoting societal improvements.

Is this a good moment to explore these questions?

It can be argued that the post-2010 UK governments have ratcheted up the politicisation of the planning system to high levels. The Thatcherite or neoliberal era as a whole in Britain (1979 to date) brought a fresh ideological agenda to planning, challenging gradually the (naturally also ideologically inspired) foundations of the planning system, set up gradually from 1908 to 1947 (Thornley 1993, Ward 2004, Bullock 2011). Planners found this drive consistently difficult to respond to. At first some resisted the idea that there was an ideological challenge, and pointed to the famed flexibility of the planning system to respond to governments of different political hues. By the early 1990s Thornley (1993) was able to give an overview of this argument, taking the position that the reforms to planning were indeed of a different order to those of earlier periods. But some academics and many planners resisted this argument, and judged that the 1990–2010 period represented a return to 'normal' planning. Others were more convinced that a genuinely different dynamic of change was underway, best characterised as within a neoliberalising order, however 'variegated' (Allmendinger 2011, Allmendinger and Haughton 2013). Allmendinger made this point more strongly than in the past in his 2016 book, titled *Neoliberal Spatial Governance*, indicating at least a firmer commitment to a broad characterisation, even if not exactly an engagement with ideological aspects in an explicit manner.

Since 2015 the UK has been seeing an intense period of deep ideological instability, generated by the leaving of the EU, but also working alongside the related global turmoil exemplified by the regimes in Russia, the US and many other smaller states. This turmoil is often related to 'populism', a term discussed a little more in Chapter 3. I consider that populism is a typical common use or media term which hides more than it reveals, especially when current tendencies within politics and ideology are the focus, as here. But what is not denied is that the forces of destabilisation are considerable, and these we can be sure will have their impact on planning, in ways not clear at present.

Certainly the unpredictability of current politics makes consideration of this subject difficult, but the ideological instability makes the task even more important. So, it can be a good time to examine the way politics and ideology play into the conceptualisation, framing and operation of planning in the UK. Alongside the swirling ideological currents, the more 'normal' continuing play of day-to-day politics may provide some more solid handholds in the discussion.

To be more specific, and at the risk of writing some lines that will be outdated by the time of publication, we may suggest crudely three scenarios for the 2020s in the UK (here abstracting, also riskily, from the likely different paths of the four parts of the UK).

- One path, apparently confirmed by the 2019 election landslide for the Conservative Party, is the continuation of the drive to strong right-wing Conservatism exemplified by the leaving of the EU and visible in the powerful commitment to cutting back the state (including local government) since 2010. This ideological drive could have deep implications for planning, implying the continuation of the post-2010 drive to deregulation and reducing the role of most kinds of planning, and probably the intensification of this drive.

- A second path might represent a forming of a new, still partially neoliberal drive, but modified by commitment to a more interventionist economic policy. Some see this as already a path partially taken since 2016, exemplified by attempts to form an industrial strategy, and a more proactive stance on housing and infrastructure. Others doubt the real impact of such rhetorical positions, but that does not mean that they might not be developed, whether by parts of the post-2019 Conservative Party or by other emerging new parties or coalitions, perhaps with New Labour elements. The implication for planning would probably be for some fresh support for certain kinds of planning, within a still broadly planning-critical governing mind set.
- A third path would be a shift to a Labour socialist approach to managing the economy and directing public expenditure. This may appear unlikely after the 2019 election defeat, but it is arguably a position which retains a strong logic, given social, economic and environmental challenges, to which the above two positions have limited answers. As in the other two cases, the effect on planning would depend much on the extent and character of such a move to left-led governments. But the rehabilitation of some kinds of planning would be very likely, particularly in some stronger steering of the geography of investment within the UK, and certainly within England.

These scenarios can be related to the recent analysis of a Danish political scientist, Rune Stahl (2019). His conception follows Gramsci in proposing that there are periods when particular projects are hegemonic, such as neoliberalism between 1983 and 2008. He suggests that there are 'interregnums' in which there are competing hegemonic projects – in the post-2008 period these are presented as economic nationalism, resilient neoliberalism and Left populism. These may be seen as broadly fitting my three scenarios. The ideological dimensions of his competing hegemonic projects are clear from the 'ism' names.

The scenarios have been characterised in primarily ideological terms, but it is essential to remember that the difficult pressures of electoral and pressure politics would remain likely to be as important as ever. Only in the event of the drive to the Right becoming anti-democratic in a more fundamental sense would this be less the case, that is, if deep constitutional moves away from elections and other national and local elements of democracy were successful, something which will be discounted here for the purposes of this scenario discussion. So, the three ideological colourings of governments would each be affected by political month-to-month pressures, which would then affect considerably planning policy and decisions.

This exercise in speculation is given simply to point out the need to develop our ability to think about planning's insertion into such big forces. The exploration of such wider perspectives is one aim of the book.

Planning

In this book it is assumed that readers understand the broad shape of town and country planning as it exists in the UK, and so that starting point is hopefully shared (planning textbooks are referenced in Chapter 2; Greed and Johnson 2014, and Rydin 2011 are nice introductions). However, it is important to remember that planning is a term with many connotations. For some brands of socialists, and for neoliberal free market fundamentalists, it may link to ideas of state intervention on a large scale, whether desirable or to be feared. The leading thinker of neoliberalism, Hayek, trained his attack in the 1940s on the terrible threat of planning. By that he was mainly thinking of the five-year plans of the Soviet Union, or even more moderate forms of economic steering, but the term became, for many of his followers, as much applicable to the urban planning which was espoused by all sorts of regimes all over the world as to true economic planning. In other words, planning has never been an ideologically innocent word. Much of the time, this may not have mattered, but whenever strongly deregulating and cutting-back-the-state governments are in power in Britain (as in the 1980s and 2010s), the old dangerous nature of 'planning' seems to drift back into the minds of politicians with a Hayekian or similar background.

This book will use examples of planning's functioning in the UK. This will be primarily within England, given the quite distinct working of planning in the devolved administrations of Scotland, Wales and Northern Ireland since 2000s. At times there will need to be some blurring of England/UK, given the complexity of constitutional arrangements, but I will seek to refer to England rather than UK or

British, wherever this is the actual focus. I will not be claiming to say much about the roles of ideology in relation to planning in other states. Ideology certainly has major national inflections, and the planning–politics–ideology relation will be quite different in other countries.

There now follow four sections, on approaches to thinking about politics and ideology, on analysing politics, on analysing ideology and a final one which lays out the approach used in this book to analysing politics, ideology and planning.

Approaches to thinking about politics and ideology

Any public policy area, such as planning, has its roots in politics and ideology. This may be camouflaged for a range of purposes. Some of the purposes, like the tradition of respect for legally justified actions by government actors, are deeply embedded in most advanced societies, certainly in Western Europe and North America. Planning is especially deeply affected by its insertion in a highly legalised system, in which discussion of ideological or perhaps class power is seen as unseemly. But these purposes and reasons do not remove the underlying force of politics and ideology in planning. The point is to stress the force of political and ideological dimensions *as well as* the elements of, in some sense, less political planning policies. Clearly, not everything is political and ideological: other materialities, technological dimensions, inheritances and 'objective' realities matter. Chapter 5 explores some of these dimensions of not-only-politics-and-ideology, including technical expertise and the role of law in planning.

This relates to classic debates on the role of ideas as against more 'material' forces. Do people, acting politically, generally follow their own interests, perhaps class interests, or interests framed in some other way, and then use ideas to justify the positions reached? Or does commitment to ideas, of whatever kind, override interests? The 'ideational turn' explored these matters (Beland and Cox 2011). Here these issues will be present only as a backdrop; the position of Colin Hay (2002) on the dialectical interplay of ideas and 'hard edged' forces will be taken as largely correct and appropriate to public policy generally and to the framing of planning in particular. Both matter, the ideas and the material, and they affect each other all the time. Sometimes material interests can appear dominant forces in planning decisions and actions, but ideas are core to a large number of important planning positions. Just think of the force of the idea of the 'free market', beyond its numerous material contexts. Or, for that matter, of the continuing force of the idea of 'planning'. So, I will not be neglecting the centrality of power and interests, but treating these as interwoven with ideas – and so with ideologies, systems of ideas.

Political scientists, or theorists, or analysts (whatever term one prefers for the academic discipline) study politics. There are hundreds of academics in UK universities teaching and researching this subject, as well as a thriving school-based subject field. But one would hardly know that from a survey of planning books, as undertaken in Chapter 2. Here I take what may be seen as a relatively traditional approach to thinking about politics and ideology, deriving from political-science thinking in the main, drawing on classic ideas of power (elites, pluralism, the faces of power), democracy and Michael Freeden's analysis of ideology.

I do not adopt some of the more academically popular contemporary approaches to politics, such as the one referred to as 'post-politics'. This has links with depoliticisation discussions (Flinders 2012, Hay 2007), as well as with the 'post-democracy' of Crouch (2004). They have distinct roots, with post-democracy coming from a thinker within the Weberian sociology tradition. Crouch presented in fairly straightforward terms the thesis that neoliberalism, above all, has been the cause of a dramatic move away from democratic government in western countries (where it had some strength for much of the 20th century). Much of this was due to systemic corruption and the overwhelming lobbying strength of a globalising capitalism – issues we will examine in Chapter 7 in relation to planning. Crouch revisited his thesis and found all the evidence supporting an acceleration towards post-democracy (Crouch 2016).

Post-politics, on the other hand, comes from a Marxist direction, especially the French Marxists Alain Badiou and Jacques Rancière, with spice added by the extraordinary thinking of Slavoj Žižek (Swyngedouw 2009). Essentially, the thesis is that increasingly authoritarian states, at all levels, have closed down options available to citizens, so that only rarely can 'real' politics appear, for a time, to disrupt the business-as-usual of national and urban management in the interests of capitalism. Put this way, the idea sounds as if it is a sort of political translation of classic Marxist understandings of societies of a capitalist kind. Those interested in such a more high-theory approach can follow up the now extensive articles, some relating to UK planning in some degree (Kanninen 2018, Walton 2018). My reasons for not using this perspective are largely to do with the level of abstraction. In this book I want to look at the visible realities of UK planning as they are manifested across many fields, and for that purpose 'ordinary' political science concepts are helpful.

Another extensive area not covered here is the more sophisticated or complex theorising of ideology. There is a switchback history of thinking about ideology, especially since the 1960s, which has swirled back and forth around Marxism, post-Marxism, post-structuralism, to name only a few dominant paths. Books such as those of Eagleton (2007), Freeden (2003), Freeden et al (2013) or Žižek (1994) will give ways into this literature for those who seek other approaches. There will certainly be readers here who will miss more discourse-theoretic approaches, or proper engagement with the classic thinkers like Althusser, Foucault or Žižek. As will be seen, my approach is 'flatter', perhaps leaning to British empiricism. This certainly loses something, particularly in relation to the questions of the degree of consciousness actors have in their (arguably) ideologically conditioned actions, and in relation to the translation and rhetorical expression processes involved in planning, as in any activity permeated by linguistic contestation. There is without doubt far more to say on these questions and much else, which is not attempted here.

Analysing politics

Power, pluralism, elitism: pressure politics

The classic questions of political analysis are about who has power over what, and what structures that power. Any politics textbook, from sixth form upwards (Andrew Heywood's many books are exemplary introductions), takes a reader through the arguments on these issues. The standard analyses of power discuss this in terms of different hypotheses, of which pluralism and elitism are the most widely known. Pluralism, often espoused by US thinkers, argues that power is widely spread in society and so all interests have a fair chance of having some influence over the future, through a range of types of political involvement. Elitism argues that in fact power is far more concentrated than this, and this can be explained in various ways. A classic statement is that of Charles Lindblom, a US academic, who said that all capitalist societies necessarily gave a stronger hand to business interests (Lindblom 1977). He was not making a grand systemic Marxist statement about the bourgeoisie being always the ruling class, and running the government. He was just saying that the tendency to elitism was inbuilt, and that efforts to combat elite power should start from that point.

It is not difficult to find evidence to support the elitist position in contemporary Britain. Marsh and Hall (2016) rehearse concisely the nature of the socioeconomic elite, formed by many intersecting features of wealth, schooling and the other ingredients of 'cultural capital'. They also show how this elite is linked to the British political tradition (BPT) through a powerful system of inequalities of access to economic and political resources, sealing together a political class located in the civil service, Parliament, the law and the world of business and pressure groups. The BPT, they argue, is based on a set of conservative assumptions about the role of the state, including the Treasury view and respect for a certain clutch of national traditions, always likely to reject radical change from the Left. Another analysis pointing up the importance of linguistic and cultural power was the article by Moulaert and Cabaret (2006) asking the sharp question 'Is democratic planning under capitalism possible?'. They were not as pessimistic as this might sound, but emphasised the very great efforts which would be needed to even begin to level the playing field for planning involvement. In other words, elites, whether in networks (their particular focus) or in straightforward old hierarchical power forms, would otherwise rule the planning roost.

Sometimes this argument is expressed in terms of democracy, how far Britain has a democratic system, how it may be made more democratic. This is surely highly relevant to planning, and these issues will appear in several places in the book, especially Chapters 6 and 7 on government and pressure groups, and in Chapter 8 when discussing what democratisation might be needed to enable effective planning. Writers as different as John Stewart, a great UK scholar of local government (for example, Stewart 2003), and Ines Newman (2014) have discussed the problems of the weak and often elitist nature of British local government, as well as its great potential because of its closeness to citizens.

There is a third position, the fully Marxist one in its various guises, which dislikes the idea of elitism as being insufficiently systemic. A classical Marxist will point out that ideas alongside material power infuse politics much more fully than elitists would normally accept. There are some traditional Marxian analyses of planning even in the present times, though probably not that many. One for Ireland (Fox-Rogers, Murphy and Grist 2011) puts the strongest position for how powerful interests structure planning practice and planning reforms (straying here a little outside the UK frame of the book). In particular these authors relate state power and property, an important move to explore in planning discussions. They argue that recent Irish planning legislation has been designed to scale back the scope for public participation, and reduce democracy in the planning process overall, in order to boost the 'business climate' in Ireland, centralising and 'streamlining' control of strategically important, especially infrastructure, applications, and making third-party appeals more difficult. Non-Marxist theorists will argue that these measures can be explained without resort to the position that the state effectively represents the interests of the capitalist class in Ireland, that it is never neutral, always biased. At any rate, the analysis of the 2000 and 2006 Planning Acts in this way is clear and refreshing.

Where one stands on the power in capitalist democracies debate depends in significant part on one's wider political and ideological position, although some academics may not like the implication that they are unlikely to be fully objective about this. What is important here is to realise the significance of this positioning when thinking about planning. It clearly makes a difference if one sees Britain as an elite polity, with a very small proportion of individuals or groups of individuals wielding most power; or if one sees power as widely diffused, leaving 'all to play for'. This applies with equal force at the local level: there is far too little recent analysis of 'local polities', whether at sub-regional (county, city region), district or neighbourhood levels. Such studies were quite common 40 or 50 years ago (Pahl 1970, Simmie 1981), followed by the locality studies of the late 1980s (Cooke 1989, Harloe et al 1990, Massey 1991). Does a local elite run planning politics in each area? Whose ideas rule? Whose terms set the shape of debate?

A long-time student of UK politics, Anthony Sampson, had his own view on the historical evolution of UK political power. In the first edition of his classic *An Anatomy of Britain* (Sampson 1962) he showed a, to some extent, balanced polity, with many forces having some power, though it was not a set of balances he necessarily liked. By his last edition, *Who Runs This Place?* (Sampson 2004), he concluded that an extremely unhealthy concentration of power had occurred in a media–business complex, leaving other interests far behind in influence. I continue to see much to support that position. This book will explore aspects of 'planning power' which support the Sampson thesis, as well as discuss possible cracks in the edifice, allowing wider influence on planning outcomes.

One further and well-known part of the politics discussion toolkit will be mentioned, one which was often drawn on in discussions of planning in the 1970s. This is the analysis by Steven Lukes of the 'three faces of power'. His idea (Lukes 1974) was that power could be examined as having three facets or levels. One was about simply direct influence on what happened, normal decision-making power. The second was about the setting of agendas, controlling what came to be discussed or not, sometimes called 'non-decision making'. The third face of power was rather about the setting of subjective preferences, in a sense prior to the other two types. This conceptualisation, which has been developed in various forms since, particularly by Hay (2002), can make a partial bridge to some discussions of ideology. Ideology, in some conceptions, can be seen as a prime force in setting the nature of the second and, especially, the third faces of power. Power is exercised by ideology by 'going behind the backs' of actors, conditioning the questions they ask and how they think. It is easy to see a connection with planning. In planning controversies one will often be aware that it is not just the discussion about the decision on the agenda which matters. Actors will often object that what they want does not even seem to be being raised. And outside observers may go further and say that the positions taken by *all actors* are set by ideological forces and other factors, very often without the awareness of the actors concerned.

Government and state: political institutions

There can be politics everywhere – families, sexualities, every aspect of social life has its politics. But here the focus is on a government- and state-regulated activity, spatial planning in its various guises, so the roles of government and state institutions are critical. The policy decisions, the resourcing decisions, the legal framings, all these are set by the governments of each country. In the UK this is, for England, the UK government, with certain constrained roles given to local government bodies or other local governance institutions. For Scotland, Wales and Northern Ireland the primary role for planning in a narrow sense has been in principle with the devolved institutions created in 1999, though these act within quite strong constraints in many policy fields, set by the UK or on occasion by EU and international laws. Here no special theorisation of these institutional or governmental spheres is given. Just two points are emphasised here, with the rest of the discussion of this question left to Chapter 6. Firstly, the power of the UK government in England is overwhelming in the planning field, as in most others. The absence of any significant element of devolved powers in England gives the central government departments a very free hand to push planning policy in the directions desired by the ministers of the day. This is related to the second point, the force of legal dimensions within the planning system. Planning is infused by the importance of legal regulation, set in Britain in significant part by case law formed by processes within the judicial system. To some degree this can constrain the role of ministers, but ultimately it is open to governments to change laws that they see the judiciary as 'mis-interpreting', and so the roles of government policy and law making and of judicial actors and processes have to be seen together.

Analysing ideology

So far it has been taken as read that we know what ideology is. This is in fact risky, as any brief conversation can reveal. There is a range of ways in which the term is used, ranging from a rather general usage meaning a mental framework or worldview, to a specific designation of systems of ideas, most commonly used in thinking about politics. There are plenty of definitions, from the very short (Flew 1979, p 150: 'any system of ideas and norms directing political and social action'), to Heywood (2012, p 5) listing ten different meanings that have been given to the term. No one meaning would find widespread agreement. Given my later use of Michael Freeden's approach to ideology, I present his definition here, without either the lengthy justification which would be desirable or the supplementary elements which Freeden adds.

> A political ideology is a set of ideas, beliefs, opinions and values that (1) exhibit a recurring pattern, (2) are held by significant groups, (3) compete over providing and controlling plans for public policy, and (4) do so with the aim of justifying, contesting or changing the social and political arrangements and processes of a political community. (Freeden 2003, p 32)

So, this definition stresses enduring systems of ideas. But this does not by itself get away from the fact that with ideology we enter difficult territory. In many circumstances, to say that someone is acting ideologically is an insult. This may draw on the deep history of the word, which very early on was given a derogatory sense – by Napoleon in fact, who accused the newly minted term of being the generator of 'ideologues', who have been ever since on the bad side. Marx and Engels had a much more complicated relation to the place of ideology in social thinking, but they too treated it (certainly in their early writings – *The German Ideology* above all) as something which was used to disguise the truth. This usage continued at least until a new approach by social scientists, led by Karl Mannheim in the 1930s, who considered that it should be rehabilitated as a neutral term. This is the way I aim to use it here. But it is important to be always aware that the pejorative valuation continues, and is unlikely to go away because of a book or what academics say. We can bracket off a 'rational' discussion, but we must remember the everyday usage which will still be in part the knee-jerk reaction of, 'all ideology is bad' and so no respectable activity should admit that it has ideological dimensions.

It is easy to get this wrong. As McLellan (1995, p 1) said: 'ideology is someone *else's* thought, seldom our own'. But really, 'we examine ideology as fellow sufferers, not as neutral observers' (Vincent 1995, p 20). It is most unlikely that this book will look as if it is written from an ideologically neutral standpoint. There is no such standpoint. My own political position means, for example, that I am a supporter of a social democratic form of public planning. I find annoying and unhelpful the attacks on 'planning' or 'planners' that I have noticed all my professional and academic life. I am probably less critical than many younger academic colleagues of the 'planning project', to use Patsy Healey's term (2007). This does not mean of course that I support all or even the majority of what goes under the name of planning in England – that will become clear enough.

Ideology underlies key dimensions of the planning and politics relation. This is not just about 'ideas' in some loose sense, though certainly ideas of all kinds are always critical in any activity – whether the invention of concepts (green belts, density, compact cities, national parks, sustainability and so on) or the promotion of arguments in a fuller sense – say, about long-term planetary survival, economic advances defined in some way, aesthetics, or ethics of governing.

Ideology is taken here to be much more than just any ideas, more than just some sort of mental frameworks. The main emphasis is, rather, on the analysis of ideology which points to the existence of clusters, families or systems of ideas about society and politics, drawing on the wide ranging advances in conceptualising ideology, especially by the British academic Michael Freeden and his morphological analysis of ideological families (Freeden 1996, 2003). He formulated a conceptualisation of ideological traditions as composites. There is no simple or pure core to any of the primary ideologies (conservatism, socialism, liberalism and so on), and this is even less the case for the numerous hybrids or variants of these ideologies. Certainly each leading ideology has some emphases which mark out its territory, prioritising some values over others, with some parts as more negotiable than others. The traditions are also naturally mobile over time and variable between political cultures, so that they may speak quite distinct languages across time and space, under the same broad heading. Freeden likens ideologies to modular units of furniture, which can be assembled in several ways – even though some ways would no make sense at all: ideological structures are certainly not endlessly malleable.

Freeden makes a strong case that politics as a field of study has often not given ideology the centrality it deserves in communicating ideas and values in a simplified form which goes far beyond the discussions of intellectuals and academics. He sees ideology as a primary mode in which politics is made, as a source of essential creativity for thought about the future, as a vital tool for communicating widely about what can be done, with ideological discussion as an activity with highly significant effects flowing from it (Freeden 2003, pp 126–128). As Finlayson (2012, p 752) says: 'ideologies are ubiquitous, intrinsic and necessary components of political life'. This argument, it seems to me, applies just as well to the field of planning, as to many others. It is those who manage to build a simplified idea of value and provide a narrative for carrying that into action who have tended to be successful in planning politics, and this is almost always based on some ideological foundations, visible or not.

One further point emphasised by Freeden is the considerable variation in the level of development of ideologies, when used in practice. This can range from, at one end, the merest of hunches which may condition much political activity, linked in fact to some idea which the individual heard some time in the past, but expressed in a highly simplified formula, or even just with symbols or at most slogans. Or, at the other end, actors may have a fully developed mapping out of an ideological position, what they are for as well as what they are against, and they may be capable of defending the position. We will encounter this variation in planning. Ideological positions can generate action by masses of people, as well as by small and generally more highly informed groups.

Neoliberalism

Neoliberalism is a widely used term to describe an ideological system, adapting the tenets of classic liberalism. The system has been successful in guiding politics, more or less worldwide. Harvey (2005) gives a history of how this was achieved by a coalition of power led by the US since 1945. He defines neoliberalism as 'a theory of political economic practices that proposes that human well-being can best be advanced by liberating individual entrepreneurial freedoms and skills within an institutional framework characterized by strong private property rights, free markets and free trade' (Harvey 2005, p 2). The role of the state is to ensure that the institutional framework is fit for this purpose. This is an ideology which has guided UK governments, to varying degrees, since 1979, and an idea of some British analyses of neoliberalism will be useful here.

I do this via three British authors whose work has connected well to urban and planning issues, and who I think should have been drawn on more in recent analysis of planning. Doreen Massey was a geographer, and books like *World City* (Massey 2007), on London, provided fine analyses of how politics mattered in the government, including the planning government, of a world city like London. Stuart Hall and Mike Rustin come broadly from sociology, but have been wide-ranging intellectuals. Two books published from article collections from the journal they edited, *Soundings*, are called *The Neo-Liberal Crisis* (Davison and Harris 2015) and *After Neoliberalism? The Kilburn Manifesto* (Hall, Massey and Rustin 2015). So their position was definitely that Britain was a neoliberalised country, even though one in crisis, especially after the financial and economic crisis of 2007 onwards. However, Hall said that 'ideology is always contradictory. There is no single, integrated "ruling ideology" – a mistake we make again now in failing to distinguish between conservative and neoliberal repertoires' (Davison and Harris 2015, p 22). So, neoliberalism was no simple, one-dimensional ideological phenomenon – like all ideologies.

A specific element of contemporary British neoliberalism was brought out especially by Massey, the extent to which financialisation has taken over this particular economy and country. Everything, from life prospects to health to pensions to university study, tends to being taken over by financial principles. 'Property and homes are a field in which the linking together of finance, landed property, geography and the production of common sense can clearly be seen ... houses and homes are now almost universally referred to as 'properties' (Hall, Massey and Rustin 2015, p 123). So a key feature of the playing field in which planning operates day to day, the housing sector, is framed by a key feature of British neoliberalism, according to the Hall, Massey and Rustin analysis.

A new twist is proposed by some commentators who see neoliberalism as being superseded by even more right-wing ideological movements, sometimes described as populism or radical versions of neoconservatism. Given that writers like Purcell (2009) and Gunder (2010) argued that planning at that moment was the servant of neoliberalism, this would, on this reading, be clearly of major significance. Both views are doubtful – that planning was a purely or even necessarily largely neoliberal supporting activity, or that neoliberalism is currently being superseded. However, as suggested above, these signs of ideological turbulence do highlight the contemporary relevance of the discussion of planning and ideology.

Ideology and pragmatism

One reaction to the claim being made here may be that British politics is less affected by ideology than that in many other countries. This may chime with a claim that consensus is the normal position in British politics: while certainly accepting that conflict is not unknown, it may be argued that a key part of the BPT is a readiness to compromise. Certainly the weight of the BPT is not to be denied, but I would argue that this is a highly ideological position, adopted often by those arguing more moderate positions (in whatever ideological camp). Nevertheless, the claim for the importance given to pragmatism and compromise may have special resonance in relation to the activity of planning. One can scarcely have a conversation with any practising planner without the concepts of balance, compromise and being pragmatic emerging. This may be a key part of planners' ideological armour, which they are unwilling to admit as ideological, given its utility. Still, I think it more useful to admit that the extents of conflict and underlying consensus have certainly gone in waves, in relation to many planning fields, but that this must include the acceptance of some very fundamental conflicts embedded in planning, These conflicts, and their ideas bases, will be part of what this book aims to expose and explore.

An approach to the political and ideological dimensions of planning

There have been attempts by academic writers to pin down one or several 'ideologies of planning'. A famous article by David Harvey (1978) took a straightforward Marxist approach to this task, arguing that planners would do better to recognise the heavy constraints imposed from working within capitalist systems. His aim was not so much to alert them to smarter ways of working within the system, although many planning academics have used the article to that effect, hoping that students, exposed to a challenging presentation of the constraints facing them in professional practice, would be able to work with more awareness and in ways which were less frustrating than an otherwise 'naïve' belief in the malleability of planning might imply. Harvey's aim was, rather, to suggest that revolutionary transformation of capitalism was the only way, in the long term, for planners to achieve their generally laudable redistributive and progressive aims. So he presented a singular 'ideology of planning' (if, he admitted, with many possible variants depending on time and place) which required planners to believe that they could act rather more effectively than was the reality, and which disguised real power and economic relations from planning actors. These ideas he saw as those embedded in professional norms and encouraged by the common sense of normal planning practice.

Patrick McAuslan (1980) suggested that there were three such ideologies in operation, prioritising property, the public interest and participation. Details of his work are given later, as it remains an illuminating approach. Nevertheless, in this book I do not adopt this approach to trying to identify and describe recent or current ideologies of planning in the UK or in England. This is because I do not find it helpful to imagine that planning in itself is something which has an ideology (or several competing ones), any more than any other professional or occupational or state-validated activities could have. Surely it makes limited sense to speak of an ideology of medicine, architecture or accountancy, except perhaps for quite polemical purposes.

Ideological dimensions of planning

The approach used here is, rather, to analyse the ideological dimensions of planning. This can be done both by taking a wider view and by looking at specific aspects – these are essentially the same, but at different levels of resolution. Both draw largely on the approach of Michael Freeden to political ideologies, described above. The wider view is given by tracing out the links between the most important political ideologies and planning, historically and up to the recent British situation. The specifics of the linkages are seen more within the shorter time-scales of planning practices and processes. So, the wider view frames the chapters on the relationship with the major political ideologies (Chapter 3 and part of Chapter 4), while the closer focus frames the ideological aspects of the analysis in all the subsequent chapters.

Most of the analysis in the book will be framed as above. However, I do now suggest that this could be developed by identifying two aspects which condition the nature of ideological dimensions. I refer to these only in Chapters 9 and 10, as there it will help with the task of analysing the different facets and fields of planning. One conditioning aspect is surely found in Harvey's argument for the importance of the constraining forces of capitalism. These are central to thinking about the role of property, law and the state. So, fundamentally important will be the nearness of the issue to the core of government and therefore to the strong forces which will always play on this – above all, the big powers in the economy and the media: some sort of capital–state nexus. One way to characterise this is by use of a version of the Critical Political Economy approach (Berry and Lavery 2017). This proposes that a basic understanding of the role of the state within the crisis-ridden nature of capitalist development is the right place to start any analysis of political processes (Berry and Lavery 2017, pp 247–248). However, it insists on the need to introduce intermediate concepts to bridge across to the agents involved in making political decisions, and draws on the simple idea of growth models for this purpose (Berry and Lavery 2017, pp 250–251). We may suggest that the planning issues which are seen by key state actors as most critical to the current growth model will be those where ideological factors will be in the forefront.

A second conditioning aspect is more difficult to pin down, being broadly 'cultural', with some link to the first aspect, but considerable autonomy. This refers to the changing *zeitgeist* of evolving sensibilities and mentalities, for example about nature, about urban and rural living, about the old and the new. I am aware of the comment by Raymond Williams in his classic *Keywords* (1976), that culture is 'one of the two or three most complex words in the English language' (Williams, 1976, p 87), and that I am therefore introducing some indeterminacy into the framework proposed here. However, I think this can be a starting point in understanding the political and ideological dimensions of planning in a way that does not overweight the perhaps most obvious material and power elements which are contained in ideological composites like neoliberalism. Planning, for example when dealing with design or ecological or heritage issues, is strongly affected by these matters of taste, habits, traditions, all of which are interwoven with perhaps more solid economic and political processes (consumerism, financialisation of individual and family lives, for example).

Political dimensions of planning

The political analysis here can be seen as having two parts. One deals with the analysis of power, the classic treatment of pluralism and elitism, of pressure groupings and oligarchies. The other deals with state and government institutions, covering central and local government, and law. Clearly the two parts are simply two sides of the overall politics, but it can help to conceptualise them separately. Details of the two parts were given above. Some chapters are more related to one part, some more to the other, though all have parts of both. Together these 'implement' the ideological directions by means of governing and political pressuring.

Ideological and political dimensions together

Schematically the above can be expressed as in Table 1.1.

The book brings together ideology and politics, showing how systems of ideas fuel and interact with government and power relations. Politics and ideology will be mediated by at least three elements, for the case of planning. One will be *the field of planning*, what sort of development sector is under discussion, whether housing, strategic or non-strategic economic sectors, or big infrastructure. Any cursory look at the public examination of plans will identify quickly the areas which take up most time and where most resources, public and private, are directed – often big housing schemes. This is where the underlying ideological forces will impinge more directly, and also where political contestation will be higher – ideological and political salience marching in tandem, consuming the planning space. The Examination in Public of the London Plan in January to May 2019 held sessions on 33 days, with 9 of these taken up by housing issues, and no doubt many other sessions with the voice of the housing development lobby clearly articulated, as this lobby sees all Plan issues through a development lens, and can afford to attend most sessions. Housing is what matters most to those with power and money, as well as to democratic majorities in London, within what can be influenced by planning. The hot sectors are more ideologically infused, as well as more heavily politically contested.

A second element will be *the facet of planning* being analysed. As against the object of development indicated by field, by facet I mean the broad consideration at the forefront in any case. In Chapter 9 I look at heritage, light-green environmental issues and design as key

Table 1.1: Political and ideological dimensions of planning

Politics	Ideology	Politics, ideology and planning
Power and pressure politics	Ideological composites (Freeden), infusing both large historical trajectories and shorter time-scale normal political processes. These conditioned by both 'material' and 'cultural' forces.	Spectrum of degrees of politicisation and 'ideologisation' of planning, mediated by pressure politics and governmental and state institutions. These affect each field of planning and the scale at which planning is operated, which generates different mixes of politically and ideologically affected planning. Together these represent the political and ideological colouring of planning.
State, governments and law		

facets of planning action, but other matters could be foregrounded in the same way. Each facet can be seen to have different political and ideological conditioning.

A third element will be *scale*, which is why that is such a powerfully important strategic choice in planning systems design. Scale can position power variably. The strong powers of call-in by government ministers, and the appeals system used in Britain, are both testimony to this positioning, as is the much-contested locus of plan making. The move of decision making on big infrastructure out of local authority hands with the Planning Act 2008 is another example of important scale decision making by governments. Northern Ireland gives an example where decision making was placed in central government for several decades because local government left decisions too close to problematic political processes. The scalar shifts post-devolution in Wales and Scotland would make other good examples. The struggles over the design and control of forward planning in England for 50 years or more can be analysed in this way – the swaying back and forth, for and against regional, central, local and very local decision-making locations.

These mediating elements involve the two parts of politics described above – the operation of pressure politics and the roles of government and state, including legal dimensions. The mediation occurs through the play of power and institutional (especially governmental) processes, which set how each field of planning is dealt with, and set the scale at which governmental action takes place. Ideologies are not something separate from such processes. As argued above, ideology acts both as overarching justifier or legitimator of systemic processes and as something deeply involved in the micro and everyday management of governing, including that of planning. So, there are '*political and ideological dimensions of planning*' in each place and period. Key dimensions are the relationship to legal systems, to governmental processes, to technical or expert processes and to participatory or deliberative processes – all covered in chapters to follow.

A final analytical element presented here relates to the *intensity of ideological and political effects*. The degrees of ideological and political influence in any planning issue or case must take the form of a spectrum in reality, but a set of possible forms can be presented for purposes of simplification. Table 1.2 gives four possible combinations, some of which may be likely to occur more often than others. Cell A may be quite frequent, where a planning case raises both ideological and political temperatures at the same time. Cell B may also be common enough, in which an issue which hardly involves deep ideological

Table 1.2: Schematic range of ideological and political situations

A. Heavily ideological and heavily political	B. Weakly ideological and heavily political
C. Weakly ideological and weakly political	D. Heavily ideological and weakly political

questions nevertheless can generate big local, or possibly national, political conflicts. Cell C may also occur more than might be imagined, in that there are indeed a good number of planning issues where the stakes are not high in these senses at all, and the decision making is likely to pass by without notice, with perhaps more technical rules of thumb being applied. Cell D may also be quite common, though again it may not be generally visible, for if an ideologically fundamental issue is not picked up politically, perhaps because of particular spatial or social circumstances (say, the fact that no one lives nearby or is affected, or because those affected are unable to mobilise any political presence), the high ideological salience becomes non-active.

What is behind the intensity in either category can vary greatly. Ideologically, the two proposed conditioning elements will generally be in play, but politically there could be as many interacting circumstances as there are planning issues and cases. I do not put these forms to work directly in the book, as it would be tiresome to keep referring to a situation being 'something like Cell B'. The point is just to suggest ways that analysis might progress in the future.

Conclusion

So, how does this book work around the knotty relationship of the three objects being examined? Readers may still be thinking, ideology is just one part of politics, why not just stick with politics as the main focus, and add in ideology as just one, more or less important, ingredient. But I believe that it is precisely important to highlight the separate understanding of ideology within planning. Yes, in one sense ideology (as treated here) is part of politics as a whole. But by separating out the two zones, 'planning and ideology' and 'planning and more conjunctural politics', we will gain in effective descriptive and explanatory power. By first separating these out, we can then see how they may reinforce or work against each other, and what sorts of blending and mutual affecting are at work.

This double-headed (ideology alongside politics) approach will be applied in each of the cuts into the topic taken in the rest of the book, after the continuation of introductory themes in the literature review in Chapter 2. Some parts of the ideology and politics combined framework will be more prominent in certain chapters – the wider ideological view in Chapter 3 and part of Chapter 4, the state and law aspects of politics in Chapters 5 and 6, pressure politics in Chapter 7. But most chapters will draw on the overall framing, seeking to show the joint operation of political and ideological dimensions of planning.

A selective survey of planning literature in this field is in the next chapter. Chapters 3 to 7 explore the modes of impact of political and ideological dimensions on planning, first historically (Chapters 3 and 4), then from different perspectives – discussion of the roles of different technical skills and knowledge (including law and professional training) in Chapter 5, and the discussion of planning and government, of pressure politics, in Chapters 6 and 7. Chapter 8 analyses the issues of communication and deliberation in relation to planning, including the role of the media. Then Chapters 9 and 10 illustrate how all this impacts across facets and fields of planning action, looking at three facets (heritage, environment and design) and three fields (housing, economy and infrastructure). These allow some probing within the ideological complexes affecting particular facets or fields of planning. Chapter 11 reviews ways to improve the planning, politics and ideology relationship.

2

Writing on politics and ideology in planning

Some planning and ideology classics

It is important first to engage with what planning thinkers have said about politics, ideology and planning, as this will also indicate major gaps in this engagement. This review is mainly focused on literature of the last 10–15 years. However it will help to glance briefly at some older classic texts. We could go back to a much-cited article by Foley (1960) on the three ideologies of planning. In fact he refers to the three philosophies of planning, which he identifies as 'sub-ideologies'. These involve making the goal of planning: reconciling competing demands for land, or improving the physical environment, or seeking directly social objectives. He notes the scope for inconsistencies between the three approaches. While he is a perceptive and influential view of British planning by a well-informed US observer, Foley's framework is primarily a discussion of the goals of British planning, rather than a discussion of any underlying ideological impacts on its activities.

Another early consideration of ideology and planning was in the proceedings of a 1973 conference (Kingston Polytechnic 1973) on *Ideologies in Planning*. In particular this led to the publication of some intriguing reflections by Patsy Healey (1974) – intriguing because she was not later to show direct interest in the area in her many writings. At that moment she shared the view of this book:

> Happily, planning and planners can no longer remain in this condition of ideological deprivation. Challenges both to the 'non-ideological' position and to the specific ideologies of planners are closing in from many directions. ... Planners can therefore no longer avoid the 'problem of ideology', and in many quarters it has been for some time a subject of active discussion ... ideology is not something to be feared and rejected, or used as a simplistic banner. It would be intellectually honest and, in the long run, a strength in the face of mounting criticism, if planners and the planning

profession attempted to be explicit about the beliefs and limitations embedded in their necessary ideologies. (Healey 1974, p 602)

Healey argued that planners, just like activists, need ideologies in order to act, and so opening up the discussion is necessary to reduce vulnerability. In some ways the work of Eric Reade, particularly his polemic on British planning and planners (1987), took up this challenge, although I have not found his admittedly acute and powerful arguments of direct use for the purposes of this book. Essentially he accused planners and the planning profession of hiding behind a professional ideology of not being political, when this was exactly what they were being, usurping the proper role of politicians, rather than confining themselves to 'political clarification'. Such a purist position could have, in my view, no practical future. Playing these views against those of an experienced practitioner like Ted Kitchen (discussed shortly) would be instructive.

Also influential, if among a smaller group of planning and law theorists, was the work by the planning and land legal specialist Patrick McAuslan, with his three ideologies of planning law (McAuslan 1980). McAuslan had the advantage, as well as being a barrister, of having been intensely involved in planning in the 1970s as a local councillor in Leamington Spa, when teaching at Warwick University. He argued that British planning was made up of two core ideologies, based on the priority given to private property and that given to the public interest, with lawyers predominant in defending the first and administrators in government and councils leading on the second, but with a more or less agreed truce operating between the leading actors in planning, depending on the period examined since the 1940s. But he identified an emerging third ideology based on public participation, highlighted as one way forward after the 1969 Skeffington Report, but in fact largely pushed aside by the first two ideologies' proponents. McAuslan favoured planning moving to adopt much of this third ideology.

As with Foley, McAuslan describes these positions as ideologies, which is not the way I use ideological analysis. I do not think it helps to identify such value positions or orientations as 'ideologies of planning'. This does not reduce the importance which the book had in raising the issue of the role of private property and, especially, the legal profession within planning. The book and some of McAuslan's articles (1971, 1974, 1975) can still be read with profit. Interestingly, a commemorative volume by some of McAuslan's students has been published (Zartaloudis 2017), showing the depth and breadth of his work. As we will see in Chapter 3, there are other lawyers who have written with considerable insight on planning, but probably none with the critical perspective of McAuslan.

Malcolm Grant, a more conventional leading academic planning lawyer, wrote on the relation of politics and planning law at the height of the attacks on planning by the Thatcher governments, and showed an unusual degree of interest in 'the forces of politics and ideology', as one section of an article was titled (Grant 1987, pp 25–28). However his discussion of ideology treated it from the perspective that 'an ideology is a belief' (p 25), without going into the role in more depth. He was critical of the 'pure pursuit of political ideology', of 'crude ideology', so his approach fitted into the normal distancing by most professionals and academics from a more nuanced analysis of ideology in planning.

Two other insightful books of this earlier period are those of Andrew Blowers (1980, 1984). From his privileged perspective as an Open University academic and a leading Labour councillor in Bedfordshire, Blowers was able to knit together issues of power and planning, particularly within a local government context. The second book chronicled the fight between a corporate interest, the London Brick Company, and Bedfordshire County Council over the economic and environmental issues involved in the company exploiting its vast land holdings in the county. A strong coalition of the company, trade unions and some Conservative and Labour councillors managed to defeat environmental activists, supported by other Conservative and Labour councillors, who had aimed to change the terms on which the company worked. Blowers does not treat ideology explicitly, but his analyses of politics, power and conflict remain under-used classics.

In the period around 1990, at the height of the Thatcherite era in the UK, there were some books which took a more strongly and explicitly political and ideological approach to planning. Two well-known examples are the books by Andy Thornley on Thatcherism and planning (two editions 1991 and 1993) and by Brindley, Rydin and Stoker on *Remaking Planning* (also two editions, 1989 and 1996). Thornley took on directly the intense debate as to whether Thatcherism (the UK-invented version of neoliberalism) had fundamentally changed planning or not. Thornley returned to the issue of the 'impact of political ideology on British planning', that is, of Thatcherism, at the start of the New Labour years, and concluded that the Major premiership 'signified a weakening of the ideological imperative' (Thornley 1999, p 183), and that New Labour indicated a return of consensus ideology. So, although admitting the instability of Thatcherism (what has generally been called since the variegation of neoliberalism), Thornley judged that Thatcherism was dead. From present perspectives that was a risky and now very doubtful conclusion.

Remaking Planning modulated the answer to the question of Thatcherism's impact by arguing that there were several different sorts of planning regime then operating in the UK, depending on local political approaches (market friendly or more planning supportive) and economic circumstances of localities. So, both Thornley and Brindley, Rydin and Stoker were taking on political and ideological questions directly, with the latter's model making the ideological position of locality actors as one of two key determinants of planning models. It was interesting that the second edition of *Remaking Planning* found less difference in models, with only two types left, one somewhat more and one somewhat less market led. In other words, ideological convergence had occurred, the authors considered – a conclusion which was to colour analysis of English planning well into the 2000s, arguably until the big changes of 2010–15 brought ideology firmly back onto the planning agenda. But after around 1990 the ideological determinants were, it can be argued, much more at national level, not so much by localities. So it was Thornley's question which remained the core one to answer: what was driving planning at national level? Several of the authors discussed in the following section have pursued this question, in their different ways, ever since.

Recent planning literature

We can assume that students get their ideas of what planning is about as an activity from many sources. A planning teacher imagines that the accumulated literature to which students are introduced during their academic degrees is one important source. Here I make a brief survey of the sorts of texts a student on a UK planning course would have been exposed to. Clearly, this is making many assumptions already about the formation of planners, but at an absolute minimum it is surely important to examine what the collectivity of the planning academy of a country imagines the subject is about, in the dimensions being studied, as revealed by academic writing.

Such a complex of literature is formed of many parts, with some being highly formalised, others being much more practice or everyday-news related. I concentrate on the former, while being aware that the assumptions and messages to a degree hidden in a report in *Planning* magazine or a local or national newspaper, or in a blog or similar conveyed by social media may be as important as or more important than the more formal area of books and articles. I concentrate here on books, and treat key articles towards the end of the chapter.

This book complex will be taken to have four parts: textbooks, general UK planning books, books on planning sectors and opinion or advocacy books.

Planning textbooks

The most obvious way in for any academic degree at either undergraduate or master's level is via the textbook for the subject. In UK planning this has in recent years come down to one core text, *Town and Country Planning in the UK*, normally called Cullingworth and Nadin, but in its latest 2015 incarnation edited by a team from Newcastle University. Other important introductory texts have been those by Yvonne Rydin (1993, revised in 1998) and Clara Greed (most recently in 2014).

Town and Country Planning in the UK does an impressive job overall in presenting the UK planning system. Chapter 3 of the book presents the agencies of planning, including all the central ministries and agencies, and sections describing local government's planning responsibilities, in total 44 pages, though much is description of the levels of government administrative complexity, from the EU downwards. The shorter Chapter 13 (17 pages) on 'Planning, the profession and the public' concludes the book, and includes sections on public involvement, and professionalism, which get into core themes of planning politics. But in neither chapter is there any explicit discussion of the political or ideological characteristics and tensions within British planning, such that a fresh-to-the-subject reader would pick up that they were entering difficult 'non technical' territory. Of course, the other nearly 500 pages of the book are full of implicitly political discussions of the key aspects of planning practice, but the deeply contested nature of planning, its ingraining in the core ideological debates of the era, hardly surfaces. This is clearly a deliberate approach. This book is the official face of planning, which every planner or person involved with or interested in planning might wish to consult, alongside planning law texts. No more than such legal texts should we perhaps expect such a text to give much emphasis to the aspects that may lessen the neutral or professional character of planning.

It is noticeable that the other books which have performed or still perform as textbooks take a more politicised approach. Rydin's 1993/1998 book dedicated one of its five Parts to 'The politics of planning', with chapters on the state, the planners and the public. Here we get much nearer to that deep contestation, with reference to 'town planners under attack' as well as to lobbying and 'values, attitudes and ideologies'. The latter section is one of the most explicit and helpful discussions, still, of the value systems and ideologies competing for planning priority, including Thatcherite, socialist, protectionist and ecologist positions, with environmentalism given most specific attention. The author did not issue further editions, so the book is no longer really current. It should perhaps be in the section on older literature, but as a prominent textbook, I include it here.

Successive books by Greed (or in 2014 with David Johnson) have also addressed politics explicitly, if briefly, with one section asking 'What is the relationship between planning and politics?' (Greed and Johnson, 2014, pp 148–149). She answers (noting Rydin's virtually parallel analysis) that there are at least three sides to the relationship:

- fights about control of property and land, and hence money and power;
- planning's position as part of national politics and ideology;
- planning's local embeddedness, with local political actors involved in a way that does not apply in many other state policy fields, at least to the same extent.

These do indeed bring us straight into the core issues affecting or afflicting planning. But it is noticeable that the rest of the book is, by and large, not at all politically explicit. Exceptions are the valuable discussion of planning as one of the built environment professions (Chapter 16), and a continuing interrogation of the gender dimensions of planning practice, a topic which should be at the forefront in thinking about planning's politics and ideology.

So, in these textbooks we find a fuller presentation of the matters of interest to me, although developed at some length only in Rydin's 1990s book.

General planning books

The second category is formed of book taking a broad view of UK planning, but being not of a textbook form – although some shade over into being somewhat textbooks-like in parts. Prime examples are books by Mark Tewdwr-Jones and Phil Allmendinger. Other books of this kind I will mention are those by Andrew Gilg, Ted Kitchen and Janice Morphet (and I am necessarily omitting several other important books of this type). Morphet's planning practice book of

2011 avoided any direct mention of politics, perhaps reflecting a firm commitment, New Labour-like, to simply showing pragmatically what would work to secure good planning. Andrew Gilg's *Planning in Britain* of 2005 was focused on evaluating what difference is made by the existence of planning, and in this frame discussed the importance of power and value systems within society (pp 51–55). The chapter as a whole discussed the underlying conflicts affecting planning action, although the book is more about trying to reach a good model for planning than explaining why actual planning is as it is. Ted Kitchen's *People, Politics, Policies and Plans* (1997) is the book which has perhaps put much stress on the significance of professional and councillor interaction, based as it is on a career at the top of local authority planning, mainly in Manchester. A prominent 20-page chapter on 'Working with elected members' valuably unravels the importance of party politics in British local authorities, and shows how critical political leaderships are. Nevertheless, the book is very close up to its subject, and does not step back to see too much of either the wider political framing of council action or the ideological currents swirling around that framing, although there is discussion, for example, of the challenge of sustainability and how this generated policy conflicts.

This brings us to the two writers who have arguably come closest to facing up to what has been going on politically and ideologically since the 1980s in British planning. Mark Tewdwr-Jones's *The Planning Polity* (2002) was an important attempt to span the changes affecting central and local government framing of planning, but it tended to concentrate on policy making and government machinery, rather than underlying political and ideological processes. A successor book, *Spatial Planning and Governance* (2012), had a broader take on the system, with a chapter on 'Spatial planning, governance and the state'. Within that chapter governance and political forms were distinguished from each other (alongside operational and implementation forms). However, the whole book, while clearly in one sense infused by political awareness, is curiously distant from discussion of big political and ideological conflicts, and in this sense not only mirrors the tendency (mentioned earlier) for British planning to keep its distance from fundamental contestation, but reflects a bit the New Labour ideas of third way, of pragmatic 'what works' approaches to public policy. Ideology hardly figures here, openly. I will note later the difference observable in articles by Tewdwr-Jones (with Alex Lord) which take on ideology more directly.

Phil Allmendinger's book-length works have been very different, as these key UK-focused texts, on the New Labour years (2011) and on the 2010–15 Coalition (2016), are looking directly at the impact of ideological approaches of these quite different political formations. They are thus, in my view, the only books which address the challenge which I think needs to be met, of relating planning eras to planning ideologies, alongside the more conjunctural politics of those eras and their sub-periods.

However, when we look closely at the conclusions, we see a strong reluctance to accord ideology an important position in the resulting planning of these periods. This is significantly more the case with the first book, on New Labour. In the conclusions, Allmendinger asks: 'Is it possible to identify coherence or discern a New Labour ideology from the experiences of planning covered in the previous chapters? The simple answer is no' (2011, p 153). He concludes that policy was driven more by events than by ideology, even while admitting that the observed ambiguity so evident in the New Labour years 'echoes the different strands of thought within the party and government over the role of the state in a global market economy' (p 154). Two pages later he concedes that perhaps the approach to planning could be best conceived as 'a form of neoliberal governance' (p 156). However, as the chapter progresses different versions of this thesis become evident, sometimes referring to a three-way split of policies, paradigms and philosophies, sometimes to 'competing ideologies gaining transitory dominance' (p 162) – meaning smaller shifts within government, not what would be really called ideological shifts. Earlier chapters foreshadow this uncertainty, with that on New Labour and planning hardly mentioning the deep differences and ongoing struggles within the Labour Party, which so affected the climate in which planning policy was formed.

The later book leads with ideology in its title, *Neoliberal Spatial Governance*, and is, overall, a more consistent attempt to blend analysis of day-to-day politics and events with the force of underlying ideological positions. The analysis is formally structured around space/scale, ethos and politics, though this is applied variably and does not articulate well with the ideology dimension (neoliberalism). In the conclusions Allmendinger says that 'neoliberalism provided the broad parameters' (2016, p 205) – and here he is extending his view to survey the 'last three decades or so', so, encompassing successive Labour and Conservative governments. But he then rather returns to the standard British fear of politics and ideology by accusing New Labour of naivety about what it could or could not do, and complaining that since 2010 'Rather than an open and respectful debate we have a series of ideologically determined stances' (p 207). In the final sections, the recipe recommended is the removal of ideology and then to look rationally at the inevitable tensions within planning, presumably to see how these could be better managed – even though they are said to be 'inherent' (p 218). The two books are full of highly illuminating analysis of these periods, and I will be treading on quite a bit of the same ground in later sections. But neither book gets fully to grips with either the ideological or the political dimensions which have been so visible (to my mind) in both of these quite contrasting UK planning eras, although the second is nearer to spelling out the ideological nature of government policy, in part perhaps because of Allmendinger's natural planner's repugnance for the measures of the 2010–15 government, meaning that identifying ideological force was easier. The aspiration to remove ideology (and perhaps even the less rational or thoughtful elements of politics) appears to go deeply against the weight of the analysis undertaken, which indeed shows the inherently ideological and political nature of planning. Surely the Allmendinger analysis suggests that the need is to understand these dimensions and choose the fruitful ideological and political paths, not run away from these dimensions – as if this would ever be possible, or even conceivable.

Books on planning sectors

A third book category examined here is that looking at particular sectors or fields of planning. Clearly this now opens up a very wide spread of books and it is only possible to take a very few examples to illuminate the kind of approaches used in important texts since the early 2000s.

One valuable contribution on the analysis of property and public policy in a wider sense, but very close to planning, is in the stream of work by Mike Raco (2013). A brief way in is in Raco (2014), where he exposes his thesis that a dramatic reorganisation of public management has been evacuating democratic control of urban projects and much of the core of the actions of central and local government. A prime example is the way the organisation of the 2012 London Olympics removed the possibility of outside influence on the key decisions, once an incredibly complex machinery of sub-contracting to a few very large corporations was set up, quite early in the process. Processes like this have been presented as ideologically neutral, fitting in with the positions of New Labour that 'what works' is the only principle of public action and that the best way to organise public investment is by Private Finance Initiative (PFI) projects. This is similar to the rolling-out of a consensual political order seen as occurring by the post-political theorists, but in considerably more straightforward terms. Planning and related processes are, it is argued, technicised and also judicialised, meaning that only expensive judicial action may be available to any outside challengers. Companies like Serco, Carillion and Group 4 take over everything from prisons to hospitals to schools, supposedly under local or central government control, but increasingly able to lead and control much of the terms of their operation themselves, and, as was seen with the collapse of Carillion in 2017, always bailed out by government if profits turn out to be less than expected.

There has been a lot of valuable work on housing, property development and planning since the turn of the century. One example of a book which gives some weight to discussion of ideological and political features is the text by Adams and Watkins (2002). Chapter 2 on the changing policy context of housing development is in part a consideration of the ideological buffeting which housing has taken, with a final section on housing provision and state–market relations. Of course, as always, policy context does not just contain ideologically driven elements, but these are brought out here fairly explicitly. Chapter 6 on the politics of planning and housing development complements this, by examining different party positions on housing, including party manifestos, and then goes on to analyse the more immediate politics of decision making, and how significantly forces within local pressure groups and national non-governmental organisations (NGOs) press on planning decisions. So, although the book is not concerned explicitly to bring out issues around ideology and politics in planning as a prime theme (it has other priorities), in this case of a sectoral study, readers will get a good idea of these forces at work.

A more recent book on housing, by Brian Lund (2016), gives a solid historical and political discussion of UK housing, having begun by saying that political dimensions of housing have been underplayed. It acknowledges the importance of ideological differences on housing policy through the last century or more, but treats ideology as an element of wider politics. Planning is largely subsumed in Chapter 2 on 'Land politics', an interesting perspective, although in the final chapter Lund refers to the 1947 Act creating 'planning politics' (p 276). In some ways he is doing the kind of job this book seeks to do for planning, but with a much fuller historical view and relatively little concern for theoretical dimensions.

Across many other sectors, such an approach is less common. There is a wealth of such books, so that whether one is interested in environment and sustainability, heritage, retailing, design, transport or whatever sub-area of planning learning, one will find at least one UK text. But, from my survey of the books known to me, most present their subjects in a primarily technical or less political way, even if with some reference to politics. Again, I think that this is a conscious decision by authors, given that, where I know them personally, I know they are capable of more politically or ideologically tuned analysis. So again, the approaches are understandable. Planning teachers know the wish of many students to have guidance of a more technical kind, which takes the pressure off them to make personal value judgements and come to terms with the fact that they have chosen a politically charged profession. The same aspiration may affect some other interested readers, though this can depend on the field and the motivation: many might also be happy to have the highly contested nature of planning action made clear to them, to help them navigate their role within the system, as advisor, activist or simply citizen.

Advocacy planning books

The fourth category is that of shorter 'opinion' or advocacy books, which have become particularly popular in the decade since 2010, presenting arguments from individual experience, whether in researching or activism. By their nature these books do tend to be more political in the normal sense of the word, but this does not mean that they are, by and large, taking the explicit approach to analysing planning's political and ideological foundations which is being argued for here. This is perhaps especially understandable for this category, as those advocating a particular revival or reform of planning, as the books mentioned here all do, generally are trying to widen their appeal. Probably avoiding 'too political' or (terrible thought) 'too ideological' an approach is considered by all the writers as the safer option. The 'most political' of the books is perhaps that of Ellis and Henderson (2014). This traces part of the problem facing planning in 'a disconnected politics', with little wider engagement in planning in many areas. The authors then stress the need to rebuild trust in planning, recreating its legitimacy, particularly by empowering local government. There is an explicit discussion of making the different forms of democracy (representative, participatory and direct) work better together (pp 93–95), an issue which has not had the clear thinking it needs.

Anna Minton's books on planning, *Ground Control* (2009) and *Big Capital* (2017), both come to planning from the outside, and ask fundamental questions of planning, focusing in the later book on the takeover of London, including much of its planning, by a coalition of interests aiming to boost its value as a financial asset. So the books are strongly politicised, but even then, they do not take a very close look at the ideological foundations of what is happening. Certainly the formation of a new neoliberal framework is identified as the core drive since the late 1980s (pp xiv–xv), but then Minton refers to 'the unintended consequences of a market-led approach to public goods', as if ideology does not work behind everyone's backs, as well as sometimes out in the open: this does not make the consequences 'unintended'. But again, this may in part stem from the wish not to put off readers.

The same logic applied to Rydin's classic short statement of *The Purpose of Planning* (2011). The concluding chapter argues how the good life can be helped by planning, dealing with the inevitable fractures and cleavages of society and putting control on market processes, incorporating all the time all sorts of public engagement. Again, the words politics and ideology hardly appear and the pattern of avoiding unnecessary red lights to readers is clearly in operation. Nevertheless, there can still be questions whether this approach does work better than being more open about the nature of the ideas battle underway in the conceptualisation and everyday operation of planning. Now that the ideological stakes are higher than probably at any time for many decades, in Europe and especially the UK, it may be time for such a more open approach, even if Rydin's one fitted the moment apparent in 2011.

The book by campaigner Shaun Spiers (2018), ex-head of the Campaign to Protect Rural England (CPRE), is naturally different from all the above. For my purposes, the interesting feature is how he treats what he openly admits is a battle of ideas. He states his position, probably one shared by many think-tanks and NGOs: 'Ideas ultimately drive politics' (p 21). 'A campaign group should not just accept that good ideas are out of the range of practical politics. Its job is also to shift paradigms and alter the frames within which politics is discussed' (p 21). Spiers refers to the ideology of Conservatism 'if ideology is the right word' (p 12). But then elsewhere, for example when discussing the failure to build houses, he says it is extraordinary that governments have fallen for housebuilders' arguments that their failure is due to planning (pp 18, 31). It is the same old phenomenon we have seen often enough now, admitting at one moment that ideas or ideology (if that dirty word can be used) matter, but then in actual analysis imagining that governments act 'cleanly', ideology free. A cynic, or I would say realist, would admit that housebuilders will naturally follow their material (profitable) interests, and that governments such as those run by the UK Conservative Party will almost naturally follow those interests, especially when, as Spiers recounts very clearly, large funding has flowed from the major housebuilders to the Conservative Party, *and* when it squares perfectly with a prominent part of Conservative ideology. Yet, reading books like those of Spiers, this link gets elided, no doubt because the hope remains that politics will get cleaner, if it is presented as potentially in that form. But perhaps a more realist approach to politics and ideology in planning would leave action with better chances of progressive effects?

Academic articles on planning and politics

Here only articles will be examined when they seem to be taking the kind of explicit view I am interested in. There are in fact, as far as I can see, *very few* such articles. One may come across an article apparently directly on the theme, but it normally turns out to be using the weakest sense of the word. As a US retired planner reflected on 'planning and ideology', he simply meant 'certain master ideas, or combination of ideas, call them what you will – patterns, paradigms, models, ideologies' (Guttenberg 2009, p 288). As we have seen, the weak sense is very common, but it is not the way I am using the concept here.

A collection of articles published in 2009 on the ideology of New Labour and planning, with my own introduction (Marshall 2009), is at least on the theme, and some of the nine articles have continuing interest. The most important recent articles are those of Shepherd (2017b, 2018). These come at the question of planning and ideology primarily by means of the theories of Freeden, and have significant overlaps with my own approach, although his use of institutionalism is not something I follow here. The first sentence of the first article is worth giving here, for its clarity: 'The institution of town and country planning rests upon ideas and concepts which will always be contested' (2017b, p 494). His main emphasis is on bringing out these concepts, which span across ideologies (liberty, property and so on), forming the dynamic ideology mosaic promoted by Freeden's approach. Shepherd also provides an extremely valuable analysis of the way ideologies affected planning during the New Labour and post-2010 years. His work is based on very full historical research and theoretical reflection, and I would commend any reader to go to these articles to get a more satisfactory treatment than they will find here on some key aspects, particularly the history of the formation and successive transformations of planning. I draw on Shepherd's work (also as taken from a Cambridge University doctoral thesis) where appropriate.

Another recent article, by Lord and Tewdwr-Jones (2018) also offers an explicit consideration of ideology and planning, and using forthright language (an earlier article, 2013, by the same authors, went gingerly in the same direction). The authors argue that the post-2010 changes in planning are 'in large measure ideological in character' (p 229). The analysis makes some use of Freeden's approach to ideology, but in the end is primarily an account of the changes post-2010, more than a deeper analysis. The words ideology and politics are used to some extent interchangeably, and the conclusion is that the creation of a 'post political' framework constraining any debate on planning futures 'has been an ideologically motivated political act' (p 240). So, although the paper very valuably brings out into the open the sort of thinking which can allow better discussion of the big alternatives facing planning, the analysis itself is not clear enough to deliver a good basis for such discussion, from a better understanding of what has been going on up to now. It is to be hoped that this is only the first of a crop of academic articles which will bring to fruition such a more openly political debate.

Conclusion

As this chapter's survey has shown, a relevant literature is beginning to emerge, particularly in the just mentioned articles. It is not surprising that the interest in these aspects of planning becomes more intense in very evidently ideologically driven periods, like the 1980s and the present time. But, as Chapter 1's survey of political science and theory approaches hopefully suggested, there is scope for using such approaches to provide valuable illumination of planning to a much greater degree than has happened so far. The next chapter introduces key ideologies and makes initial links to British planning.

3

Ideologies in Britain, with initial linking to planning

This chapter explores the main ideologies and their links to planning. It therefore starts to detail the ideology-and-planning connections. Chapter 4 gives a historical overview of Britain's planning development as seen through the conceptual lens used in this book, as well as a more detailed history of one recent government's management of planning reforms.

The primary ideologies in Britain, and initial linking with planning

We now look more carefully at the range of ideologies with influence in Britain, and begin to make connections with how they have affected planning. We have to get to grips with the 'ideological landscape' (Berry 2011, p 2), a term which usefully highlights that at any moment there is a spread of ideological influences in play, pressing on day-to-day policy formation, and with relational effects – if one part of the landscape changes, that can have knock-on effects on other parts, over time.

A first decision needed in all surveys of ideologies is which ideologies to cover. Textbooks make varied choices. The massive handbook on political ideologies edited by Freeden, Sargent and Stears (2013) has 20 chapters in the section on specific ideologies, although around half are not on 'isms', having a more topic or geographical character. Shorter treatments are likely to limit themselves to the big three of the 20th century, liberalism, conservatism, socialism, plus whatever extra ideologies are seen as key at the moment of writing – communism and fascism in the post-war decades, new movements such as feminism and environmentalism from the 1980s. Freeden (2003) considers the distinction between 'thick' and 'thin' ideologies. The classic 'thick' political ideologies are seen as having a depth which allows some view to be taken across most of the core questions facing societal action, and so governmental policies. These have typically been the motors behind successful and enduring political parties or political regimes. On the other hand, a whole range of movements of ideas, while in many cases developed and influential, are 'thin' in that they do not have the capacity to resolve key issues likely to need governmental and party decision: environmentalism is strong on green issues, but Green parties have struggled, at least in many countries, to present themselves as possessing equally coherent positions on, say, the economy or the schools system – or planning, though there a strong dose of environmental prioritisation can go some way to a confident position. The same applies to feminism and nationalism, ideological positions which pick up issues as crucial in many ways as those at the root of the Left and Right split characterising the differences of conservatism and socialism, but which do not map easily onto those Left versus Right clusterings. However, this thick and thin division is in itself open to challenge, as will be seen when we come to discuss the (apparently) thin ideologies.

In a way, the thick ideologies work as core ideologies, the thin ones as counter-ideologies, working against certain parts of the core ideologies, but in the end likely to, at best, be able to combine with a core and so have powerful impacts that way.

My own choice is to foreground the thick ideologies, Left versus Right, as I think that these still characterise core decision areas which are critical to planning. This matches what has been a century-long reality in British politics, a two-party system fighting around issues set by socialist and conservative ideologies. Clearly, the Left versus Right idea of an ideological spectrum does not catch all that is going on in the busy development of ideologies since the French Revolution introduced this dualism (Leach 2015, pp 10–13). Freeden (2003) is often keen to stress that there is a continuum of ideologies, with general types blending into each other, often in a very untidy way. But for a state activity like planning, the different emphases given by blocks of thinking that can still be called broadly Left and Right make a great deal of difference. The Right has more scepticism about collective, including state, activity, while most kinds of Left thinking, including those most behind the forming of planning in Britain, favour state and collective activity, under proper democratic control. These are profoundly important for any sort of planning, including that of places, town and country.

However, I do also think it important to note the significance of what might be called 'non-class' cleavages in society and in ideas, particularly around matters of gender and race and nationality. Partly because of personal capacities, these will tend to be more in the background in the great majority of the pages of this book. The ideologies associated with these cleavages have been variably influential in Britain, but they have made headway since the 1970s, affecting the way planners, and the political and social actors they interact with, pursue their roles. This is also so, and generally much more obviously, with the environmental movement. Green ideology clearly has affected UK planning politics a great deal, and it too has not mapped terribly neatly onto the thick ideological camps, though in Britain an alignment with Labour and Liberal forces has often been common.

We will see how each of the political parties draws on Freeden-type composites. It is important to realise that there is never a neat mapping of ideologies onto political parties. This may make much of the following analysis more messy and rough edged than might be desirable, but that is how things are. A further important point is that I do not include any separate treatment of liberalism. I have already explained what I take neoliberalism to mean, and its most significant impact is via the Conservative and Labour parties taking on some or all of its ideological force. Certainly the Liberal Democrat Party has also been affected by neoliberalism, particularly in a change of leadership in 2005 which opened the door in 2010 to collaboration in government with the Conservatives. Liberalism remains an important ideological force in Britain, but for the purposes of this book I omit a separate treatment of its relationship to planning.

Given its dominance since 2010, I start with the ideology of Conservatism, looking at some of its recent guises. I refrain from attempting to analyse in any detail the changes emerging during the transformations of the May- and Johnson-led governments. Clearly these are critical to the future, but it seems too soon to say much about them, given the evolving situation. The ideological turbulence seems too great, making changes quite unpredictable.

Some may see this two-ideology choice as too binary. Certainly there are more than two ideological currents, as will soon be clear, and certainly there is no simple and universal rule historically that Labour equals pro-planning and Conservative equals anti-planning. But, as the history will show, a binary understanding is a good starting guide to the political ideologies of planning in the last century. After this starting point, we can add, for example, that often neither Labour nor Conservative positions were green or feminist to any degree, nor liberal on race, and so on. But even then, a broad generalisation would be that Labour has promoted more progressive policies in these zones than Conservatives have. But equally both parties have supported, in a fundamental sense, the continuation of capitalism in Britain, even if Labour had doubts on this score in the mid-20th century.

Conservatism

We will see that Conservatism is not a simple and coherent whole – just as we would expect from Freeden's perspective. Ideologies give overall directions, and a range of options which can be drawn on, in 'pick and mix' style, and Conservatism has always exhibited these features. British Conservatism is often seen as a historically peculiar animal, able to change its spots in order to maintain power, adjusting more or less easily to each era, whether of aristocratic or industrial bourgeois dominance, mass democracy and the era of the welfare state, or the present period of driving back to the pre-democratic era (Crouch 2004). That may be so seen in the very long run, but the situation in the relevant recent period is perhaps rather simpler (Moran 2011, O'Sullivan 2013). Writers on Conservative ideology have struggled with the shifts in the ideological core of British Conservatism since the Thatcherite transformation of the party in the late 1970s. Evidence of this can be found in the academic output on the party in the period 2005–10, when discussions often seemed to accept at face value the transformed image which the Cameron leadership was presenting to the electorate (Lee and Beech 2009). However, such confusions were understandable, as this was a period when different ideas were being tried out, and it is only with the benefit of hindsight after the actual performance of the 2010–15 government that we can give a more confident account, backed by recent discussions (Heppell and Seawright 2012, Griffiths 2014, Page 2014, Leach 2015).

Moran (2011) argues that the myth of Conservatism as a 'non-ideological' party, though in fact never true, has been profoundly misguided since the 1970s. The Thatcher doctrines, which permeate the party, are based in major part on clear ideological positions, derived from a blend of Hayekian economy and US New Right sources. It is the neoliberal elements which have been most identified with the impacts on planning in Britain. But there have been different strains of neoliberal influence on British conservatism, which may be simply summarised as the 'full version' stemming most directly from Hayek, implying massive cut-backs to the state and abandonment of as much welfare and planning content in government as possible; and the modified version, evident in key Conservative figures like Michael Heseltine and Ken Clarke, who were not only strongly pro-EU, but supported the continuation of some, suitably reformed, parts of the welfare state, and considerable intervention in social and economic policy. It was the vying between these two strains since the 1970s which we can see, especially with hindsight, to have been the key struggle of Conservatism, one clearly won after 2010 by the more virulent Hayekian strand. The impacts on planning since 1979 have been profound, and we will encounter them throughout this book, in different extents and characters. But of course neoliberalism has not been the only ideological force impacting on British Conservatism in these decades.

O'Sullivan (2013) also identifies other elements of the New Right reformulation of Conservatism since the 1980s, including the organic idea stressing national sentiments, and an associationist strand supporting 'Big Society' ideas. As Pautz points out, examining the 2010 election manifesto, 'The three interdependent major principles were the "Big Society", "localism" and "compassionate Conservatism"' (2013, p 364). These have turned out to be decidedly secondary elements when Conservatives are running government, but almost certainly gave essential support before 2010 in broadening the appeal of the harder New Right positions. As Griffiths concluded, 'Cameron's account of progressive conservatism was part of a change of image, not substantively of policy or ideology' (2014, p 38). The dominant Thatcherite-based positions combine a deep suspicion of the state in relation to most economic and social issues, a commitment to strong 'law and order' (here a longer Tory history is certainly evident) and a profound nationalist and (in the 21st-century sense) global imperialist understanding of Britain's traditional status in the world (again a long-standing traditional element). McAnnulla (2012) stresses the strong persistence of anti-statism in Cameron's ideological pronouncements throughout his leadership of party and government, despite the softening of rhetoric in some secondary areas. All this is mixed with an equally established reflex link to the upper classes of British society, both old established and new wealthy. The nationalist and internationalist strands of this package imply a strongly Atlanticist position on economic and foreign policy. The Conservative support for the EU has been slowly whittled away since the 1970s, and after the 2016 referendum the Conservative Party conference gave a dramatic example of being able to turn its policy on the EU in the opposite direction, without, as far as could be seen, very great stress to the core ideology of the party. In other words, the party drew on different parts of Conservatism, in a way that made the enormous volte face for most Conservative MPs, and probably most party members, more or less digestible.

So, this is indeed a classically composite ideology, but, as Freeden implies we should expect, one with some priorities which appear very deep seated. The commitment to cut back the state, particularly the welfare state, is one such ideological commonality probably held now by nearly all active Conservatives, and this is linked to pressing deregulation, in favour of private business forces. Values espoused by other British parties (except the UK Independence Party – UKIP – which had quite similar ideological positions to the current leading edge of British Conservatism – compare their 2015 manifesto with Conservative government practice), are in contrast outliers in Conservative ideology, particularly any concern with social equity or environmental sustainability. When Conservatives have said they are concerned environmentally, or green, it has become clear that this has meant the traditional support for a traditional conception of the English landscape, built around some farming interests, protecting key commuter belts where Conservative political strongholds are based, and, normally, interest in avoiding change in the relevant countrysides. Another core element of Conservative ideology, brought out by O'Sullivan's (2013) survey, is the profound scepticism about democracy among key thinkers inspiring the Conservatives, particularly Hayek. This fits logically with their attachment to social and economic elites.

The above analysis depends on sources dating to before the explosive changes being generated within Conservatism by Brexit and then the massive election victory of the Johnson-led government in December 2019. Some analysts are arguing that the presence of significant numbers of Conservative MPs in Midlands and Northern 'left behind' urban areas may generate a shift in government policy, possibly back towards the interventionist economic centre. Reflections on the evolution of global Far Right politics lead to questions about which way the post-2019 Conservatism will evolve: 'Where does Britain's Conservative Party stop and the United Kingdom Independence Party (UKIP) or Brexit Party begin?' (Mudde 2019, p 23). Mudde identifies three features of the current Far Right landscape internationally: nativism, authoritarianism and populism (the latter defined as a claim to be against the entrenched elites). There are certainly elements of this mix in current UK Conservatism, but the success in taking over the established right-wing party (as in the US) is likely to make the mixture different in the UK case, with any claim to be against established British elites likely to look thin rather quickly.

It is simply too early to comment further on this at the time of writing, in the midst of the 2020 COVID-19 pandemic as well, although the strongly nationalist and often xenophobic drive behind Brexit is hardly likely to disappear and will colour the new Conservative blend. At any rate, some classic tensions will surely persist within the British Conservatism composite.

Some of these tensions surfaced during the 2010–15 government, as they did during the Thatcher governments, and as they are likely to do again in the post-2019 government. Countryside protection and deregulation are not easy to work together in practice. Stripping back the state has to be balanced against going too far against certain interests, such as support for big farming, or the need to protect landowners with coastal property from erosion, or in low-lying areas from flooding. All this, though testing for politicians, is negotiable. Business supported, by and large, staying in the EU, but with that issue resolved, it will surely remain with its traditional support for the Conservative Party and press its normal agendas. Deregulation will apply where critical Conservative interests are not infringed – it is a core part of the ideology. But the package does have multiple strands, is subject to continual struggle by the key actors present in each policy field, and so there is not necessarily a completely clear position deriving from the ideology as a whole for any particular field.

Socialism and Labour

Although textbooks have traditionally presented socialism as a less slippery object than conservatism or even liberalism, it is true that in the case of British socialism it has covered a multitude of positions. Inheritors of the socialist tradition have a very wide repertoire on which to draw, and hence enormous scope for disagreement. In Britain, those forms have been corralled into the evolving institutional tendencies of the Labour Party since its formation in 1906. This is not to say that socialism does not have some independent existence in terms of ideas in Britain, to varying extents in different periods. But, in terms of political impact, it has been almost exclusively the Labour Party which has promoted more or less socialist policies across the spectrum of the activities of government, centrally and locally. Planning in the shapes it has taken since the 1940s has depended greatly on the creative pushes of Labour politics, for good or ill, alongside the normally constraining Conservative government policies. So, above all, we need to look here at this Labour version of socialism.

However, this does not necessarily make pinning down the ideological essence of Labourism any easier. Political scientists have emphasised the multifaceted nature of socialism, with some core positions but then big variants in almost any direction. Principles include sympathy for classic values of community, equality and fraternity, with an awareness of class position and the importance of supporting people in the most need. Key markers are views on the role of the state and the attitude to more or less constrained capitalist economies. The generally greater support for collective action, often but not always with a large state component, does point to interventionist actions, and that has formed a foundation for the big steps in setting up the planning system in the 1940s, and continuing actions under Labour governments since that time, under any number of headings – new towns, national parks, council house building, urban renewal schemes, collaborative urban regeneration, regional and strategic planning, using public landownership and so on. While other parties (mainly the Conservative Party) have certainly at times promoted actively programmes in all these areas, they have rarely been that active in starting new interventionist drives in these fields. Even in areas like historic conservation it was the activity of the Labour government in the 1960s which set the main outlines of the field since then.

Socialism and Labourism before the 1990s

Planning as it has operated in the UK since the 1940s has been in large part the result of ideological drives from socialism. This is an unpalatable statement for those in the Labour Party who, for some decades, have been trying to distance themselves from the socialist tradition. It is also unpalatable for many planners, whether active in practice or in academia, who wish to present the activity and profession as non-political, or at least non-ideological. We can trace this socialism–Labour–planning link through examining a spectrum of policy fields important to planning.

Property and the state

One core part of planning relates to the limitation of property rights. Socialist ideology has been much more ready to limit the rights of owners to do what they like with their property than Conservative and classical liberal ideological positions. The Planning Act 1947 had at its foundation the so-called 'nationalisation' of property rights, in that from the date of the Act's coming into effect owners could no longer expect to build or develop their land without planning permission, unless such development fell within certain constrained 'permitted development' rights. Since 1947 this principle has broadly endured, and this endurance is critical to such impact as any planning can expect to have. As one can see in the long and the recent history, Conservative governments have done what they can to reduce the impact of this foundational feature, in particular by very early on cutting back strongly the betterment and taxation elements associated with the bringing of development under public decision making, and then by 'liberalising' the planning regime in various ways, strikingly so in the 2010–15 government reforms. While in their detail these swaying struggles have been conditioned in part by momentary political circumstances, they are essentially ideological battles about the nature of state action.

Land

The gains arising from development were taxed at first at high rates, normally taking all the gain for public use, but the gain was progressively returned to developers by Conservative governments. Each Labour government since then has attempted to reinstate some kind of regime to secure community benefit from development gain, but the first two efforts (via the Land Commission and the Community Land Act 1975) were rapidly abolished by the succeeding Conservative governments, while the New Labour governments struggled to find any resolution to the land question. In the end they fell back on continuing use of the planning obligations approach used since the 1980s (locally negotiated deals between authorities and developers) and a watered-down system, the Community Infrastructure Levy, which has since struggled to have any useful effect. At the time of writing the theme of land value taxation is again a popular one for reform proposals. As in the New Labour years, the various schemes are presented as if they are ideologically innocuous, but hard-headed and ideologically attuned politicians will no doubt look at them as in the past and resist the temptation to take on this ideologically intense area. Certainly, recent Conservative governments have shown no interest in such zones of reform. Some planning may be acceptable to them, but only if within the deepest commitment to private property, in land, buildings and infrastructure systems.

Housing

A socialist approach to housing was crafted during the early 20th century in the shape of housing built by local councils. For a while this became acceptable across parties. The long-term cost of council housing was carried by council tenants, with well-managed housing revenue accounts always able to provide housing at well below market rents. However, though council housing was, taken as a whole, a success story for those living in the houses, it constituted an ideological threat that Thatcherite Conservatism was not prepared to accept. Since 1979 the sale of a large part of the council housing stock, at very large discounts in relation to market values, and the transfer of most of the remaining stock to housing associations, now largely commercially driven, removed the financial basis of municipal housing.

Other elements of planning for housing were not so obviously ideologically coloured. Councils of all political parties had to negotiate with private developers to meet local demand or need. But this distinction, whether the council should take into account social need, or simply allow market-led building models, did raise large distributional questions. Even after 1979, Labour councils were more likely to press for some forms of social housing, using the scope for planning obligations, or exploiting their remaining land stocks (built up in the previous decades, little added to after 1979) to lever social housing gain. In general, Labour governments spent more on public housing and urban policy and regeneration fields, and dedicated more time to worrying about the root causes of poverty, riots and similar expressions of societal stress. This came from the value base of Labourism as much as from the practical need to take notice of the urban areas where Labour support was concentrated.

Transport

Again, there was a tried and tested approach to transport which fitted a socialist approach to planning new towns or developing existing ones: promoting forms of public transport – rail, tram and bus systems. Again as well, this did not have to be seen as intrinsically socialist, but as just part of the normal provision of urban infrastructure, pursued by Liberal or Conservative councils in the early 20th century probably as much as by Labour authorities. Increasingly though, after the Second World War, Conservatives preferred private forms of provision, with massive promotion of car and lorry transport, and a tendency to run down tram, rail and bus forms. Until after 1979, this distinction was far from black and white. There were considerable areas of convergence of Labour and Conservative policies in government, on interurban roads and on airport and port expansion, for example.

After 1979 socialist-led councils pressed strongly for cheap fares and for investment in public transport (the Tyne and Wear metro, or the free or cheap fares schemes in London and South Yorkshire are examples from the early 1980s). At the same time the Conservative response was to privatise and deregulate bus services, eventually to privatise the rail system (as well as most ports and airports), and to build roads, but not to invest in public transport. There were exceptions, such as

Margaret Thatcher's support for the Channel Tunnel (though only if it was built with private finance).

There were significant changes *within* government periods, notably the retreat from large-scale road building under the Major governments, and the abandonment of a more radical attempt to change travel behaviour under the Blair government, after 2000. To some extent these were generated by shifts within the ideological coalitions making up the two big parties. But a range of political pressures 'beyond ideology' were equally or more important in both shifts, including the (strongly green influenced) direct action movements against road and airport expansion of the 1990s, and the fuel tax protests of 2000. So, as always, it is not a matter of arguing that only ideology matters, in this any more than in other fields.

Transport planning has always been understood as a critically important lever in managing development, whether in existing towns and cities or in building new settlements. So, another core part of the planner's tool box is based in part on a struggle between an approach flowing from socialist ideology and one originating in neoliberal (small state) ideology. The pretence that transport planning is non-political and non-ideological may have been useful, but is not based on a clear look at the deep differences between the approaches to transport taken by the two main parties, over the post-war period.

Integrated planning

One more element of socialist ideology's impacts will be mentioned here. This is the drive for an integrated approach to planning places. This may sound quite innocuous, something which any sensible person might be able to support, when considering the complexities of making human settlements work well. This does not seem on the face of it to be something deeply affected by ideology. However, the experience of planning since 1979 has revealed that the previous approaches to planning in this way, based on models of looking forward into the future and then mobilising societal resources to achieve set goals, were in fact strongly coloured by socialist thinking. This was what has made them often so objectionable to all recent Conservative governments. Market-led planning is not easily made compatible with integrated planning, if at all. This has been the evidence of several decades of planners trying to square the circle of a system led by private investment, with a limited planning toolbox to pull the disparate actors together. Under the 2010–15 government the tension was, somewhat unusually, openly admitted, with the very idea of planning seen as unhelpful.

One minister lauded the importance of chaos in the place of planning. The promotion of neighbourhood planning springs in part from the same source, with the idea that initiative from the bottom up, with little coordination, will be superior.

From the 1940s to the 1970s, it was very generally accepted that it made sense to think about the future of a city or county or, at times, larger regions together. Since the 1980s this has been much less the case, with 'silo' type planning much more common, whether promoted by government ministries (investment in transport, or energy, or science, or universities) or by local authorities (under more pressure to present a joined-up picture, but often now deprived of the resources and institutional supports to achieve the joining up). The abolition of strategic and regional planning and governance institutions in 2010 was as clear a rejection of the value of integrated planning as one could expect to see.

Planners, and planning academics, may often not be aware that in this key process dimension they are immersed in ideological struggles between the two primary British political traditions. Planning theory of recent decades has used the language of collaborative and communicative planning, or institutionalism, or discourse theory, to try to negotiate the minefields of 'the best way to plan places', in part because planning theorists, as well as most planning practitioners, prefer to depoliticise discussion of planning alternatives, which they see as only feasible if ideology is kept firmly out of the picture. Several of these approaches fitted in quite well with the drive to remove as much of the socialist language and core values from planning and managing cities as possible, and so had a considerable consistency with the emerging tendencies of New Labour. This is of course not to say that planning theorists have some direct responsibility for New Labour's failures (or achievements), but it is important to note when academic ideas and government drives reflect and reinforce each other. This happens in planning, as in other fields.

New Labour

All commentators agree that the takeover of the party leadership by Tony Blair in 1994 marked a big shift in the ideological direction of the party, even if several elements of the move towards the centre ground of politics had been evident since at least 1987. This change is generally called New Labour, the phrasing promoted by Blair and other influential leaders. It was given some intellectual backing by figures like Tony Giddens, labelling this shift as something international and with the name 'the Third Way' (Giddens 1998). The fairly strongly socialist approach of the 1980s, itself representing overall a shift to the Left in relation to the 1970s, disappeared from the majority discourse of the party and, after 1997, from the government. Minority support for socialist positions remained, particularly in the person of John Prescott, deputy prime minister to Blair, but became increasingly sidelined. An early and perceptive treatment of New Labour by Freeden (1999) stressed how classic an ideological operation was underway, part of a surge of ideological experimentation by the New Labour leadership and their thinkers. This was fashioning a typical ideological amalgam, using parts from all the classic traditions, but above all, in his view, from liberalism and conservatism, forming an 'ideology reassembled' (Freeden 1999, p 48).

There was at the time and has been since a great deal of analysis of the intricacies of Labour political battles during the 1994–2010 period, in part centring on the disagreements between Blair and Gordon Brown, the powerful chancellor of the exchequer till 2007, who then took over for three years as prime minister. Some took the view that Brown had a more interventionist approach than Blair. However, for present purposes it is not necessary to enter these labyrinthine discussions. It is the net result of the government positions that matters here, made up of varying ideological currents certainly, but playing out in some reasonably consistent compromise policy stances, taking the period from 1997 to 2010 as a whole. What is most important for a consideration of planning is that there is an overall New Labour character to the dominant stances.

The period of Labour opposition from 2010 to 2015 was one of continuous heart searching within the party as to how far new directions should be taken, abandoning some elements of the now widely established positions of New Labour, whether to socialist programmes or in some other ways. The leadership of Ed Miliband, broadly a supporter before 2010 of Gordon Brown, smoothed over these debates to a large extent. Miliband did attempt to shift some of the language, in particular emphasising the commitment to equality more than Blair and Brown had done. By the time of the 2015 election manifesto, these shifts were noticeable, with slightly more interventionist positions on economic issues, but with no radical break from the New Labour direction.

After New Labour?

The election of Jeremy Corbyn in 2015 as the new Labour leader changed the nature of the internal party battles. At least the higher parts of the leadership adopted openly socialist positions on a number of issues, with the 2017 and 2019 general election manifestos reflecting these choices in several areas. One was the commitment to gradual renationalisation of the utilities sectors privatised in the 1980s and 1990s, primarily rail, energy and water. However, the emphasis was on gradualism. In other ways these manifestos were fairly moderate, certainly compared with the socialist positions of, say, the 1974 Labour government, which proposed to take shares in many of the largest industrial companies. The period since 2015 has seen continuous struggles over the direction of Labour, not only because of the extreme difficulty faced by the leading opposition party after the EU referendum of 2016, but because most of the parliamentary party could be characterised as still largely New Labour in its ideological positions, as against the more socialist ideas of much of the new party membership. The replacement of Corbyn by Keir Starmer as leader in April 2020 is likely to change the balance back to more centrist positions – however that is conceived. But the new composite Labourism which will emerge in the early 2020s is unlikely to be any kind of exact reproduction of New Labour positions.

The other ideologies

It may seem to play down the importance of all other ideological currents to refer to them as simply the other ideologies. However, this relates to difficulties in dealing with ideologies which are not the classic heavyweight types, of which conservatism and socialism are examples. It has been noticeable that every few years Michael Freeden writes another article trying to pin down the nature of a particular ideas set or movement (New Labour, nationalism, populism), in which ways they are ideologies (thick, thin or otherwise), reflecting not only these definitional issues, but the extent to which ideologies, classic or otherwise, can usefully be thought of separately.

Here I suggest that it will help to explore the way in which the other ideologies knit into the major, more extensive ideologies. These can then be seen to be acting in the real world as composites, not only within one ideological family as Freeden stresses, but across the spectrum of ideas sets as a whole. It will be seen in each of the three cases dealt with here that there is a drive to heighten the significance of the ideology, and that this may be done by generating a deep historical analysis of the relationship between the big families, the more specific ideologies, and real historical change. A further feature important for planning is the way in which localities or regions will have their own composites, related to an extent to local and regional cultures. There is not space in this book to do real justice to this, but some references to this will appear, and this could be a valuable theme for future research.

Environmentalism or green ideology

Since its emergence in the 1960s green thinking has made a strong claim to form an ideology, rather than just a general perspective on the importance of a better relationship with the natural world. This gradually led to political formations, in Green parties, which were able to get governing positions from local to national levels in countries with proportional representation systems. The core of the ideology remains the very high priority given to humanity's need to remake its way of living on the planet, to achieve more harmony with the natural world. This has included support for reducing pollution from all kinds of production and consumption activities and, since the 1990s, pressing for an effective response to climate change and transitioning to a low carbon society, within each country and globally. Parties fighting for electoral success have naturally also policies across the full range of issues. Most Green parties are positioned on the liberal and Left side of the political spectrum, but this varies considerably between countries and periods. In Britain the proportional representation systems in Scotland, Wales and London have helped the Green Party to have a sometimes significant presence in those polities. At UK level and in English local government their success and impact has been much less, and this has been a factor in reducing the maturing of policy positions and wide knowledge of these positions.

In green thinking, there is a major strand that challenges the superior reach of the classic ideologies. This would argue that the whole of western (and now global) civilisation is based on a particular highly exploitative form of use of the planet, common to the new Anthropocene era, and especially founded on high carbon systems of industrialisation. A more recent critique argues that the Anthropocene, while a helpful term, is less important for the understanding of planetary development than the Capitalocene, which traces the threat to the planet from the beginning of intensive capitalism in the late 15th century (Moore 2017, 2018). These analyses can be seen as introducing critical new terms into the debate on the present situation. Those who support the analyses of the Anthropocene, and even more so the Capitalocene, would say that these cannot be treated as sideline additions to, say, socialism or liberalism, but have to become a central marker of these ideological worldviews, if they are to have any relevance to steering future politics. No doubt different ideological currents have gone some way to taking this on board. Ecosocialism is one which can claim to have developed a full and quite coherent ideological position (Pepper 1993, Lowy 2015). Believers in these ideological composites may well feel that their preferred model is one which can apply well to planning thinking as a whole. It is probable that several such formulas have had influence in recent decades, from the short-lived promotion by Margaret Thatcher of the inheritance metaphor for environmental guardianship in 1989, to the engagement of the Labour Party with ecosocialism when in opposition in the 1980s and 1990s, and in its municipal socialist ambitions when running councils such as the Greater London Council (GLC) in the 1980s.

The situation for green thinking in Britain and the impact on planning is somewhat contradictory. On the one hand, the influence on the mainstream political parties has been considerable, with all parties, if to differing extents in different periods, picking up at the least 'light green' positions on issues like biodiversity, transport and energy. These have influenced the making of planning policy at national level, keeping, for example, the rhetoric of 'sustainability' present in national guidance, even if the reality of the effect on planning is often much less. However, most of the mainstream parties have maintained other priorities at most times, above all holding that economic growth, however conceived, is more important than trying to meet green goals, particularly a serious transition to a low carbon and low impact society. This does tend to drive the core of planning efforts to stop at light green efforts, unable to press for more fundamentally transforming or transitioning movement.

This double-sided character can be the fate, for good or ill, of ideologies which do not have full 'thickness' and which, because also of their situation (highly problematic in the UK electoral system), do not have any real power at national level. They can be influential by affecting the programmes of the core parties, but the risk of policy directions only being rhetorically or superficially supported is high. Nevertheless, the impact on planning has probably been greater than this situation might be expected to have generated. There are at least three reasons for this. One is that green ideology may have a particularly good fit with the structures of feeling and everyday activities in planning. Planning has always had a significant environmental strand, particularly in relation to countryside protection, and also holistic thinking about ways of living (the utopian strand in planning's formation in Britain). So, it was perhaps natural that the ministry containing planning should be named the Department of the Environment in 1970, and that this ministry produced the first UK environmental strategy in 1990, *This Common Inheritance*, with a strong read across to planning policy making in the next two decades.

A second reason may be more a matter of the culture surrounding planning, which has meant that both planning academia and planning practice have had a broadly greenish tone ever since the emergence of green movements in the 1970s. This may follow on from the first factor, but adds to it from below, in giving many of the leading activists in planning practice and in influential NGOs a strong set of ideas: the agency of these individuals may have mattered a lot in planning, in a way that has perhaps not been so evident in many other professions.

A third reason, again in part connected, lies in the difficult situation in which British planning has found itself since the 1980s. Both Conservatism and New Labour had at least strong reservations about the legitimacy of planning in these decades. It was natural for planning to look for a possibly more acceptable set of ideas to justify its existence when the implicitly socialist basis I described earlier came under sustained attack. Green ideology, on the other hand, was a rising force from the 1970s, with even an apparently far from green politician like Margaret Thatcher feeling obliged to accept some of the language of the ideology at the end of her period as prime minister. The Major, Blair and Brown governments all put some stress on planning's green credentials, so one can argue that the approach had beneficial effects for planning. The language of sustainability was very commonly used from around 1990 to 2010.

Feminism

Even more so than environmentalism, the women's movement since the 1960s has had one overriding priority, to remove the exploitation of women in its myriad forms, and promote more well-being across society, for men as well as for women, by this means. Feminism, as the varied and far from united set of ideas animating women's movements, is therefore best treated as a thin ideology. Clearly, its core agenda has implications across every sphere of human life, but it is not easy to add this up into a comprehensive ideological position and programme. With occasional exceptions, feminism has not expressed itself by forming separate political parties, and its influence has therefore been even more a matter of influencing the mainstream parties and the wider climate of thinking and action.

As argued earlier for green thinking, it should be remembered though that there are thinkers who do not accept that feminism is a thin ideology. Radicals in both camps would argue that the ideas presented by these movements so overturn accepted approaches of classic ideologies that they at least point to the need for completely fresh ideological wholes, even if not necessarily yet forming such wholes. In particular, some feminists (perhaps most of all some radical feminists) claim that if the full weight of feminist thinking is accepted, everything else changes, literally rewriting all other ideological frameworks. Inevitably, decisions on what is 'thick' or 'thin' in the ideological categorisation business are partly ideological.

Feminism's influence within planning can be argued to have been significant, as it has been in society as a whole. An example of an area where feminist thinking has been more visible has been in urban design, including the design of the public realm, paralleling to a degree the strong influence of feminism in architecture. There has also been stress on areas traditionally most associated with women's work, such as retailing and caring for young and old. Some element of change has been gradually evident in the previously very male-dominated field of transport planning, again in part associated with the micro design of streets and public spaces. Such progress as there has been stems in part from the very extensive publications work and campaigning since the landmark reports of the GLC in the early 1980s. This work, mainly by women planners and those in related areas, has presented the needs in each zone of planning work. Particularly in many London borough plans, women-friendly policies have been present for many years, following to some extent the model policies laid out by GLC publications in the early 1980s. This suggests that, in some aspects, the planning system can be partially shifted to respond to gender issues. However, there was resistance from governments (via the Planning Inspectorate), which often did not allow 'women's policies' to stay in statutory plans, because they were seen to be 'not land use matters'.

At any rate, the many areas where progress has been very limited have been quite visible to the planning academics and practising planners working from a feminist perspective (whether explicitly or implicitly), as presented, for example, by Greed (2000) and Greed and Johnson (2014). Greed and others emphasise the failure to implement gender-friendly policies across planning, attributing this in part to the failure of governments to prepare wide-ranging guidance in this area. The guidance which did exist was swept away with the 2012 publication of the National Planning Policy Framework (NPPF), which was silent about gender issues, though a very sympathetic reading might find some trace in the short section on healthy and safe communities. A more radical explanation of the failures for feminism to establish strong gender-attuned policies and practices in planning might find the answer in the continuing domination of historically embedded patriarchal understandings across dominant ideological frameworks, despite apparent rhetorical shifts.

Given the almost universal relevance of feminist thinking, it can also be argued that the failures mimic and are bound up with the fields of wider planning and societal failure in housing, the provision of good jobs in conditions in which parents can participate comfortably, and the maintainance of good services to support the kinds of work that most women do more than men. European countries with stronger Green parties have experienced greater progress in many of these areas, because feminist influence in these parties has been generally strong. This is not a route available in Britain, except to some extent in Scotland and Wales. Certainly, feminism is, like environmentalism, a zone where international experience can be especially valuable. A survey such as that on 'Fair shared cities' (Sanchez de Madariaga and Roberts 2013) has impressive accounts of the work to promote women-friendly planning in the Netherlands and Austria, to place alongside UK experience.

Nationalism, racism and multiculturalism

I put under one heading these rather distinct sets of ideas, as they overlap to some degree in terms of their influence on planning. In standard political science books on ideology, each may have a chapter to itself. All can make claims to be ideologies, if of the thin variety and so needing to attach themselves to one of the core ideologies in order to be functional, under normal conditions. This is, again, disputed. Freeden (1998) considered whether nationalism should count as a distinct ideology and, though not coming to a firm conclusion, gave a sympathetic hearing to the idea that nationality and nationalism have more affinity with kinship or religion than with the classic 'isms', and so it might be best to see nationalism as a component of other existing ideologies, not even as a thin ideology.

Nationalism, in its various forms (one being racism-based nationalism), has had powerful effects on states and politics for at least a couple of centuries. Multiculturalism, though only badged that way since the 1970s, has been present for perhaps as long, and as an internationalist and tolerant approach can also be said to have been influential on state policy, if less dramatically and forcefully than nationalism. This is not the place to enter definitional discussions on these, any more than on the other lesser ideologies. Here the purpose is simply to accept that these bunchings of ideas exist, sometimes in quite coherent terms, often just lying powerfully under everyday politics.

Their links with planning have generally not been explored that much, though a few scholars have been persisting in examining the relationship of racism and planning (see Beebeejaun 2004 and 2012 for relevant commentaries). Above all, Huw Thomas (2000, 2008) and Richard Gale and Thomas (2018) have continued to point out the importance of what is called the racialisation of public and governmental activities, particularly applying this to the situation of planning. Thomas and Gale's question in recent years has been: why has the push to raise the importance of considering race and ethnicity issues, which began with a landmark Commission for Racial Equality/Royal Town Planning Institute (RTPI) report in 1983, made so little progress? The surveys they and others have made at intervals have given a picture of planners taking some apparent interest in the issue, but then failing to incorporate race equality measures within nearly all practice, despite occasional bouts of central government encouragement (such as after the 1999 MacPherson Report identified institutionalised racism in the police). The answer given draws on Critical Race Theory (CRT), a set of ideas developed in the US. CRT argues that 'a deep-veined racial ideology ... runs through the very foundations of US society and economic and institutional life (Gale and Thomas 2018, p 467). This has been extended to suggest that 'race is historically foundational to the edifice of the modern European and North American nation-state' (p 467). Gale and Thomas then suggest that planning has simply continued to operate on the basis of enduring professional presuppositions, which themselves rest silently on such deep ideological foundations. 'Planners are more likely to understand the significance of racialization within planning itself if the embeddedness of planning within wider racialized structures is grasped' (p 471). Such grasping would be, as they say, a long-term political project, but it would be helpful, they consider, to place planning within a wider political struggle for radical social change. We might think of this as part of and similar in some ways to the centuries-long struggles for democracy in Europe. They also stress the need to link up the intersecting force of other structural inequalities, such as class, gender and race. In other words, rather as in the cases of green thinking and feminism, the drive here has been to go deeper into structurally embedded historical forces. The Grenfell Tower fire in London in 2017 generated stronger thinking and activism among many academics, which highlighted the links between the roles of class and racialising politics in North Kensington and the planning and housing policies affecting the area over many decades (Bulley, Edkins and El-Enany 2019).

There are clearly implications for the ideological composites I have been referring to, in that it would be important to go beyond thinking of multiculturalism or racism or internationalism on their own, to make links to the big ideological programmes contained in the classic ideologies, about (genuine) democracy, equality and liberty. Understanding change internationally would in any case still be key to making progress, as the big struggles over immigration to Britain from the EU and the rest of the world have made very clear.

This links on to the (possible) ideology of nationalism, whose role has been most noticeable in two ways since the early 2000s in the UK. One is in the boost that Scottish and Welsh nationalism have given to new governing forms, which has brought with it the opportunity to experiment with new approaches to planning within Wales and Scotland. While the struggles within both countries, and above all Scotland, are in part tied up with the issue of independence from the UK, the focus for planning has simply been on the scope to do things differently at a sufficiently strategic scale, with a good number of the levers of statehood. Examples have included the promotion of national planning frameworks in all parts of the UK except England, and a bigger emphasis on long-term sustainability in both Wales and Scotland. The stances of the devolved governments towards local government have also been significantly less hostile in Scotland and Wales, taking the period since 2000 as a whole.

The second channel of nationalism's influence has been in the rising force since the early 2000s of a right-wing and often xenophobic form of English nationalism, which became a motor behind the growth of UKIP. This is turn led to the shifting of the Conservative Party, most dramatically after the EU referendum of 2016. There has as yet been no useful study of the impact of UKIP's existence on local planning. At most there have been references to the influence within some local authorities where UKIP councillors held power, or at least positions with impact. The suggestion was that this led to an extreme form of rejection of all development in these areas, beyond even the often anti-development stance of many Conservative-run councils (*Planning* magazine 22 April 2016). However, the bigger-picture effect of such a right-wing movement is no doubt potentially much more important than such local impacts. It remains to be seen what the big election victory of the Johnson government in December 2019 will do in potentially incorporating even more nationalist elements within Conservatism, as UKIP activists feed into the redirected party.

This discussion has often been blended with one on 'populism'. It can be argued that the kinds of ideological amalgams represented by parties like UKIP or like the Trump US presidency represent a different phenomenon, a kind of nativist, normally right-wing idea of 'the people' (Muller 2016, Sager 2020). Freeden surveyed the term and its evolution, considering that 'it is emaciatedly thin rather than thin-centred' (Freeden 2017, p 3) and that it hardly bothered, often, to join with other ideologies to form a more coherent whole. Eatwell and Goodwin (2018) provide a much stronger defence of the importance of what they call 'national populism'. While their book is more about national populism as a kind of politics or a movement than as an ideology, they are effectively arguing that something with deep roots going back several decades (perhaps to the 1970s) has now forced its way onto the political stage, and that this will be durable, and that there is some ideological coherence, despite the international and temporal variety. Equally, Crouch (2018) finds that populism can be identified as much of the vehicle for the advance of post-democracy. However, his treatment also does not present populism as some kind of consistent ideology, but much more as a way of doing politics, based very much on nation rather than class. On balance, I am happy to omit discussion of populism, which can be a confusing rather than illuminating term, even though it is clear that the kinds of movements and parties it is used to describe could have big impacts on planning's evolution, as Sager (2020) argues.

One evident issue is how anti-immigrant state policies work out at local and national (UK) levels. The risk is that the racialisation identified by Thomas as a consistent strand in state reaction to non-white people in Britain since the 1950s will become embedded in new governing formulas. The sharp rise in hate crimes since the 2016 referendum, due to the imagined greater acceptability of attacking immigrants or those perceived as alien, is one marker of the way that actions are affected by attitude change. How far this is playing into planning in micro or macro terms is as yet unknown.

Conclusion

Turning to the joint operation of these ideologies, we can consider composites at the national level, changing over time, and in localities. So, one locality may combine socialist positions on equality and communal support with racist and patriarchal ideological standpoints, while another, perhaps because of the long-term presence of large immigrant populations, may form a polity where anti-racist views are essential for normal political success and convivial living – such as in cities like Birmingham or Leicester or, in different ways, London. It has doubtless been impossible for the three mayors of London since 2000 to adopt strongly racist or anti-feminist policies, whatever their personal political positions, given the demographic and political make-up of London. On other policy areas, such as the economy, they have probably had more leeway, although it is clear that the first mayor, Ken Livingstone, felt unable to adopt any more socialist economic positions. However, this may have been more the result of having to deal with a New Labour national government, than from local political pressures.

From a wider perspective, we could identify different eras of ideology-influenced planning, picking out especially the importance of key figures, and making clear their ideological backgrounds. An example I am familiar with would be Pasqual Maragall, mayor of Barcelona from 1982 to 1995. He had a background of struggle against Franco's dictatorship in far Left socialist groups, studied law and political economy and led a group of councillors imbued with years of practice in community and trade union struggles. So, he came to the mayoralty equipped to understand the circumstances of land markets, popular mobilisation and state roles from a particular ideological position, which chimed with the wider political landscape of forces in Spain at that time (Claret 2017).

In this way, we can analyse ideological and political situations, which then guide planning possibilities. A further issue in this discussion of the pulls within ideological composites is how far the big drives within the classic ideologies are constraining what is happening within the other ideologies. This is the issue of the relative autonomy of, say, gender issues within neoliberalising capitalism. Is it inevitable that the kind of neoliberalising and generally right-wing capitalist drives since 1980 will have constrained moving forward in the directions hoped for by green, feminist and anti-racist ideologies? Or is it best to see this conditioned, as CRT and some kinds of green and feminist analysis do, by the deep structures within the dominant ways of thinking, common to some degree to all the dominant ideologies, at least in practice? Thus patriarchy, racialised approaches and high resource exploitation modes can be seen as embedded in the reality of conservative, liberal and socialist ideologies, despite claims to the contrary which each may contain.

No doubt no clear answer can be given to how the pressures between the big and lesser ideologies play out. Certainly, right-wing political drives have been vigorously incorporating attacks on all three of these 'other ideologies'. It is now a standard part of current far

Right movements in Europe and elsewhere (US, Brazil) to attack all progress made by the women's movement, to promote openly racist agendas and to rebut claims of humanly induced climate change and fundamentally oppose the values of green movements. This is a clear sign that the tectonic plates of the various ideological composites have been moving in a big way since the 1970s, and at the time of writing in far from desirable directions. Even the limited progress reported in recent decades by those planning academics supporting feminist, anti-racist and green movements may well be under strong attack if these trends continue.

4

Planning history, planning reform and politics and ideology

This chapter starts with a brief history of the relationship between the long-term transformations of planning and politics and ideology. This is followed by an equally brief examination of the top-steering of planning in one case example, the 2010–15 government. At this very important national level, we can get some sense of how ideological and political dimensions worked together.

UK planning history and ideology

Historians have taken a strong interest recently in the role of ideas and of ideologies (Blackburn 2017). Since at least the 1990s historians of Britain in particular have explored more complex accounts of the role of ideas, especially for the 20th century. Such accounts benefit from looking at ideologies and their mixes and ebbs and flows more carefully than in the past, and with less stress on unmediated 'material' forces. Blackburn's survey in fact takes its cue from an article by Freeden (1990) on the absence of serious consideration of ideology by historians. It cannot be said that planning history has always been very aware of ideological elements in what it is studying, but these have been present to a degree. What follows is a very preliminary overview.

We can divide the history of planning for present purposes into three large blocks, one very briefly on the pre formal planning period, one on the movement to the 1947 Act system and the third covering the life of that system and its many ups and downs. The reader must use a real planning history book (such as Ward 2004) to get more than the very bare frame presented here. A further point which is played down here is the significant element of international learning and borrowing, throughout the periods, meaning that the play between ideology and planning thinking should really have this international dimension built in as well.

Before 1914

The 'prehistory' of planning in the 19th century saw decisions on land and development oscillating around the relative sanctity of property rights and the struggles within corporations and central government over how far those rights might be 'infringed' by one kind of public intervention or another. Put like that, the integral role of ideology in the broad development of these discussions and the political struggles drawing on them is clear enough. Laissez-faire in economic and social terms was justified in this period by classical liberalism, which resisted all extensions of state power, at whatever level, until the pressure for such extensions became irresistible. Urban issues at the core of what was later called planning were then usually addressed in terms of sanitary reform, health and sometimes housing, but they depended essentially on large numbers of property decisions. Gradually, the right of private owners to do exactly what they wanted was cut back. This was partly done by the transformation of ideological emphases, in which liberalism came to accept that, particularly given the widening electoral franchise, raising the living standards of urban majorities was a goal of value, alongside the defence of property. This affected most the Liberal Party in Victorian Britain, but Conservatism moved at times in this direction, drawing on certain traditions of paternalism, so that prime ministers like Robert Peel and Benjamin Disraeli undertook reforms in more or less the same directions as the Liberal governments. The result was the gradual emergence of an undergrowth of regulatory systems, via building control regulations, municipal 'gas and water' socialism in the big urban authorities and, ultimately, the first Housing and Planning Act in 1909.

Towards the 1947 planning system

Standard histories of planning recount the slow building up of planning laws nationally and planning practice locally, which over the decades from around 1900 up to 1945 formed a portfolio of experience and an agenda of calls for an improved national framework for planning. From the 1890s there emerged the 'famous names' of British planning, Ebenezer Howard, Patrick Geddes, Raymond Unwin and Patrick Abercrombie, all of whom could be characterised as somewhere in the radical and liberal camp politically, although Howard had elements of a utopian socialist past. We can contrast this, looking forward to the post-1947 years, with a marked cadre of socialist and communist planning practitioners (if not so much theorists) influential from the 1940s (Ward

2012), and then probably a more social democratic generation, with Peter Hall an outstanding figure, from the 1960s. One could write this history partly by highlighting the ideological positions of these core figures, but I do not attempt that here.

The enthusiasm for extending planning made much more progress first within the Liberal Party, before 1914, then in the Labour Party. Shepherd (2018) sees a three-way overlap of New Liberal, One Nation conservative and state socialist thought making the forming and evolution of the system far from seamless, with significant tensions. In my view, socialism and modified liberalism were at the heart of the making of the multifaceted 1947 system, which consisted of a framework of statutory plans, public decision making on applications to develop land (both these led by local authorities), arrangements for state intervention of numerous kinds (new towns, national parks) and financial systems for feeding value gain from development to public use. Most of these elements sat easily enough with most varieties of socialism which were in strong positions in the 1940s, with support for a central state role and for strong local authorities at the forefront. However, for the pre-1939 years, there was considerable tension between the competing ideological positions, with socialist, Liberal and protectionist as well as property-supporting Conservative forces pressing often in different directions, and so causing some stasis on most potential change areas.

The Liberal Party was ever weaker from the early 1920s and its ideological position generally moved towards the Left, under the influence of the economic depression and Keynesian thinking, with leading Liberal figures like Beveridge and Keynes effectively legitimising programmes led by socialists by the 1940s. The Conservative Party was divided on planning issues, with much of the party adhering to classic liberal defence of private property rights, but with influential figures like Neville Chamberlain pressing forward both certain planning reforms and support for measures to deal with poor housing and depressed areas – again, approaches easily squared with Labour or emerging Liberal positions. The wartime coalition and the official reports prepared during the war made the ideological positions comprehensible to key actors, clearly preparing the ground for the post-1945 government.

The result in the key years of the passing of planning legislation in 1945 to 1948 was that the Labour and Conservative parties were on opposite sides on many issues, but the ideological high ground rested largely with Labour. This was, as always, in part due to other factors affecting the overall political climate, and particularly the nature of the immediate post-war years, when the momentum of continuing state intervention – which had clearly won the war – helped to carry through reforms which, though ideologically validated, might have been difficult to carry under different political circumstances. In particular, the private development sectors were in a weak state after the war, unable to carry through very effective lobbying work, as tended to be the case in subsequent periods of the post-war era.

The life of the 1947 system

Over 70 years have now passed, with Britain living under a planning system with many enduring features, and there are naturally several strongly distinct periods within this era. But it will be convenient here to take this period as a whole and consider what were the main ideological pressures being exerted on the system, standing back well from the year-to-year changes. The main competing positions throughout are those based fundamentally on Conservative and Labour ideologies, as each changed. The picture would get more complicated if I attempted to sketch in as well differences emerging at local government level (the same would apply equally in the earlier periods), but I will focus my generalisations on the UK government level. It should be noted that in all of the governments it was as much the struggles within the parties which conditioned how far reforms and practice evolved.

There will be some overlap here with parts of the chapter on ideologies. But the focus is now on the overall history, so although each ideology will figure again, they will do so as parts of the evolution of planning as a whole.

Conservative governments generally cut back the 1947 system, whether in generally less dramatic ways (before 1979) or in more fundamental forms, as neoliberalising ideology transformed Conservative positions. A key example in the 1950s was the gradual removal of the betterment provisions of the 1947 Act, meaning that no community gain flowed to the public from private development. Labour governments tried other ways to try to regain the principle of recouping parts of the gain, through a Land Commission (1960s), a Community Land Tax (1970s) and a proposed Planning Gain Supplement (2000s), though all were either abolished by subsequent Conservative governments or never got going, beaten back by well-organised property lobbies.

Labour governments, on the other hand, broadly supported what they had created in the 1940s, and extended this in some ways, though in quite distinct forms in the three periods of Labour national rule. An example is the greater Labour support for strategic and regional planning. This took different forms in each government period, but each saw a flowering of sub-national planning at levels above cities and counties – and in each case the institutional and policy innnovations were removed by following Conservative governments. This is a case where there is an element of common building across the two parties, as in the early 1990s the Conservative government, led by figures on the more interventionist wing of Thatcherite Conservatism like Chris Patten and Michael Heseltine, did set up regional structures, which New Labour then developed after 1997. Nevertheless, with the swing of Conservative ideology, and so the party, to the right after 2010, this regional machinery and the associated policy stances were promptly abolished.

Another example of some degree of converging policy positions, based on a mix of ideological overlap and enduring political pressures, was the promotion of green belts around many of the major cities. This was a policy first emerging from the London County Council, then Labour run, in the 1930s, but the solidification of this planning tool emerged under a Conservative government in 1955. It was then promoted by local authorities of all parties for the following decades, with most activity in designation of green belts in the 1970s and 1980s. All national governments have, then, supported green belts as a core element of planning ever since. We may judge that the protectionist wing of Conservatism has been very strongly in favour of this planning instrument, reinforced by overlapping perspectives with key lobbyists like the CPRE. Labour support may have been less whole hearted on occasions, but Labour had always had a strong interest in countryside recreation and, at least for some decades, in food production, and, in addition, the green belt was clearly a strong publicly accepted formula which meshed with interventionism, and so it could meld with several parts of socialist inclinations and tolerances.

The biggest changes came from the increasing force of neoliberal ideology in both parties, through Thatcherism from 1979 and through New Labour after 1997. Handing as much power as possible to private sector actors was at the core of neoliberal thinking, and this fitted a reorientation of planning. This did not, however, mean a wholesale retreat of the state. Both Thatcherite and New Labour governments maintained strong programmes of support, if in different forms, for urban regeneration. Only after 2010 did this support start to seriously decline, in terms of investment of government funds, as part of the assault on public spending of a much more intense scale than ever before.

Other parties were generally much less influential, during these 70 years, but certain ideologies, of the thinner variety, did have important impacts. Green ideology gradually built up its force from the 1970s, so that by the 1990s it made a powerful mark, especially by the setting up of 'sustainable development' as a core planning goal, in varying degrees of reality, as against persistent rhetoric. The main impact of green thinking was of a 'light green' form, supporting programmes to protect green spaces and to deal with pollution and waste. But the arrival of climate change as a major agreed challenge in the 2000s promoted some degree of deeper green policy making, even if this again varied across moments and governments. The absence of a powerful Green Party to take forward these agendas strongly, at either local or national level (the result of the non-proportional electoral system, in part), was one factor reducing the impact of these ideas on planning, but this by no means removed that impact.

Nationalism as an ideological force has had significant influences from the 1970s on. The main emphasis of this book is on England, and so I do not say much about the impact of Irish, Scottish or Welsh nationalisms, but these were significant in various ways for planning, from their first flowering in the 1970s through to the obtaining of devolved administrations in 1999. This is especially so in Scotland, where, since 2007, Scottish Nationalist Party administrations have governed the country, pursuing distinctive planning policies (as had the Labour-led administrations of 1999–2007, if with different emphases). Within England, nationalism has been influential, and this linked to varying degrees of racism, in itself a deeply rooted ideological phenomenon in British (and Irish) history (Fryer 1984, Craig 2012). The force of nationalism, and potentially of institutional racism expressed within governmental practice, has been most evident at moments of high immigration, as in the 1960s and 1970s, and again in the early 2000s. This affected above all Conservatism, which adopted more nationalistic positions from 1979 onwards, and this became a core element in the success of nationalist ideology in 2010 and afterwards, led by UKIP, as well as by sections of the Conservative Party. This was determinant in securing success for the anti-EU campaign (Brexit), leading to the UK leaving the EU. There have already been analyses of the relationship of Brexit and planning (Cowell 2017, Morphet 2017), but I do not try to trace through the impacts here, partly because they will depend very much on other, wider ideological and political developments, as indicated in the three scenarios discussed in

Chapter 1. The influence of ideas about race and planning has been well studied by Huw Thomas (2000, 2008; also Gale and Thomas 2018), and this can be conceived as a significant current affecting planning practice, especially at the local level, though impinging on national policy making in certain zones, particularly in planning for Gypsy and Traveller sites, a highly controversial issue, especially under Conservative governments, as shown in the 2010–15 government study later in this chapter.

One centrally important movement of ideological mould breaking of the last century has been feminism. Especially since the 1970s, this influenced political programmes and practice, especially of the Labour Party, and filtered into planning practice in a variety of ways. The effects on policy and practice have certainly been less than many campaigning groups would have wished, but in some fields, such as urban design, the influence has probably been powerful (Roberts and Greed 2000, RTPI 2003, Greed and Johnson 2014). Unlike environmental and nationalist movements, feminism has not had (in Britain) any significant separate party presence, nor the chance of effective pressure within Green parties, as in some other countries. So, it has had to depend on its ideological force, winning by ideas and linking with other 'thick' ideologies. The difficulty with this necessary approach is that some, perhaps most, of the existing political parties do not wish to give central prominence to many women's demands. This has been especially so in the Conservative Party, despite two of its last five prime ministers being women.

This long-run history has been presented in terms of the relation between ideologies and planning, without referring to the distinct relationship with politics, in the way I am conceiving that. The main reason is that, in a more than century-long overview, it is not possible to zoom in on the detailed relationship of planning, politics and ideology. That can be done only by looking at particular periods in more close up. A brief example of how such analysis might proceed is now given.

Planning, politics and ideology in the 2010–15 UK government

Politics and ideology are mutually infused in the real history of making policy, with shorter- and longer-term pressures, both forming the evolution of the ideological landscape and steering the stress on different facets of that landscape. In Gramscian terms, the analysis of the 'conjuncture' and the underlying ideological drive have to be thought through together (Hall and Massey 2015, Hall, Massey and

Rustin 2015, Inch and Shepherd 2020). In fact, the Gramscian use of conjuncture is normally applied to long periods in which major shifts in class power and ideological functioning can be detected, as in the practice of seeing the 1970s/1980s as dividing one conjuncture from another. However, there is no reason why more subtle shifts cannot be identified even with a five-year period; it certainly feels as if such shifts occur, giving different scope to different social actors and arguments, even year by year. Thus the 2010–15 government was not free to do precisely what its ideology (or varying ideological currents) might have wanted, because pressures from 'outside' had to be dealt with; for example, elections in a democratic state had to be won.

The UK government for five years from May 2010 was a coalition of Conservatives and Liberal Democrats. The Conservatives probably dominated in most policy areas, the Liberal Democrats having only three cabinet-level ministers, as well as the party leader being deputy prime minister. It may be that the junior partners had a restraining influence on policy making, but a reliable indication of the extent will have to await the work of historians.

The dominant policy direction of the government was about cutting back the state, with two linked strands. One was the pursuit of massive 'austerity' policies, above all in areas linked to the welfare state that had been built up in the early and mid-20th century. By cutting the size of the state in Gross Domestic Product back from the levels reached in the late 20th century, using as justification the need to reduce the national debt accumulated in bailing out the banks in 2008–09, the Conservatives found a simple and consistent narrative. This also involved shifting taxation from the richer to the poorer parts of society, and removing public support for the poor and middling social segments (Hills 2014, Toynbee and Walker 2015).

The second strand was 'deregulation', cutting back elements of government regulation related to any social or environmental objectives, 'freeing business' from the burdens of state interference. This was an accompaniment to the first strand, allowing cuts in government roles and therefore the dismantling of central and local government, gathering speed during the five years.

It is not difficult to see how critical the intersection of these policy drives was likely to be for planning. Planning depends on a range of public resources for many of its ambitions or effects, and is a publicly oriented intervention in what profit-making businesses would otherwise do. It has been part of the mindset of state action since the early 20th century. The key planning acts of the century were passed in the core reforming governments of the Liberals before 1914 and the Labour government after 1945. More and more openly the Conservatives were intent on removing most traces of both reforming periods, to take Britain back to a more Victorian-style state and society. This was perhaps not clear to most observers at the start of the 2010 government, but it became clearer as the years passed.

The five years saw shifting political conjunctures, with the strength, self-confidence and main goals of the government moving around somewhat. This was particularly affected by the economic arguments and the perceptions of the success or failure of the government economic strategy. The year or so before the 2015 election was naturally a period heavily affected by the more direct areas of political contestation (as viewed by Conservative strategists). There is no doubt that government policy was developed in part through contestations, especially the quite bruising encounter with parts of the Conservative heartlands (including a big campaign led by the *Daily Telegraph* newspaper) over the NPPF. As Finlayson says in discussing the role of rhetoric in ideology and politics: 'Political thinking, then, is part of strategic action called forth by concrete experiences of contestation' (Finlayson 2012, p 257). Nevertheless, it is argued here that underlying ideological directions were broadly maintained through these shifting conjunctures, even if arguments had to be tailored and adjusted according to particular narrative or rhetorical shifts.

Planning policy was influenced by the personal positions of the key ministers involved, including the prime minister, the chancellor of the exchequer, the ministers directly involved in planning and a coordinating minister, Oliver Letwin, who had a cross-government role in pushing core ideological drives. I will not go into the details of the backgrounds and positions of these men (they were all men) here, but will simply summarise that strong ideological positions on what would at least until recently have been seen as the radical right of the Conservatives were shared by all the key actors, with one minister, Greg Clark, being a possible exception. At the same time there were politicians involved who had particular 'everyday political' positions, from their experience or preferences, with Eric Pickles and Brandon Lewis perhaps representing a more visceral backwoods Conservatism, closer to the feelings of typical UKIP supporters. UKIP became a more and more open and threatening force during these five years of government, and so was putting some pressure on the government (as senior Conservatives saw it) to respond to these feelings. So, within this set of politicians one can also detect a mix of more underlying ideological dimensions and more direct and electoral concerns, both of which could drive planning policy development. Table 4.1 gives an overview of names and policy initiatives for the period.

Major planning dimensions, 2010–15

The overall drive with two strands described above framed the government approach to planning, but with extra features specific to planning layered onto this. One part of this was 'localism', while another consisted of some political hotspots or passions on onshore wind farms, provision for Gypsies and Travellers and managing green belt planning. The analysis seeks to bring out the connections and disjunctions between these elements, and so illuminate the relations between ideology and planning in the making and implementing of Conservative planning policy during these years. In particular the importance of political conjunctures will be evident, affecting the selection and highlighting of ideological facets as much as the commitment to particular areas of 'low politics'.

A further feature of the ideological nature of this government was the policy-making style, marked by bringing in outsiders to make key policy advances (as with the drafting of the NPPF), the dependence on (primarily) one right-wing think-tank (Policy Exchange) and certain development industry lobby groups, the reduction of effective consultation and a lesser resort to studies and using evidence.

'Localism'

Chronologically, 'localism' was the first policy zone. From here on the inverted commas around localism are omitted. But it is important to remember that this is a construct, just as was the localism promoted by New Labour in the early 2000s, and it should not be assumed that it translates to a clear political commitment to 'local control' for some agent identified as in some sense 'local': by speaking in these terms, we immediately become aware how deeply confusing, contestable and ideological the idea of 'local' is, and therefore how suitable it can be for particular political uses (Layard 2012). It is essential to divide rhetorical intention from reality, however important rhetoric is, especially in recent Conservative policy making (Finlayson 2014). This particular localism was developed by the Conservatives in 2008–10 to encapsulate a narrative about New Labour having been in favour of central control, top-down structures, in planning as in many other policy fields. Several Conservative policy papers published in 2008–10 developed the story, with *Control Shift* of October 2008

Table 4.1: Key ideological and political drives in the planning sphere in the 2010–15 UK government

Years	Key events	Ideological drives	Political drives
2010	Eric Pickles secretary of state 2010–15; Greg Clark planning minister 2010–12; Regional Spatial Strategies abolished 2010–12.	Oliver Letwin minister of state in Cabinet Office overseeing deregulation across government 2010–15. Local government cut back massively throughout – estimated that planning services reduced by 40%. 'Localism' as primary driver from work in opposition, primarily during first year of government, but continuing as one theme throughout.	(The empty cells 2010–12 do not imply an absence of politics, but the predominance of 'purer' ideological drivers.)
2011	Localism Act 2011; NPPF made 2011–12, major battles over contents for 12 months.	'Growth' as key theme from 2011 onwards, given as justification for cutting back planning system from that point onwards.	
2012	PPG prepared 2012–13 (online so continuously revised); Nick Boles planning minister 2012–14.	Alex Morton special advisor to David Cameron 2012–15 (previously specialist on planning and housing at Policy Exchange); 'Deregulation' as primary aim from 2012, with both legislation (three Acts) and much action through policy guidance (NPPF, PPG, ministerial steering). Planning system reach and effectiveness cut	

(continued)

Table 4.1: Key ideological and political drives in the planning sphere in the 2010–15 UK government (continued)

Years	Key events	Ideological drives	Political drives
		back dramatically from 2012 to 2015, through changes to the General Development Order and Use Classes Order.	
2013	Growth and Infrastructure Act 2013		Especially from 2013, increasing intervention by secretary of state to call in planning applications or recover appeal decisions, to make decisions personally, in 'hot spot' areas.
2014	Brandon Lewis planning minister 2014–15		This intervention affected above all decisions on Gypsies and Travellers, onshore wind farms and development in the green belt.
2015	Infrastructure Act 2015; Deregulation Act 2015.		This intervention was done largely by personal interpretation of cases, though in the case of Gypsies and Travellers, backed by special guidance issued in 2012. Legal challenges appeared on these interventions, seen by some as arbitrary and bringing the independence of the Planning Inspectorate into question.

being the most significant (Goodchild 2010). Bullock (2011) argues that the policy making of the years before 2010 created a new link between decentralisation (some sort of localism) and deregulation (an old Conservative instinct), seeing them going hand in hand, in a way that Conservative ideology had probably often felt but had not made into a plausible narrative before. This fits with the Freeden model of ideological evolution or reassembly, whereby dormant or unclear parts of an ideological inheritance could be called on and rearticulated to fit the political moment and policy field. The party probably owed this trick of ideological mechanics most of all to Letwin, alongside Clark.

The main ingredients of this localism were the abolition of all regional structures in England (remembering that this whole account of planning is restricted to England), and the installation of a statutory layer of 'neighbourhood planning' at the level of parishes in rural areas, or some other small division in towns and cities. These were core parts of the Localism Act 2011, alongside several elements not so linked to planning (Ricketts and Field 2012 have a full account by lawyers). Slade (2018a) reveals that initially Oliver Letwin and Policy Exchange were pressing for the complete abolition of the local plans system, and that it was only subsequent discussion, particularly motivated by the fear that this might cause enormous disruption in the development industry for years, that pushed ministers a little more sympathetic to planning (Bob Neill, Greg Clark) to agree to keeping statutory Local Plans.

State cut-back: austerity and deregulation

The aim here was to remove regulatory parts of government action which would restrict the 'liberties' of business, whether or not these might have purposes in public interest terms, as of course most parts of the planning system have had in the last 70 years or more. The Open Source Planning policy document continuously presented planning as 'bureaucratic', and this remained a consistent theme of Conservative policy. While localism served to weaken any general steering frameworks that existed, by removing regional guidance and confusing the layers of planning below that, deregulation progressed on two complementary paths.

The first path was to press what regulation there was into more business-friendly tracks, mainly by the remaking of the central government advisory or guidance machinery. Before 2011, this had consisted of a mix of Planning Policy Statements (or some remaining Planning Policy Guidance Notes) and circulars or advisory notes from ministers. By 2014 it was formed of the NPPF, finalised in 2012, and an online system (subject to regular revision) of Planning Practice Guidance. Between them, these were more pro-development, and with much less social and environmental content, than the previous central policy package. It can be seen that this work was the result of efforts over an extended period, virtually taking up the entire parliament.

Some might argue against this interpretation – that this was at its core an ideologically driven reform of the planning system. The main rhetoric of the reform was that this was shortening and simplifying guidance, but this appears as a smoke screen for quite radical change of the political content. It is far from clear that the new guidance has brought any advantages as a result of being shorter, with many commentators agreeing that the NPPF is ambiguous and confusing in key areas, and a prime factor in slow Local Plan production. One highly controversial area has been the stress on viability, which is seen as increasingly overriding other considerations, but on an intensely contested and untransparent evidence base. Another important pro-business drive was to cut back the chance for councils to get Section 106 contributions, particularly for social housing: a system was created whereby schemes already approved could be altered to remove 'burdensome' contributions by developers.

The second path of deregulating reform was to remove the amount of changes, whether in development or use, which can be controlled within the planning system. Many observers saw this as undermining the effectiveness of planning to a critical extent. Between 2013 and 2015 several changes to the General Development Order and Use Classes Order meant that many changes of use, particularly from offices or retail to residential, no longer needed planning permission (Smith 2015b). This fundamentally undermines the strength of any Local Plan, as these plans depend on the designation of areas on maps which are allocated for particular uses – as well as the development control process as a whole, even if no plans exist. These changes were introduced gradually, within several pieces of legislation, and were sometimes presented first as temporary measures, largely when Nick Boles was planning minister, and have been seen as part of the drive coordinated by Letwin to press deregulation across government. They figured in the Growth and Infrastructure Act 2013, the Infrastructure Act 2015 and the Deregulation Act 2015. The justification presented on this side, as well as the normal Conservative stress on freeing business from state shackles, was related to the growth agenda promoted particularly by Osborne from 2011 onwards, when the government was under heavy criticism for failing to promote growth in the UK economy. This is again highly controversial, as no evidence base exists to suggest that reducing the reach of the planning system will encourage economic growth, whether generally or in particular sectors or localities (Adams and Watkins 2014). However, 'growth' probably served as a quite effective narrative, only very weakly challenged by the Labour opposition and most commentators.

Despite the usefulness of the deregulation and growth agenda to this government, taken as a whole, and within the broader ideological landscape driving the core of the government, particularly in the core executive of Cameron, Osborne and Letwin, it generated some difficulties, given the other strand of localism. The tensions sometimes appeared also in relation to the political hotspot areas discussed later. While the Treasury publications from at least 2012 increasingly referred to the need for local planning authorities to allocate much more land for development (especially for housing), and whenever possible to say 'yes' to planning applications (as the NPPF was supposed to facilitate – the presumption in favour of sustainable development, with 'sustainable' left unclear and underemphasised), this could easily clash with the localism narrative. This became ever clearer to most observers during the middle part of the government, and caused real tensions in both policy development and ministerial decision making (as Bullock 2011 predicted it would). Should local authorities be able to refuse applications (as localism surely could imply) or did growth or deregulation trump that right? Would the Planning Inspectorate and the secretary of state impose decisions, so removing the force of localism? How could localism sit with the early decision to remove permissions for 'free schools' from local authorities, to be decided by central government? The period from 2013 to 2015 became ever more tangled around these issues, with ideology and certain business pressures pulling strongly one way, and some political and increasingly (as the 2015 general election neared) electoral considerations pulling equally strongly the other way.

Political hotspots within planning

It can be argued that senior Conservative politicians rarely see planning as having much value – hence the often hostile approach to it as a system. At most they see planning as giving the chance to block changes which are particularly threatening to them or to their more vocal constituents. There can be change from one time to another as to which are the areas at the top of their 'to be blocked' agenda. During this government there were three main forms of development which formed the hot areas for planning ministers: housing in sensitive areas like green belts, onshore wind farms and Gypsy and Traveller sites. It is not possible to give here details of all three – just some analysis of the first two is presented.

One difficult area was one which can affect all governments to some degree, trying to tread the path between central control of housing decision making and letting local authorities keep this role, especially when green belts are involved. This was strongly influenced by the NPPF and the shifting of power away from authorities and toward developers, given the tangled effects of the NPPF regime as it evolved. This led to more planning by appeal, and this was backed by significant use of powers for recovering appeals, though without quite the dramatic shifts visible in the other two hot zones. Another complication coming from the localism reforms was trying to get a balance between supporting neighbourhood plans as well as local plans, given that neighbourhood plans were by the later part of the government starting to come on stream, often in the absence of an up-to-date Local Plan. This raised precisely the dilemma that critics had said would emerge, with neighbourhood plans starting to lead the Local Plan process, rather than being consistent with local plans.

A second area was onshore wind (Smith 2015a). In 2010 the Conservatives had presented themselves as even handed, wishing to make wind farms more acceptable by offering incentives. By June 2013, and boosted by UKIP raising it as a campaign issue, alongside the general pressure built up by many years of media criticisms from sources close to climate change sceptics, a decision was taken to ratchet up government opposition to onshore wind (Toynbee 2014) by requiring more pre-application consultation on all onshore wind applications and by the secretary of state recovering more appeals.

The effect was clear 18 months later. An analysis by *Planning* magazine of 28 recovered appeals on wind farms in 2014 showed that 25 were dismissed, with 11 of these going against the recommendations of inspectors (*Planning* magazine, 16 January 2015, p 8). A consultant acting for wind energy developers said that this level of going against inspectors' advice represented an 'extreme politicisation of the planning process in this sector' (*Planning* magazine, 16 January 2015, p 8).

The 2015 Conservative manifesto stated its intention to halt the spread of onshore wind farms by cutting subsidies for this kind of renewables, as well as giving residents direct right of veto over proposals. An early government statement confirmed that onshore wind consents would be taken out of the Planning Act 2008 regime and 'given back' to local authorities (and so to the secretary of state for Communities and Local Government, not the secretary of state for Energy and Climate Change).

Recovery of appeals increased as the 2015 election approached, with neighbourhood plans and housing, and fracking, being added in July 2014 to the types of development to be recovered. It was as if a new election tool had been discovered by the Conservatives, to deal with UKIP threats in possible marginal seats.

Thus these areas were thoroughly politicised within central government, moving away from any localist approach. The secretary of state's interventions became ever more intense as the 2015 general election got nearer.

The 2010–15 government: concluding comments

The politicisation and centralisation of decision making discussed in the last section went against the broad lines of any narrative of local or independent decision making, in order to intervene in areas about which the Conservatives felt very strongly. The message that a secretary of state can in effect rewrite policy in this way, if politically convenient, left many planners and lawyers uncomfortable, given the unprecedented degree and consistency of the interventions, which were not based in policy or existing case law.

We may conclude on the balance of the relationship between ideological underpinnings and political and conjunctural imperatives in this planning policy period: the two were consistently intertwined. There is an intersecting flow of political and ideological determination of planning policy trajectories visible during these years. Conservative ideology was drawn on in different ways at different times, though with an underlying coherence set by the nature of the ideological fix reached through party struggles and experiences since the 1980s.

Conclusion

We have now examined both the long-term historical relationship of the main ideologies and planning and one recent period in more detail. We now move away from a historical approach, to analysing different dimensions of the political and ideological character of planning. In fact, the next chapter starts with a consideration of the *extent* of the infusion of planning by politics and ideology, by examining law and expertise in planning. There follow chapters on government processes and planning, pressure groups and planning, communication and deliberation, and then examinations of particular planning dimensions and fields.

5

Planning expertise and planning law: autonomy from politics and ideology?

This chapter is about the 'other side' of the argument – how planning is certainly not all politics and ideology. The chapter examines how two important aspects of planning practice affect the relationship to politics and ideology. These aspects are the use of technical skills and expertise, and the strong foundations in legal processes. We are therefore going here into the 'instrumentation' of planning, the many tools and procedures and knowledges used in the art of planning. Further important aspects of this instrumentation relate to planning's organisational location, for example how far it may be seen as a bureaucratic function, and how it relates to the world of pressure politics. These, though, are major areas in their own right and will be the subjects of Chapters 6 and 7.

One question at issue here is how far planning can be seen as autonomous. To argue that it is strongly so would, to a degree, go against my stress on politics and ideology. The chapter therefore considers this, with one conclusion being that planning certainly involves much beside politics and ideology, but even these parts are not so very politics and ideology free. There is of course much that is not *directly* ideological in planning – for example, spatiality, the force of material objects, the power of 'purely' self-interested behaviour, if such a thing can be abstracted. There is not space to discuss the extent of politicisation or ideologisation of all these aspects. But the matters discussed in this chapter are perhaps especially important in grasping the nature of planning.

This chapter does therefore belong in the 'political and ideological dimensions of planning' box of Chapter 1, even though the topics are not at all fully consumed by these. I start with the issues of skills and expertise, before tackling the weighty and, in my view, much less effectively discussed issue of planning's links to the law.

Technical and knowledge dimensions

To those working as planners, it is clear that there is an extensive base of knowledge, technique and experience which underlies this work, just as it underlies any skilled activity. Some academic critics have been less sure of this, citing a much weaker technical base than in some professions, normally citing law, medicine or engineering as being 'real professions' in comparison (Reade 1987, Evans 1993). I am certainly going against Reade's view (and that of some radical critics of planning) that planning technique is simply camouflage for real political (and ideological) purposes in planning. As will be clear, I am happy to agree that technique is infused by politics and ideology. This, however, far from removes the experienced expertise which any competent planning involves. This position may gain support from the recent Parker and Street (2019) paper, which reviewed the long-running debate on skills and knowledge in planning and suggested that it was time for the RTPI to reconsider whether planners could be expected to cover such a wide range of skills as current guidelines proposed.

The discussion is extended by the consideration of the forms of knowledge which can support effective work, as in the ideas of Flyvbjerg (2001), that there is a kind of expert experience, which he calls phronesis, that practitioners build up, often over many years. I, no doubt starting from my own experience as a practising planner who then taught planning students for many years, take it as a certainty that there is a real basis to the skills planners need to gain, even though I am happy to accept that this is less easily specified than in some other professions or work areas.

I would point to perhaps the best book written on planning skills, by Ted Kitchen (2007), as support for this view of planning as having a strong technical, knowledge and experience base. Kitchen was a highly skilled and experienced planner working at the top of English local government, in his final years as city planning officer of Manchester. He then moved to teach planning, and to write up his experiences. His book on skills orders the types needed as: technical; planning system and process; place; customer; personal; organisational, management and political content; and synoptic and integrative. It is clear that here Kitchen is stressing what might be seen as softer skills, beyond the more technical ones which most planning schools prioritise, such as urban design or planning law.

Another book I could call in support would be that by Duncan Bowie (2010) on the experience of putting together the early London Plans during the Livingstone mayoralties. Bowie worked specifically on housing issues, and particularly on the management of the instruments for assessing housing capacity (land) and housing markets and housing need. No one reading this book could be in any doubt of the considerable skills needed in managing this process through its whole life cycle (research, calculation, working with politicians and other interests, presentation in public examinations, implementing with the actual housing actors and so on). Attending the Examination in Public of the latest London Plan in early 2019 was a reminder that this has not changed. Days of debate on technical detail took place, which to the great majority of observers would have been impenetrable. Just as with the Kitchen book, this clearly raises large issues of accessibility and political democracy, but recognising that does not remove the facts of knowledge and skills involved.

Other books, such as those mentioned in Chapter 2, will put the emphasis on other skill sets, or perhaps more generally on wider approaches to thinking about planning's nature and goals. Different planners, academics and observers would set the priorities differently, perhaps to a degree greater than with many professions. There is of course a broad core curriculum required by the professional validating body, the RTPI, but this allows considerable flexibility, letting undergraduate and master's courses in different universities choose their own formal balance, which is then strongly affected by the interests and capacities of staff.

Given this view, I naturally accept that planning as a knowledge-based activity has a clear partial autonomy in how it works, separating it off from political and ideological dimensions. It is perfectly understandable that planners and those training them (formally in universities, day by day in planning offices of many kinds) will state that this base is predominant in much of their everyday practice. But we need to go further into what this skilled autonomy may really mean. A recent example from published research in Wales will help to clarify aspects of this working (Harris, Webb and Smith 2018). Guidance on planning in Wales is given by Planning Policy Wales (Welsh Government 2016), and Welsh local authorities have to prepare their local plans within this guidance, including that on setting housing numbers. One aspect of this work is deciding on the use of the household projections released regularly by the Welsh Government – how far each council will follow these, or propose reasoned divergences from the housing provision implied by the latest projections. This, though, as the article makes very clear, and is fully known to all the actors they interviewed, is a highly politicised process. Many politicians and local action groups will see this element as the core focus for their involvement in the Local Plan preparation. There is therefore inevitably a powerful and conflictful convergence of technical work with political decision making, in this particular element of plan making.

The researchers found considerable current variation in the ability to carry out this step of plan making, given the often slim and declining resources available to planning authorities. Some councils outsourced the work to consultancies, which had the disadvantage of leaving the planners relatively weakly prepared in the discussions and negotiations required in the public examination stages of plans. But the consultancies could build up their skills, because they could specialise in this element of planning work, repeating roughly the same exercises from one council to the next. Some planners found it simpler to follow the projections to the letter, not having the skills or time to argue the case for other numbers.

We see here therefore a typical component of UK planning practice being carried out under often demanding current circumstances. What is certainly a significant element of the planner's skill base is in fact very difficult to navigate, partly because of the structuring political circumstances that have driven in recent years to more and more outsourcing of demanding elements of plan making or to planners being forced to adopt a 'slim line' approach to plan making, and partly because of the normally locally conflictual politics of this part of plan making, which requires management, communication and political management skills of a high order, to reach an approved Local Plan. We see the apparent autonomy of planners being hemmed in by these varying political constraining realities, which generate in their turn the need for well-honed skills in other dimensions of the planning process.

Of course, at a deeper level, the Welsh planning system is affected by the ideological structuring of the whole challenge being tackled. As will be analysed further in the section on the relationship of housing planning and housing provisioning as a whole, the tasks imposed on planners emerge from particular political economies of how houses are produced, and how the public administration is structured nationally and locally to deal with the tasks allocated. So, again, the apparent autonomy can be seen to be constrained, if here at a deeper level which hardly impinges consciously on practice from day to day or even year to year.

It is also important to notice the segmentation of planning practice and technical work underway, as consultancies have taken on more of the technical areas of plan making, in particular, (Raco 2018). While not yet fully studied, it is clear that this has big implications for the nature of planning work, how individual planners relate to the local political process, how their day-to-day work is structured, how the responsibilities to clients, public and other actors are evolving and what are the varied ideas in the heads of planners about the purpose of planning activity, as impacted upon by such outsourcing. Parker, Street and Wargent (2019) see the rise of a new 'consultocracy' (p 159), with the use of consultants naturalised, reducing the reach of democratic local steering of planning.

The provisional conclusion from this discussion of technique and the space for autonomous action available to planners is two sided. Yes, the autonomy is there, and the skills are real and demanding skills to acquire and perform. But this acting out is at the same time both political at the fairly obvious level, as is appreciated to varying degrees by all actors in this planning task, and also ideologically conditioned. The form that this two-sidedness takes will vary greatly between fields. There are some fields where planners do have a fuller and less politicised space of action (we may think of minerals planning, or some aspects of conservation planning), even though political and ideological considerations are never fully absent. The 'hotter' fields of planning action are probably nevertheless more common, under current UK circumstances.

Planning and law: reviewing the literature

So far, I have not given explicit attention to one critical feature of planning work, its deep entanglement with the legal system of whatever country is being studied. In one sense this is just another element of the skills base of planners. Many planners, especially those in more senior positions dealing with planning application decision making, including appearing at public inquiries, will have a good knowledge of planning law. Many others will depend on legal advisors, whether within the council or consultancy or government agency, or brought in from the now large planning sector of the law industry. But there is more to planning law than it being another skill element, though it is certainly that. A discussion of planning law sheds further light, at a deeper level, on the relationship of planning to politics and ideology, and how complex the structuring of these relationships must inevitably be. In examining this area we will see a kind of parallel between the relative autonomy of the legal system and that of planning. So this will help to further the goal of this chapter, to give a more satisfying answer to the question as to how far or in what ways planners' work does have a real autonomy.

The nature of law as a whole

Thanks to several decades of academic work in varied critical disciplinary areas, there is now a vast literature considering the nature of law in the broadest sense. This exists within legal academia and outside it, in philosophy, politics and sociology in particular. Here I take my cue most of all from the one sustained engagement with the law of the French sociologist Pierre Bourdieu (1987), supplemented by other inputs from critical legal studies and critical legal geography.

Law and sociology: Bourdieu

Bourdieu is mainly concerned to pin down the apparent independence of law as a feature of societies. He sees law as 'an entire social universe ... which is in practice relatively independent of external determinations and pressures' (1987, p 816). His sociological analysis establishes how a social division between lay people and professionals is created, with strong internal cohesion in the law's cadres and a monopoly conferred by the state to interpret and act on the state's decisions. This is policed by certain behavioural and intellectual formulas performed, to a degree, by all legal practitioners, though also with clear hierarchical distinctions maintained within the profession.

The core effects are achieved linguistically and in practice to create a neutralisation effect, and a universalisation effect, together setting the law apart from and above other kinds of utterances.

> Far from being a simple ideological mask, such a rhetoric of autonomy, neutrality, and universality, which may be the basis of a real autonomy of thought and practice, is the expression of the whole operation of the juridical field and, in particular, of the work of rationalization to which the system of juridical norms is continually subordinated. This has been true for centuries. Indeed, what we could call the 'juridical sense' or the 'juridical faculty' consists precisely in such a universalizing attitude. (p 820)

There are differences between the European and Anglo-American traditions, but the basic forces of law work to the same effect. A legal canon is created, and a set of juridical professional tools are manipulated to fit this canon to circumstances. Interpretation allows the required polysemy, so that ambiguity and elasticity can be built in as needed. Bourdieu is particularly insistent on the role of language, which allows practitioners to maintain a distance from the matters they treat, as well as from ordinary non-lawyers, generating a kind of aristocratic and ascetic mode of being or at least seeming. He notes the closeness of interests among lawyers in most circumstances, arising from similar family and educational backgrounds (p 842). Judges are, he notes, almost always from the dominant class. There is a 'non-aggression pact that links the magistracy to dominant power' (p 843). 'Thus, one of the functions of the specifically juridical labor of formalizing and systematizing ethical representations and practices is to contribute to binding laypeople to the fundamental principle of the jurists' professional ideology-belief in the neutrality and autonomy of the law and of jurists themselves' (p 844). Bourdieu's theoretical system designates law as a key element of forming the 'doxa', those invisible cornerstones of normalcy in any social order. The relationship between the juridical field and the field of power is subject to what he calls 'miscognition' (*méconnaisance* in French), a deep ideological process which cannot be subjected to superficial analyses.

> The alteration of mental space, logically and practically contingent upon change in social space, guarantees the mastery of the situation to those who possess legal qualifications. They alone can adopt the attitudes which allow the constitution of situations according to the fundamental law of the field. Those who tacitly abandon the direction of their conflict themselves by accepting entry into the juridical field (giving up, for example, the resort to force, or to an unofficial arbitrator, or the direct effort to find an amicable solution) are reduced to the status of client. (p 834)

Bourdieu also gives some analysis of how the evolution of the legal 'demand and supply' allows adjustment of the profession, for example by enabling the emergence of young lawyers who will fight for new kinds of rights. Even the 'semi-professional mediators' (p 837) can participate in the process in a technical way: we may imagine planners under this formulation, but one also thinks of the action groups in planning inquiries who have to get rather expert, learning the ropes of language and norms.

Underlying the whole field is the relation to the state: 'Law consecrates the established order by consecrating the vision of that order which is held by the State' (p 838). Planning is of course a state-regulated activity, but it is doubly state-enthralled, given its high legalisation.

Law and geography

A slightly less general take on the same connections is from Joshua Barkan (2011), a US geographer. He tracks through the way in which legal concepts create a taken-for-granted institutional landscape. '[T]he fact that policy projects or diffuse ideologies are instituted through specifically legal processes, including legal forms of reasoning, evidence, argument, and adjudication, has relevance for understanding the political constitution of economic globalization' (p 592). For 'economic globalization', substitute 'planning', and the sentence still makes sense.

Barkan is concerned with 'the ways that individuals and social groups – including lawyers and judges, but also lay people – think about, engage with, contest, and reproduce legal concepts, formal law, and legal ideologies' (p 591). He sees law as a means for the incorporation of ideologies into legal conventions and tribunals, taking the law of the sea and on fishing as an example. In the process of privatisation, 'ideologies are translated into the legal claims of states, companies and indigenous groups' (p 593).

Like Bourdieu, Barkan points to the role of language and concepts, with law as a kind of translation process.

> Blomley (1994) has described this process as legal 'closure', in which law-makers continually attempt to bracket law as a rational, stable, and clearly bounded set of rules governing politics within specific territories. Closure works, in part, by translating political claims and social interest into a new idiom. For this reason, when groups and individuals enter legal institutions, they reposition their arguments into a different linguistic and rhetorical form. (p 599)

It is particularly important that the legal system requires, formally, 'the distinction from politics to be at least rhetorically significant' (p 599). Equally important is 'the legal demarcation of the economy as a sphere beyond law and politics' (p 600). So, law is 'a discourse and practice that not only bounds itself, through practices of legal "closure", but also polices the spheres of politics and the economy while mediating their interrelation' (p 603).

A US legal geographer, David Delaney, argues for the need to focus on the fine grain of the constitution of the law, for example to see how it is infused with 'technical internal "rules of engagement" such as "standing", "mootness", and "ripeness"', whose deployment will have important spatial (as well as other) impacts (2015, p 97). More simply, 'power and law are two facets of the same thing' (Delaney 2016 p 268).

A current example is the struggle of academics and activists to see how far the legal system can be used to secure justice for those affected by the Grenfell Tower fire in 2017. They have been divided on the options practically open to those confronted by the weight of state power. Tuitt (2019) argued that putting much faith in the law would work against the long-term struggle for justice, noting in her support that the public inquiry instituted by the government very soon declared as 'non-justiciable' (outside the inquiry's terms of action) many of the activists' demands for justice.

Law and politics

A consideration of the overall weakly developed relationship between law and politics argues that it remains problematic, with a significant gap between the disciplines (Campbell 2012). 'The disciplinary separation of law and politics is an institutional fact with considerable ideological overtones. For many lawyers, law is respectable and politics is not. To some of these the very idea that law is a manifestation or type of politics seems almost offensive' (p 228). Most work is done from a point of view internal to the process of law. Campbell does find relevant work which critiques the law's claims to ideological neutrality, for example by feminist and race theorists in US political science. However, an examination of UK politics textbooks does not suggest that such theoretical work is very present in UK academic political thinking. This wider deficiency, arguably affecting the law and social sciences interface in several fields, has no doubt bolstered the weaknesses of planning's consideration of law.

Law and property

A major concern of critical legal studies has been to explore questions of property. As a Marxist theorist, Sol Picciotto, put it:

> the individual legal subject is essentially the bearer of commodities, the owner of economic assets producing a revenue. Hence the bulk of law is concerned with property. Even aside from substantive law, this characteristic

> is embedded in the nature of legal procedures ... Legally protected interests boil down to the individual's person or property. (1979, p 172)

Nick Blomley has looked at the 'difficult character of property' from a geographer's perspective. He analyses the way in which US planning became primarily focused on land use in the early 20th century, which allowed the emergent planning profession to escape the deeply difficult ideological ground of property and ownership, and concentrate on the apparently neutral and safe idea of the use of any piece of land. The US Town Planning Institute set its goal as 'the orderly disposition of land and buildings in use and development' (Blomley 2017, p 360). As a result:

> land use planning appears detached from many of the ethical dimensions of property. Questions of the power relations that course through property – exclusion, dispossession, rights – do not figure ... Re-zoning hearings in inner city neighborhoods, struggling with marginalization and gentrification, hear residents' claims – centered on collective rights to not be excluded, and appeals to indigeneity and colonialism – politely but totally rebuffed by the depoliticizing discourse of setbacks, building heights, and car parking requirements. Density, it seems, nullifies justice. (Blomley 2004, p 361)

Other US planning academics have pursued the same line of argument, pressing for the development of a better language for discussing property in planning. Krueckeberg argued that the 'problem with "land use" is its presumption of neutrality and appearance of objectivity' (1995, p 301). He says that 'concepts of use rights and income or profit rights in property are at the heart of planning questions' (1995, p 308). Jacobs and Paulsen (2009) start from the view that in the US 'planning has been used to secure and protect the property right interests of the affluent and influential classes and races' (p 134). Jacobs and Paulsen are mainly responding to the growing force of the property rights movement driven forward since the 1980s by conservative interests, to lessen even further any potential impact of planning regulations on private property. As they argue that planning cannot escape its relationship to property rights, they propose a reorientation of language towards community and away from individual property rights, and suggest that a property rights impact statement as part of the planning process would help to make visible and debateable the property dimensions of planning (p 141).

The importance of property to a consideration of planning's political and ideological nature may seem self-evident. Property matters, in every planning case and in every statutory planning process. In many areas most voters are property owners, large or small. Defence of private property is a root element of liberal and conservative ideologies, and a core ingredient of the constitution of capitalist systems. Yet property is remarkably invisible in the great majority of planning writing, discussions and practice.

The literature on planning and the law

This literature is much less extensive than that on law as a whole, and is marked also by having a lesser critical component. The vast majority of writing on planning law has a purely practical purpose, to make progress on an area of legal application, and this is contained in the regularly revised textbooks of planning law, in the continuously updated encyclopedia of planning law and, in Britain, in articles mainly in the *Journal of Planning and Environmental Law*. One will generally look in vain in any of these sources for reflection on the relationship of planning and law, in an underlying and general sense. This is of course indicative in itself, suggesting a field of knowledge and skill which is sure enough of its role and importance not to engage in much navel gazing. Self-reflection or even self-criticism is more likely to emerge when an activity is challenged. Planning law is, taken as a whole, not strongly challenged, however intense debates may sometimes be on specific issues.

However, there are two areas of discussion which are useful for my purposes. One is rather old, resulting from the engagement of the planning and land lawyer and academic Patrick McAuslan with the field, largely in the 1970s. The other is the work of Philip Booth, a planning academic who spent many years reflecting on UK planning law and its differences from such law in other countries, especially in France. This is supplemented by some ideas in a recent planning law textbook which for the first time contains some elements of reflection (Sheppard et al 2017).

Patrick McAuslan and Malcolm Grant

Patrick McAuslan wrote two books (1975 and 1980) and two articles (1971 and 1974) on British planning from a lawyer's perspective.

The 1980 book, on the three ideologies of planning, I have already mentioned. The work came in part from his role as a local councillor in Leamington before 1974, giving him hands-on knowledge of the British system, in addition to his teaching and research interests. The 1971 article gave a valuable history of the relationship of law and planning since 1947, arguing that lawyers had staged a fight-back against their relative exclusion from the 1947 system, using the Franks report of 1957 to introduce elements of judicialisation previously absent, by opening up the inquiry system.

The 1974 article makes a strong criticism of the effect of the law on planning, and of the defeat of attempts to promote the inclusion of public participation in the Planning Act 1968. McAuslan suggests four themes which have impeded a more positive evolution of planning: the stress on property as the focus of legal attention, the increase in discretion given to officials, the emphasis on formal procedures and the complexity of the law. He argues that lawyers invariably take the perspective of their property-owning clients and that the planning process is biased towards the rights of property owners, given their relevant 'standing' or being invariably 'aggrieved persons'. Planners have reacted against 'the lawyer's property-oriented strait-jacket' (p 138), but this has brought its own problems of over-mighty public officials. He argues that the stress on formal procedures has weakened the hand of all outsiders, and that this is worsened by the great complexity of planning law, referring to the *Encyclopedia of Planning Law and Practice*, then a three-volume work over 8,000 pages long. He regrets the 'virtual demise' (1974, p 149) of the Skeffington Report. He also regrets the legalisation of development control which stemmed from the provision of rights of appeals and hearings for landowners; 'the legalisation or judicialisation of development control is a story of the triumph of the ideology of private property espoused by the lawyers over the ideology of public interest espoused by public officials' (1980, p 147).

McAuslan's books extended the critique in these articles. But although his 1980 book is much cited, it did not leave overall a long or significant impact on planning thinking. A memorial volume on his life's work as a whole appeared in 2017, but the major emphasis is on his work in Africa, rather than on his British planning writing (Zartaloudis 2017). There may be various reasons for this relatively limited impact, beyond the historical circumstances following the 1980 book publication, with planning under attack and any radical reorientation to a public involvement ideology being driven off the agenda. One reason may be the failure of McAuslan (or perhaps colleagues) to persist with a theorisation of the planning and law relationship, which is arguably only taken a little way along the needed path by these published works. Another may be the effective response from the 'establishment' to the criticisms. Malcolm Grant, a very respected academic planning lawyer, for years editing the planning law encyclopedia, responded to McAuslan, as well as to John Griffiths, another lawyer radical (Grant 1978). While accepting some parts of the criticisms (including the complexity of the law), Grant essentially put the blame on the system of laws, not on the behaviour of lawyers. If the system wishes to support the status quo (for example, in relation to property), the lawyers will follow that. He would probably have agreed with McAuslan's characterisation of the view of planning lawyers: the law 'provides a neutral framework for the exercise of power but is not in itself biased in any way for or against a particular philosophy or ideology governing that exercise of power' (1980, p 1). Rather, Grant argues for a more constructive approach to judicial review, as well as changes to the content and values of legislation on planning.

A later Grant article (1992) returns to some of the themes, with an overview which gives a picture of the planning system as all powerful, and highly politicised as well as highly centralised. It is worth quoting his concluding section in full, as it shows how the perspective of probably the leading British planning law commentator showed little signs of the challenges of McAuslan of years earlier:

> British planning law is in operation a highly complex and technical system, and the aspects discussed in this article have been chosen to give a general impression of how it works in practice. It is above all a system of procedures, to which substantive controls are subordinate. Issues of principle are reserved to politicians and officials, not to lawyers and courts, and political battles shape both its procedures (through constantly changing planning legislation) and its substantive outcomes. It is peculiarly a British phenomenon, centralised, secretive, pragmatic, flexible and critically dependent ultimately on political morality and official incorruptibility. But if either of those two characteristics is missing, it has the capacity to become a particularly dangerous system of concentrated political power which is only loosely accountable. (p 12)

Again, there is no sense of lawyers presenting any sort of problem, and there is a great self-confidence in commenting on the system. The commentary is very much from a legal standpoint outwards, not thinking more broadly. In all these ways, it no doubt foreshadows how important lawyers have become in planning since that time. As far as I am aware there has been little critical commentary from within the planning law field since McAuslan's time.

Philip Booth, planning and law

The work of Philip Booth is that of an architect planner, but one with considerable legal knowledge. He has studied planning history in depth, in order to extract the importance of the relationship with the British legal system, which he thinks has been much underplayed. This has resulted in original and powerful writings (especially Booth 2003), both on the deep history of the state's engagement with urban development, back to medieval times, and on the detailed evolution behind the 1947 system, with its roots in the law of nuisance and then local government regulations, and the micro history of the approach to development control in the 1930s and 1940s. In a sense, he is confirming some of McAuslan's analysis, in stressing how the common law, the courts, private property and the legal profession all retained influence through the continuing British legal tradition, and so crafted the particular approach to planning which emerged in Britain in the 20th century.

Booth's main reflective engagement with the planning and law relationship is perhaps in a 2016 article on planning and the rule of law. He discusses how he distanced himself only very slowly from the planner's normal instrumental view of law, which saw the law as simply a set of tools that planners could apply as they wished. But he came to see that the reason why British planning was so different from that elsewhere was the different legal tradition, based on the common law and particularly the law of nuisance. He argues that public administration had already taken its core form when planning, a latecomer, arrived. The basic categories such as 'development' emerged from case history, not from an academic legal process of reflection, as in France and Germany. In the end he comes out very much on the side of the legal system's approach to rational argument, basing decisions and policy on clearly enunciated principles (as, for example, sustainable development could be, if so specified). Again, I quote Booth's final paragraph to show the way in which he conceptualises the planning–law relationship:

> The rule of law has shaped spatial planning and spatial planning has inherited the modes of thought and the

> processes of the law. The degree to which this has happened is not always acknowledged by planning professionals or the politicians that they serve. The understanding of that legal inheritance is important because it helps to explain the underlying rationale of the processes of spatial planning. This paper has argued from a largely English standpoint, that the working through of the rule of law and its impact on spatial planning in England, and by extension in the rest of Britain, takes a particular form. It may be argued that what is true for Britain is substantially true for other countries, too. The law has shaped spatial planning, and its modes of thought and processes have been transferred to and internalised by planning practice. But the significance of that understanding is not simply academic. The argument of this paper is that the legal inheritance also points to ways in which practice might be improved. We can learn much from the way in which law has evolved, and the quality of thinking that lies behind its evolution. (p 358)

It will be noticed that there is no sense here at all of the importance of politics and ideology to the substance or processes of planning. The analysis and the prescription is very much on the importance of the legal foundations and the value of developing these using legalist approaches. My own approach, as will be clear shortly, is to stand back from the law and planning relation in a different way from Booth, seeing the scope for more radically different approaches if better planning is to result. This is partly based on the judgement that historical forces can be more malleable than such an approach as Booth's may suggest. There are, in my view, considerable limits to arguments based too much on path dependency.

The planning lawyers

What about the lawyers themselves? McAuslan says that 'lawyers have always stood aloof from planning, and a mutual suspicion exists between planners and lawyers' (1975 p 31). I can certainly testify to this statement from my own experience, though since the early 2000s the overwhelming power of the lawyers mobilised by development interests has perhaps generated a more mixed reaction among local authority planners, blending envy, respect and resentment in various measures.

What is clear from any reading of *Planning* magazine is that lawyers are now a core part of the planning industry, and planning is a core part of the law industry. Commentaries across a spectrum of articles in this magazine are, if anything, now more likely to be by a planning lawyer than by a planner. This has been particularly noticeable as lawyers have virtually taken over the highly complex infrastructure planning field since it was separated off after the Planning Act 2008. Given that this excluded local authorities to a large extent, developers have to write their own development consents, and the processes introduced even more intimidating thresholds of knowledge than in the normal town and country planning regime, it was not surprising that the London planning law firms geared up quickly to absorb this new source of business. It is now clearly the case that the great bulk of expertise on the infrastructure regime is in these law firms, and if government consulted on changes, as it often has done in the decade or more since the 2008 Act, it was these firms, grouped for convenience in the National Infrastructure Projects Association (NIPA), who could give the most helpful advice on the need, from their perspective, for legislative revision. It is true that NIPA contains developer, local authority and academic members, but the leadership has been consistently from planning lawyers.

It is hard to provide solid evidence for the increasing presence of lawyers in planning. Just looking at the barrister members of the Planning and Environment Bar Association (PEBA) does not show a rapid inflation of numbers – 307 members in 2006–07, 311 in 2009–10, 341 in February 2019, to cite the only data obtainable (thanks to PEBA's secretary for these). Numbers of planning solicitors do seem to be rising faster, with 502 solicitors found in the 43 largest planning law firms in *Planning* magazine's 2017 survey, 607 in 2018 and 672 in 2019. So, larger practices had 20, 30 or more professional lawyers, an impressive weight of expertise when one compares this with the normal professional planning presence now in government agencies or councils. This may match the relentless growth of the solicitors' profession in Britain as a whole, with numbers of practising solicitors rising from 120,000 in 2010 to 142,500 in 2017. It also must match the growth of the planning consultancy sector overall. Much more research would be needed to reveal the full extent and nature of this professional force.

An approach to the planning and law relation

My approach to this area has some similarities to that discussed by Sheppard et al in their planning law textbook, which they describe as a political economy approach. They stress the need to see how politics, economics and law interrelate in a society: 'debates over planning law inevitably involve the power and influence of property rights … the nature, form and purpose of planning law will be determined by which political viewpoints and ideologies hold sway' (2017, p 29). However, they do not go much further into their approach.

My conclusion from the above survey is that there are convincing pointers to analysing the way in which law affects the politics and ideology of planning. The primary visible impact of the law's core role is to depoliticise and deideologise (if the rather unpleasant word is allowable) planning. This flows directly from Bourdieu's case for the neutralising and universalising effects of law. An observer outside the planning law tent will feel that the law has the capacity to take the planning situation they are dealing with outside politics, and apply universally valid principles. The result is, at least initially, disempowering for anyone who does not have access to good legal resources. This applies just as much to the field of planning, now that it is intensely legalised and judicialised, as it does to an area like criminal law, where the dominant presence of state power and legal expertise is much more obvious.

In other words, the general belief in the rule of law and the everyday reality of the permeation of planning by legal concepts pose a strong challenge to the argument being made in this book. On one level, law really does remove political and ideological dimensions from planning, as it seeks to do in all fields it deals with. But, from my perspective, this understanding is a gain, because it explains in part why the political and ideological sides of planning are to an extent hidden, pushed under a legal veil. It may also contribute to the difficulties that observers (such as myself) have in analysing the relationship of planning and ideology: the failure to integrate the law question into planning theory may exacerbate how academics struggle with this issue. Thinking outside the legal mental stranglehold is simply hard. Booth found this as he explored the history and carried out comparative work, though in fact he broadly accepted the framing of the rule of law in any case.

The veiling effect must also contribute to the widespread support in the planning profession for a politics-free practising of planning: not in the sense of planning being outside everyday politics, which all agree it is not at all, but in the sense that planners do and should strive to be politically neutral – like the law is.

But it is essential to go further than emphasising this gain in understanding, to go beyond seeing the effect of the legal veiling. What Bourdieu and many other critical analysts are also saying is that the process of banishing politics and ideology is socially constructed.

However real it is, it is only real in certain ways and at certain levels, because it has been created, instituted, historically and politically and ideologically. Just as real as the depoliticising and deideologising effects of law are the tendencies it generates (under contemporary political economic circumstances) for conservative and elite supporting understandings of how planning can be done – in other words, its also heavy political and ideological effects. This stems in large part from the law's relation to the state and to property regimes, evolved as many have now described in varying ways in each state. How often is the effect of the immense power of private property 'called out' in any planning case? That property power remains invisible, normally, behind a legal wall.

Together, both the apparent depoliticisation and deideologisation, and its real opposite, the chaining of planning to broadly conservative interests of property and state, impact on how non-lawyers and non-professionals can engage with planning. Depoliticisation and deideologisation obstruct the option of engaging with fundamental underlying issues in any planning case. The conservative tendency means that all practice starts from certain assumptions about legitimate structures and values, that is, the equally real and existing politics and ideology. This generates an underlying tendency for planning to be inaccessible, to be outside the reach of ordinary citizens, however well organised.

Given the social construction of the planning–law relation, there remains, however, the potential to challenge this situation. A new or lesser form of veiling might be developed. This is in a sense what McAuslan was arguing for in the concluding chapter of his 1980 book. He admitted that his general conclusion, that 'the ideologies of planning law mirror the ideologies and practices of government and society' (p 265), was hardly surprising. But he then explored the way in which the status quo to which most lawyers were attached might be changed. He suggested that at least a minority of lawyers might support the challenging ideology of public participation. At this point, the book ends, and clearly the different times of today would point in other directions or other possibilities. But McAuslan certainly went some way in revealing the links of law, politics and planning in his period, and, by using the word ideology, implied (without much real analysis) that the issues were deep rooted.

We will need to discuss the possible alternative trajectories further in Chapter 11. A starting point is the extreme complexity of the UK planning system. This was a core finding of a recent full review (Raynsford 2018a, 2018b) of the system, which described the chaotic accumulation of reforms since the last consolidating Acts in 1990–91, which are confusing to planners, let alone to ordinary citizens. The complexity is extensive, as to understand it fully we have to include the legal regimes sitting alongside the main planning areas, including the major body of environmental law, and the special regimes for conservation and some other fields, as we will explore in later chapters.

The complexity is admitted by lawyers, but it provides part of the base of their business, as only they have the time and skills to interpret and deploy the legal frameworks, in applying them to development projects. Any attempt to democratise and open up the planning system would need to work out how this complexity might be reduced. Clearly, a full consolidating Act would be one starting point, but this would risk just consolidating a still enormously complicated and legalistic structure.

Planning education

This book is about the activity of planning, much more than about how it is learnt and taught. But the education and training of planners clearly relates closely to the issues considered in this chapter. Planning education is based on the assumption that there is a lot that can be learnt, partly of a technical and legal nature, to make planners work more effectively. There is a large literature on planning pedagogy, but it is a reasonable guess (without an exhaustive survey) that little of that is prioritising the issues examined in this book. But a recent article by Huw Thomas (2017), drawing on earlier work, explores the links between the powerfully ideologically driven transformation of UK universities and the experiences of planning teachers. He makes clear the effects of the neoliberalisation of British universities since 1990, with the increase of competition between universities, the introduction of New Public Management techniques, and the resultant subjection of academic practice to the drivers of Key Performance Indicators, for both research and teaching. This fits well with the reflections on 'the neoliberal university and its alternatives' by Rustin (2016), where he discusses the classic alternatives which universities face (as public educators, industrial trainers or traditional humanists).

Thomas describes the big tensions created for the varied traditions of planning education, with a broad perspective on a liberal education, and on the values of planning at risk of being eroded by these managerialist transformations. So, in this area as well, ideology is very prominently and (for university academics) very obviously in action, alongside the natural politics of any institution such as a university and its links with governmental policies. In Chapter 11, when possible ways forward are discussed, some words will address this important aspect of British planning.

Conclusion

This chapter has explored two aspects of planning – its skills base and the permeation by law – to progress thinking about how far these are part of the political and ideological dimensions of planning. These parts of the instrumentation of planning do, I have argued, have genuine zones of autonomy in which planners operate. This is in part positive for planners in many situations, giving scope for creativity and securing successes. But the autonomy is only partial, as politics and ideology infuse how planning techniques work in real situations (like housing numbers calculations), and the planning and law relation is ideologically conditioned. For those radicals hoping to change planning's impacts, this can be positive, as it points to ways to open out and reform, perhaps fundamentally, planning's set of instruments and relationships with the political process. Communication, another dimension of the instrumentation, comes into this, as only with a more democratically functioning media system could some moving away from excessively blinding and distancing legalism and technicism become feasible. This will be covered in Chapter 8.

6

Ideology and politics in government, central and local

Chapter 1 proposed that politics could be considered in two parts, consisting of institutional and governmental forms, and of pressure and group politics. This chapter and the next explore these two (in reality intertwined) political zones. This will not, of course, exclude the treatment of ideological influences at the same time, as the governmental and pressure politics activity in planning is heavily infused with ideological dimensions.

As planning is part of the activity of the state, governmental matters are enormously important for how planning works. This chapter examines this working at central and local levels. Quite distinct governmental structures now rule the four parts of the UK, and, as elsewhere in this book, I concentrate on the UK government which rules England, directly. This is done in four sections. The first surveys the structures of government, central and local. The second explores how thinking about planning as part of public administrations or bureaucracies can reveal more about the relationship with politics. Third, I give an overview of the operation of politics and ideology in local government in England, by means of some, admittedly limited, examples. A section on neighbourhood planning follows, to see how this new area of formal planning relates to the themes of this book.

Government structures

There being no constitution, governmental structures can change significantly under the policies of any UK central government, or, within the devolved administrations, by their government decisions, within certain limits set by the devolution Acts. However, there are certain fixed points which have applied for several decades, as well as areas of change. This brief survey will identify both continuing features and some significant changes.

It can be argued that both Conservative and Labour ideologies have large components of centralism within them. In the case of Conservatism this relates to the need for strong authority at the centre of the nation (and, until the 1960s, the British Empire), especially in fields of special importance to Conservative conceptions of government, such as defence and law and order, as well as maintaining the integrity of the UK. In the case of the most powerful strands of Labourism, normally dominant for the whole century of Labour national importance since the 1920s, this has connected to the importance of having the strength in central government to take on the big challenges of steering the otherwise partly independent capitalist economy, as well as having a chance to promote an idea of a reformed society, against strong media and cultural forces going against socialist or progressive thinking. In both cases this supported the existence of a strong government machine based in Westminster, and the sovereignty of the elected part of Parliament against any other forces (such as the judiciary, the House of Lords – always a potential problem for Labour, as it had been for reforming Liberal governments – or the royal prerogative). In planning this meant, from the 1940s, a position within a strong ministry, first, until 1951, called the Ministry of Town and Country Planning, then with various names but a significant planning presence, at least till the 1990s.

There were indeed elements within the ideologies of both parties pushing for strong elements of local control over planning, and these coincided with the historical, organic, growth of planning responsibilities, in which local government had a leading role as maker of bye-laws and primary implementer of regulatory procedures in many fields of domestic policy, particularly in those of public health and housing which led into the formation of planning in the early 20th century. Conservatives drew on their tradition of limited intervention controlled by elites in each locality, normally of a safe conservative colour in most areas until the 1920s. This thread of localism has had a continuing presence which has supported the maintenance of planning as a major local government function. One can point, for example, to the reforming of planning legislation when Chris Patten was secretary of state for the Environment in 1989–92, when locally plan-led decision making was promoted, seeking to reduce the role of ministers and the Inspectorate.

Labour approaches to government also contained a significant element of localism, drawing on the traditions of municipal government built up in, especially, London and the big provincial cities since the 1920s, which by the 1960s saw most cities and towns of any size having had significant periods of Labour rule. Some of the strands of socialism had important local emphases as well, including the Cooperative Party and guild socialism, alongside strong trades councils linking with the partly locally organised trade union movement in some areas. These strands competed with the powerful central elements visible in the periods of Labour in power in the 1940s, 1960s, 1970s and 1997–2010, when the activities of reforming ministers like Morrison, Silkin, Crossman and Crosland all put emphasis on central steering at national and regional levels, using instruments like New Town Development Corporations, the Housing Corporation and strong redistributive taxation to support poorer areas of the country. Regionalism was strong within Labour thinking in this way in the 1960s and 1970s, laying out regional strategies coordinated with central government investment in transport and other utility spheres as part of attempts at regional 'rebalancing' away from the richer southern England. The 1997–2010 governments saw a pull between those supporting the regional drive of John Prescott, arguing for a devolution to English regional assemblies, against the centrally committed core of the government, including those with strong regional bases like Jack Straw and David Blunkett, who consistently opposed what they saw as a potential weakening of the central hold of Labour on the UK machine. The centralist strands of the Labour tradition were comfortably successful in this struggle. The arguably best attempt to build a locally coherent and responsive regional planning got caught in this ideological crossfire within Labourism.

It can be argued whether this tussle over the organisation of planning as a state activity was the result of the ideological orientations of the two main parties, or whether it stemmed from the gradual path-determined accumulating of power positions, which meant that local government maintained and in fact built up its role as a key implementing actor, until at least the early 1980s. Certainly there were historical and 'practical' reasons behind the presence of planning decision making within local councils, as well as the counter force very visible, especially from the 1940s, in the shape of the appeals system and ministerial and regional steering of the priorities of planning. But I would argue that ideologies, though as always not that visible, played important parts. Ideological conservatism, embedded in some respects in both the main traditions, supported the continuation of the Westminster model of governing, with no written constitution and no defence of the powers of local government on a long term-basis. None of this would have been acceptable in the very different traditions present in some continental systems since the 1940s, where subsidiarity is constitutionally embedded in some cases (Germany, Austria, Spain, Italy), and where political (as against ideological) traditions normally maintain systems of rough equality across governmental levels, in countries as different as France, the Netherlands, Belgium, Denmark and Sweden.

This centralism of the two ideologies has perhaps been especially visible since the 1980s, with the victory of Thatcherite Conservatism empowering the central government as the key actor in UK planning and related spheres, gradually reducing the significance of local government as an independent actor, most dramatically in the massive slimming down of local government resourcing since 2010. Equally, the New Labour version of Labourism was not especially sympathetic to local government, taking the whole government record together, fitting with a similar faith in the role of the private sector in local development, house building and in many other spheres. This was a long way from the 'municipal socialism' espoused by much of the Labour Left in the 1980s. At that time, when radical socialists controlled a good number of councils in London and most metropolitan areas, it was thought that socialist policies, including in the fields close to planning in economic development, housing, transport and the environment, could be built from the bottom up, even when central government was controlled by a government with opposite policies. This option was blocked by the Thatcher governments, which were able to stamp out this challenge by using the easily-to-hand strengths of the core UK state, abolishing authorities, including the GLC, in the vanguard of the local municipalist movement, and crushing the financial independence of other councils. This may have been one experience pushing most leaders of the 1997–2010 governments back to the centralising traditions of Labourism, when themselves in power.

The components of planning government

A listing of the elements of the planning polity reveals the location of planning work, in formal terms. Again, this is just for the UK government and England.

Central government

The Ministry of Housing, Communities and Local Government supervises the planning system, deals with applications called in by minister, prepares any legislation, sponsors the Planning Inspectorate. The number of professional planners has declined since 2010, within a ministry mainly now focused on housing matters. Several other ministries are also very important, including the Treasury (now containing the National Infrastructure Commission) and Transport, but they do not have direct planning roles.

The Planning Inspectorate (PINS) is a major employer of professional planners. It deals with appeals, manages public examinations of local plans and manages examinations within the major infrastructure planning regime.

In the past, several other important state agencies have employed significant numbers of planners and have effectively contributed to government capacity to plan. However, given the large cuts to most of these agencies since 2010, this is less the case than in the past. These agencies include the Environment Agency, Historic England, Natural England, Highways England and Network Rail.

Regional government

This has been largely non-existent in England since the abolition of regional institutions in 2010, but it existed for most of the previous 50 years in various forms, including voluntary regional associations to undertake regional planning (1960s to 1990s), and more formal regional governmental offices, regional development agencies and regional assemblies (1994–2010). Some elements of regionalisation have been beginning to reappear in a limited form, including bodies sponsored by the Department for Transport (DfT), such as Transport for the North, and Midlands Connect (since 2015). Local Enterprise Partnerships (LEPs) have existed since 2010, as business-led bodies at regional or sub-regional level, responsible for leading on economic and industrial promotion.

Local government

The main planning authorities are 237 district councils, 55 unitary councils, 10 National Park planning authorities and 32 London borough councils. These are the primary decision makers on planning applications and the primary makers of statutory local plans, although neighbourhood plans may be made by parish councils and neighbourhood forums.

In addition there are 27 English county councils, with some transport and environmental planning responsibilities, but, since 2004, relatively few direct planning powers, and so employing rather few professional planners, in most cases.

There are also the Greater London Authority and London mayor, with powers to make the London Plan and to intervene to some extent in London planning issues, and with control of Transport for London (TfL) and a London housing budget. Both the London mayor and

TfL are significant employers of professional planners. In contrast, the emerging combined authorities, a weak form of collaborative agencies for mainly metropolitan areas, have direct planning responsibilities in only a few cases, and the number of planners employed is small, even compared with the last generation of regional planning of 1990–2010, which depended on limited planning staffing.

The resultant shape of the planning polity

It will be seen that the great weight in terms of day-to-day planning is at the base local authority level. This is matched by a large planning consultancy sector which mainly works to extract development permissions from this base local authority level, and to some extent to support Local Plan making. The other pole of planning expertise is in PINS, although, following steep cuts in resources since 2010, this is also under great pressure to simply deliver the minimum requirements imposed by central government in relation to targets for decision times. Neighbourhood planning is the third arm of planning activity in England, developed since 2010 in statutory terms, though present in other ways for many years. This also consumes significant planning resources, in part professional and in part self-trained local actors (or retired planners). It is important too that there are special regimes for landscape protection, with wholly separate planning authorities in the ten National Parks, and advisory boards for the 34 Areas of Outstanding Natural Beauty (AONBs). The National Parks and AONBs between them cover large areas of England, and naturally force planning policy in directions appropriate to their designation in those areas.

Public administration, bureaucracy and planning

Planning is an administrative activity, and in some sense a field of bureaucratic action. There is a large academic field dealing with public administration (Peters and Pierre 2012). This literature discusses among much else the forms which such administration takes, including the forms of bureaucracy as these have been theorised since Max Weber's classic writing. The literature also has as a central theme the relationship of public administration and politics. Clearly, private administrative, managerial and bureaucratic activity does not have the same relation to politics. So, planning consultancies, now such a core element of planning activity, are related to politics only in a more external manner, via their links with local authorities and central government and its agencies, though this does not remove the politicalness of their planning activity. Local council planners, on the other hand, are inside the political process, as are in slightly different ways civil servants working in central government or those working in PINS. These publicly employed planners are both internally and externally affected by their links to political processes.

The rhetorical framing of bureaucracy is a significant one for planning. When politicians, particularly those on the Right, say that planning is bureaucratic, which they have frequently done in Britain, they are making an ideological statement. They are contrasting the supposed rigidity, insensitivity and slowness of such action with the supposed flexibility, responsiveness and speed of market-driven, private sector action. Planning is part of 'red tape', and one of the core zones where Conservative governments, and to a lesser extent New Labour ones, have pursued deregulatory programmes. This line of rhetoric is often used to justify privatising and commercialising activity, and lies behind the overall drive to slim down the state, pursued fairly consistently in Britain since 1979, though in varying forms and different rhythms. So it will be helpful to discuss the nature of 'planning bureaucracy'.

Bureaucracy, and how far planning is bureaucratic

Two dimensions are examined here. The first is the overall evaluation of bureaucratic and public administrative activity, of which planning is a part. A well-known book by Paul Du Gay (2000) argued that the attack on bureaucracy (nearly always public bureaucracy) which had driven the New Public Management often made public administration less effective. He argued that the values behind public administration remained essential for achieving fair delivery of public programmes, and that trying to mimic private management approaches simply distorted the possibility of achieving efficient and effective action. A Dutch text on public administration came to the same conclusion (De Vries 2016), arguing that it was time for academics to stress the positive achievements of public administrators. He admitted the perennial risks present in any kind of bureaucratic activity, public and private, but pointed out that these had been being tackled for several decades, often finding a good balance between regular, fair and efficient service, and the flexibility and responsiveness to the customers or clients of public services. He pointed to the new ideas for reforms from around 2000, moving away from New Public Management to the 'Neo-Weberian State'. This suggested 'reaffirming the crucial role of governments as the main facilitator of solutions to the new problems. Central are the administrative law in preserving its basic principles and a public service with a distinct status and culture' (De Vries 2016, p 98). Peters and Pierre argued that 'a strong bureaucracy is characterized by the rule of law. The law-governed nature of the public administration is a safeguard against clientelism, corruption and favoritism … A strong public bureaucracy is critical to sustain core democratic values like equality, legal security and equal treatment.' (2012, pp 6–7).

These views chime well with the discussion of Ted Kitchen (2007) of these roles in planning, in which he shows how planning authorities were evolving new approaches to meeting the needs of their multiple customers or stakeholders. So, I would support the general drift of Du Gay's viewpoint, that bureaucracy does not have to be a dirty word, a term of abuse. The ideological nature of such use of this language can be exposed, and the value of public administrative work, in its various forms, some more and some less bureaucratic in the classic Weberian sense, can be celebrated.

A second dimension relates to in what way planning is close to the classic bureaucratic form. That form can be taken as having two components. One is the macro character of bureaucracy as carried out by a hierarchical body of officials, appointed on merit, and expected to be neutral. The other is the frequent characterisation of the activity as strongly rule conditioned, with repetition of tasks in a relatively automatic way. While planning and most central and local government work is broadly bureaucratic in the macro sense, it can be argued that planning is too varied an activity on the micro component to count as strongly bureaucratic. Some areas of planning work do have some of the characteristics of tightly rule-following and repetitive work which may be seen as conforming closely to the micro dimension of a classic bureaucracy. These could include the assessment of small schemes or applications, to see whether they meet certain criteria. But it is difficult to find many types of planning work of this kind. Larger and more complex planning applications absorb the greater part of the time of planners working in development management (DM), and these all need very careful attention to particular circumstances, and so require skills and judgements which do not fit the idea of bureaucratic action. The same applies to work on enforcement, where site visits and communicating with the public are core elements, as well as in other areas of work in conservation, landscape or design. Planning policy work is even less easily made to fit within general rules, with the plans prepared for sectors or localities and regions needing creativity and fitting to unique circumstances, almost always. Of course there can be regularised elements, with local plans copying or adjusting wording, for example, very often, from neighbouring authorities or similar contexts.

So, there are elements of rule following and relatively simplified work in planning, and the public administrations as a whole (with planning as part of these) have macro-component features of the classic bureaucracy. But most of the work itself is not strongly rule dominated, that type forming a small proportion overall of planning work in either councils, consultancies or central government and the inspectorate. So, the label 'bureaucratic' operates, in this sector, as in part an ideological designation, implying criticism of the nature of public sector activity, rather than a reasonable description.

Public administration, politics and commercialisation

It is much more interesting to examine directly the core issues in planning work, which include, as in all public administration, the relationship to politics, and also, especially given the increasing commercialisation of planning, the growing risks of clashes of interest and corruption (Jones and Comfort 2019). The two issues, politics and the danger of corruption, have of course been historically close. The invention of modern forms of public administration, emerging in Britain from the mid-19th century, was a response to this very issue. It will be important to examine here how far recent reforms and tendencies may be returning administration to a more pre-modern character. A major part of the point of rule following, and some elements of modern public administration like appointment on merit, has been to act as a bulwark against commercialisation and corruption.

Part of this relates to the roles of discretion and political decision making and delegation in current planning, including the drive to hand over planning administration to consultancies or big service conglomerates (in Britain most commonly at present, the company Capita). Current research is finding that this is changing planning culture across much of the planning sector, encouraging local authority planners to think in terms of income-generating activities, rather than a wider sense of the public interest.

At the local level, most councils delegate most decisions on planning applications to planning officials. Also, the expertise and complexity involved in plan making means that only the broad lines of plans are likely to be determined by politicians. There are naturally tensions to be negotiated in this relationship. A study in a southern English town (Tait 2012) found that the approaches to professionalism varied considerably between council-employed planners, who were keen to maintain good relations with their councillors, and private sector planners, who considered that a harder-edged idea of expert practice should guide all professional planning work (in the case studied, this was seen as favourable to the decisions on their clients' projects). Tait describes the necessary ambiguity in the role of council-employed planners, who do not have a single client like private sector planners but have to bear in mind many stakeholders, although 'the relationship between planning officers and elected politicians is central to the professional identity of local authority planners' (p 613).

Equally fundamental in the changing relationship to politics is the drive to outsource council planning to the private sector, supported by successive UK governments but especially since 2010. This means that a company like Capita may be writing the reports on planning applications, taking delegated decisions and preparing local plans all over England, thus breaking the link between locally employed planners and local councillors. This contractualisation has been studied extensively by Mike Raco, looking at the management of the 2012 Olympics project as well as other regeneration or urban development schemes (Raco 2013, 2014, 2015a). Raco argues that one effect of such complex contractual arrangements is to remove the possibility for any public or community input after a very early stage of project development and in fact to similarly weaken the scope for input by elected councillors or MPs. Commercialisation therefore tends to weaken democratic guiding of planning and its related fields, although clearly the forms of commercialisation will affect the nature and degree of this removal of democracy, and thus the restructuring of the relationship between planners and politics.

At the central government level, slightly different issues arise, as planning roles in the central ministry have not yet been outsourced. However, the reduction in the numbers of trained planners in this ministry since the early 2000s, and the bringing in of more staff with business backgrounds, can have problematic effects in the nature of support for ministers and the creation of new planning policy. A study of PINS examined possible conflicts for civil servants dealing with some of the case work, when in effect PINS has to act on behalf of the secretary of state, as well as be a neutral semi-judicial actor on appeals and called-in applications (Sheppard and Ritchie 2016). The article explored the different model in Northern Ireland, where there is a Planning Appeals Commission (PAC). The PAC is separate from the ministry and is funded by another part of the Northern Ireland Executive, giving, it is judged, a better chance of full impartiality, with less risk of political influence over decisions. While the article does not reach firm conclusions, it demonstrates the significance, at this sharp end of decision making, of alternative ways of institutionalising the relationship between planning decisions and central government politicians. The case study in Chapter 4 on the 2010–15 government showed how significant the personal interventions of the secretary of state can be at times, and so the clear scope for the politicisation of decisions that the arrangement of ministers, department and inspectorate can facilitate.

Another nice study emphasising how important central processes and networks are, even in apparently 'local' matters, is that of Rozema (2015) on opposition to the High Speed 2 (HS2) rail project. Local interest representation was seen to have strong limitations, unless allied with national groupings and using the levers of central governing, especially MPs and other party mechanisms. Central power in the UK unitary state was what mattered most, and most local groups found it hard to engage with or reach this power nexus.

We see here, therefore, issues particular to the difficult zone that the ideologically stressed field of planning constitutes for the state, at all levels. These have existed for the whole history of British planning in different forms, and have been negotiated variously, depending on the institutional and ideological characters of each period. The 'classic' period of the 1947 system no doubt allowed the working out of certain arrangements for managing the politics and planning relations at central and local levels which combined, broadly, scope for overall political steering with space for effective expert work by planners. The present period is one where, for various reasons, those modes are more challenged, by commercialisation, by the cutting back of all public administrations related to planning and by strongly anti-planning ministers being in power, at times. This means the planning and politics relation now is probably evolving into uncharted territory. It is for the moment also uncharted by adequate research. What we can be sure about is that the nature of this evolving political infusion of the administration of planning will be having effects on the outputs of planning.

The operation of planning in local government

The 'coalface' of planning activity in Britain is managed to a significant degree by local government. Is ideology less determinant here, and is everyday politics, or even a more technically controlled process, more likely to have the leading role? The answer will inevitably have an impressionistic element, given the absence of extensive research on the working of local planning in Britain for many years. A valuable exception is the work on local planning cultures by Valler and Phelps

(2018), which explores some of the same issues of enduring patterns, though without an explicit emphasis on politics or ideology. They also use Oxfordshire and Hampshire case studies, though my own take on these areas has some differences.

We need first to survey briefly how local planning works. Within the institutional forms described above, the pressure is on district and unitary councils in England to make or revise local plans and make decisions on planning permissions, among other, lesser responsibilities. Both of these major roles are policed by government, with quite strong incentives or penalty systems. The so-called 'localism' of the 2010–15 government did not touch this powerful directive system of central government over local planning. Most planners would say that the main actions of that government made achieving success in these primary roles harder, especially given the heavy loss in planning personnel in local government: the cut in planning budgets of local government is estimated at 53% in these years (Gray and Barford 2018).

Here the focus is on plan making, the area most known to me. But DM is at the core of everyday decisions on planning applications. DM was previously named development control, and the name change reflects the development-friendly 'culture change' of the early 2000s – in itself an indication of the ideologically charged nature of the activity. Clifford (2018) gives a clear if depressing picture of contemporary practice, showing a system under extreme pressure, with pressure to do ever more (speedier decisions, with less refusals) with ever fewer resources. Clifford examines the dilemmas experienced by council planners. All those interviewed had less than half the staff of ten years ago and the scope for public involvement was being driven out by the stress on viability of schemes and time pressures. This is often leading to a neoliberalised practice, where whatever the personal values that planners may have, or have been encouraged to promote (perhaps concerns about equity, climate change issues, or design), they are forced to prioritise business development and 'growth' as defined in governmental documents like the NPPF. So, Clifford suggests that local politics may be significant up to a point, but the whole system is driven most of all by national ideological and political forces, especially by the national framing of guidance and the continuous cutting of public resources.

Planning Oxfordshire

We can begin to get some idea of how local government planning works by looking at the panorama in Oxfordshire, a context of which

I have knowledge over many years. Every locality has its distinctive characteristics, and so, although there are features which Oxfordshire will share with, particularly other southern, counties with two-tier local government structures, each area will be unique. Other localities may well be less stressed than Oxfordshire. An example would be the Cheltenham, Gloucester and Tewkesbury sub-region, which, by the accounts of those familiar with recent planning, has managed to cooperate quite well to agree future housing development areas.

Since local government reorganisation in 1974, Oxfordshire has had a county council and five district councils. This structure replaced an autonomous Oxford City Council, a county council and numerous small urban and rural district councils. Other than causing Oxford City Council to sometimes hark back to its days of imagined independence of the county council, the large geographical change in 1974 was to absorb a large area of what had been Berkshire county area, this becoming the new district council, Vale of the White Horse. The rest of the old Oxfordshire county area outside the city was divided between three large districts, called Cherwell, South Oxfordshire and West Oxfordshire (see Figure 6.1). The Conservatives had outright control of the county council from 1973 to 1985 and from 2005 to 2013. During the other years, there has been formally no overall control, though in practice there have been only short periods of non-Conservative rule. For example, Conservatives have held control since 2013 with the help of four Independents.

Planning since 1974 has been divided between county and district levels, with the districts always responsible for most decisions on planning permissions. The county council guided the overall shape of development through making a Structure Plan (to 2004), and then by input to the Regional Spatial Strategy for the South East (to 2010). Since 2010 the county council has direct powers only over planning transport, minerals and waste, though it can use its coordinating power. The councillors who manage these authorities are all directly elected, so there is no 'democratic deficit' in these arrangements, at least formally. Other bodies such as parish and neighbourhood councils are also elected, though normally on extremely low or uncontested polls. A creation of 2011 is the Local Enterprise Council for the county area, which has control over significant central government funds. It is made up of business representatives and members of councils, in the main, with no direct democratic legitimacy. I do not cover the most recent phase of planning, since 2017, including the preparation of a Joint Strategic Plan for the county, as this would enter into contemporary issues which remain thoroughly unresolved.

Figure 6.1: Oxfordshire showing district council areas

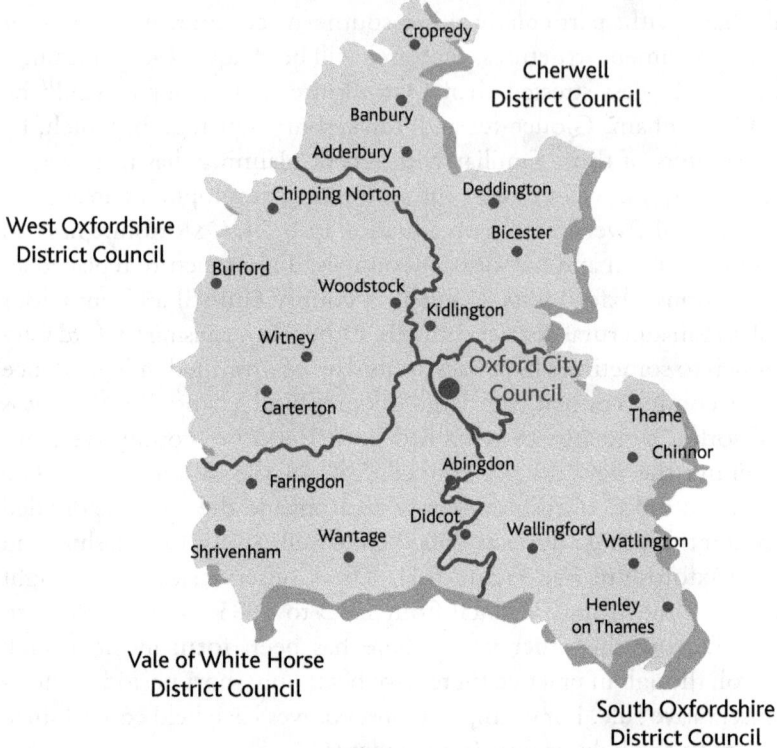

Source: Thanks to Dave Valler (Oxford Brookes University) for permission to reproduce this figure, and to Lisa Hill (Oxford Brookes University) for the redrawing of the figure

Planning in Oxfordshire since the 1970s has always been intensely politicised, with many planning decisions making the front pages of the local press week after week, year after year. This has included all the successive revisions of the Structure and Local Plans, as well as the struggles over housing allocations, road schemes, and proposals for other infrastructure, like that for a vast new reservoir south of Abingdon, often mooted since the 1980s, but never progressed.

Since the 1974 redrawing of boundaries, the county forms a reasonably coherent sub-region, centred very much on Oxford city, though with other significant urban centres, and much commuting to urban areas beyond its borders, to Reading, Swindon and, to an extent, London. The population in 2018 was estimated at 682,000, up from 606,000 in 2001. Oxford city has about 150,000 of this total, but the real urban reach of the city is larger than this suggests.

Against this structural and degrees-of-democracy backdrop, how can the process of governing planning within this sub-region be characterised? In the broadest terms the fights over planning can be described as pre-eminently political, taking place within each local authority in relation to planning applications and the making of forward plans, and between authorities (within whatever structure exists at the time) in relation to overall directions of growth and of infrastructure investment. The politics is first and foremost organised around party-political competition, with the presence of two tiers and varied arrangements for council elections meaning that there are elections somewhere every year. The party spectrum has included normally four parties: Conservatives, Labour and Liberal Democrats in all areas, and significant Green presence in Oxford city since the 1990s. On the other hand, since the 1980s, Conservative councillors have had almost no presence in Oxford city. Most councils have had varying control, with several periods of coalition in most councils. But, since around 2000, the dominant pattern has been Conservative control of the four less urban districts and often of the county council, and Labour control of Oxford City Council. To avoid too much entry into the complex patterns of the earlier period, I will now concentrate on this more recent period of around two decades from the late 1990s, which presents to some degree a simpler picture.

So, how far are the ongoing struggles over planning priorities ideologically based, as against formed by essentially interest-oriented politics? To give at least a tentative answer, we need to say a little about the main areas of contention over this period. To a large extent, these come down to the prioritising and locating of types of growth, mainly housing growth. But they can take varying forms. The growth strategy pursued since 1974 has been that of the 'country towns' strategy. This involved accepting a certain level of urban growth, modulated depending on the locally perceived needs of the period and central government pressures, and distributing this mainly to four main towns, in addition to Oxford city. This was designed to preserve the large Oxford green belt and, equally important, to protect the vast majority of rural areas and villages, including the large AONBs skirting the county on three sides. This was the formal strategy of successive Structure Plans up to 2004, and effectively, given the continuing influence of past allocations, up to the present.

But this broad strategy was always intensely contested, above all in its detail. Until 2004 this contesting was contained within a democratically functioning system managed by the county council. Between 2004 and 2010 a similar process was set within the making of the Oxfordshire part of the South East Regional Spatial Strategy (RSS), but when the RSS system was abolished in 2010, this work was lost. We can focus in on a heavily divisive element of the RSS to get nearer to a judgement as to the role of ideology and politics, the proposal to allocate land on the south side of Oxford for an urban extension, at Grenoble Road.

Grenoble Road proposed urban extension

Oxford had used two large urban extensions since the 1960s to provide new housing areas, extending beyond the Cowley car factory area (see Figure 6.2). It was proposed from the 1990s onwards that a third extension should be made, beyond the current urban boundary at Grenoble Road, but as this was within the South Oxfordshire District area, the agreement of this authority was needed, which had not been forthcoming. A further effort was made to allocate this land for housing within the South East Plan drawn up from 2003 to 2007. The site was included in the Plan, following general agreement, including of the county council, and the recommendation given after the Examination in Public of the Plan, but with South Oxfordshire still unhappy. This allocation was the subject of one of several legal challenges to the final approval of the Plan, which meant that when the 2010 general election came, this Plan was still not finalised. The change of government meant the abolition of the regional planning system and, in this case, that the allocation of the Grenoble Road site did not go ahead. Oxford City Council has continued to press for the need to provide more sites for its 'unmet housing need', and to argue that

Figure 6.2: Grenoble Road area in wider Oxfordshire context

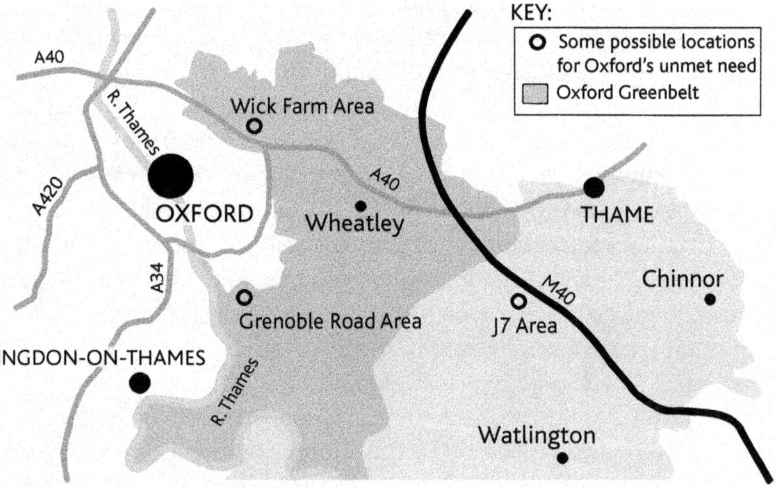

Source: Thanks to Dave Valler (Oxford Brookes University) for permission to reproduce this figure, and to Lisa Hill (Oxford Brookes University) for the redrawing of the figure

this site is one which can help to fill the gap, and South Oxfordshire has continued to resist the allocation, despite being under intense pressure to find large sites to meet the requirements of the NPPF system.

This particular site struggle was magnified by national political struggles. We have seen how Conservatism was positioning itself from the early 2000s as the opponent of New Labour's big state interventionism. In part, this was to be expressed for electoral consumption in planning terms, as the reconfiguration of 'localism' was carried through in 2008–10 (Tait and Inch 2016). Grenoble Road was the sort of site that fed into the construction of this narrative, against regional planning in particular, but against, in general, any leadership or interventionist roles by central government. This multi-scalar interweaving of political and ideological threads works differently in each English context. But for the 2000-onwards period in southern England, with Conservative councils surrounding the rare phenomenon of a Labour-run authority, this constitutes a privileged case. Labour leaderships may see southern England in part through the lenses of the few cities they control, from Oxford, for example, looking outwards. Equally, Conservative antennae may be oriented particularly to cases like Grenoble Road, rather than to the wide expanses of blue-coloured map covering so much of England.

In part this was therefore a party political feud. South Oxfordshire has been in Conservative hands since 1973, with the exception of 1995 to 2003, when there was a Liberal Democrat and Labour coalition, and since 2019, when it has been Liberal Democrat. Oxford city has normally been controlled by the Labour Party (in coalition with the Greens 2000–10, and with one Conservative administration 1976–80). However, the urban extensions were seen by South Oxfordshire councillors as the incarnation of the problems generated by Labour approaches to housing since the 1940s. The second extension, built in the 1990s, called Greater Leys, was mostly housing for sale, with some housing association development as well, so did not quite represent the original threat that was identified with earlier Oxford expansionism. But the sense of South Oxfordshire councillors seeing the erosion of their area by unwanted urban pressures went beyond the details of history. Even compared with threatened extensions on other sides of Oxford, Grenoble Road seems to be felt to be exceptionally unacceptable to Conservatives (as against protectionist groups, which appear to be even-handedly opposing all). This is no doubt related to its class connotations near to Cowley and Blackbird Leys: for Conservatives, these areas were associated with everything negative that had happened in Oxford since the 1930s, with the large car factory in Cowley and the council housing estate at Blackbird Leys.

This has surely been in part an ideologically coloured struggle, as well as in part being fuelled by the more widespread political struggle led by protectionist interests like the Oxfordshire branch of the CPRE. The CPRE have maintained a consistent defence of the green belt over decades, arguing that any cutting into it is a step which will be followed only by more intrusions. The fact that the Grenoble Road land is not seen as especially high-grade countryside (it is much affected by overhead power lines and the sewage plant covering much of the site), is not judged as relevant in green belt policy by CPRE (understandably, given the stated policy objectives of planning for green belts, taking these as a whole over the last half century). This consistency has given undoubted strength to this pressure group (and associated forces).

As we are beginning to see in different cases, there is a merging together of different levels of political and ideological arguments and energies in this case. Conservatives, and to a good extent Liberal Democrats in this context, adhered to a defence of the countryside position which fitted their ideological grounding in an image of independent communities formed around privately owned houses (and cars, and where possible schools and other facilities). So the politics of the kind of Conservatism present in South Oxfordshire is not simply following a calculus of pressure: 'the electors will not allow us to cede any ground on losing green fields to development'. Certainly this calculus is there, and is especially important near election times. But this political pressure model has an underlying ideological base. The argument works similarly the other way round. Oxford Labour, and to an extent other parties within the city (Liberal Democrat and Green) have urban-ness in their political make-up, and so act 'naturally' to press for some development to provide for their housing needs. But this rests too on a grounding of a completely different imaging of the part of Oxfordshire in which the city is set, and also on an ideological broad canvas of seeing planning for longer-term social purposes as a core part of a local authority's job, and with this having a significant component about social need.

We can thus note that the spatial imaginaries of the actors, the 'geography in people's heads', is understood here as part of the local ideological constitution of groups of actors, and as having some significance, in the planning context at least. These imaginaries vary strongly in the Oxford sub-region, depending on the actors' standpoints.

Of course the ideological components I am referring to here are not necessarily visible all the time. But they appear often enough for one to be pretty sure that they are present in the default positions of the key actors. Nor is the aim to present the struggles as having a neat simplicity, with, say, all CPRE supporters signing up to the same ideological positions as the most committed Conservative adherent of private provision in all possible spheres and the cutting back of the state. Clearly, here Conservatives and CPRE alike are exploiting the power of the socialist-crafted planning system to stop the free play of development or market forces. The green belt is anathema to some free market Conservatives, as the continuing attacks from think-tanks like the Adam Smith Institute make clear. But this does not matter: ideological core positions do not have to rest on a fully coherent and 'theoretically correct' idea of capitalism and society, and how the state should act. So again, Freeden's morphological conception of ideologies helps: one part of CPRE's ideological position can slot in with one part of the Conservative council leaderships' conceptions, and this is enough to ground a concerted politics.

Politics and ideology in South Hampshire

There are many studies of UK planning and locality change if one takes a broad definition of that term, even though, as argued in the literature review, little of this focuses on political or ideological dimensions. One area which has benefited from at least some focus in that sense is South Hampshire, though here both studies refer to the period of planning before 2010 (Buser and Farthing 2011, Phelps 2012). Buser and Farthing focus on the emergence of a consensus constructed around a sub-regional partnership, PUSH (Partnership for Urban South Hampshire), in the early 2000s. This rested in part on older cooperative efforts in the Solent area, but equally had to overcome years of conflict between the Conservative-dominated Hampshire county and normally Labour-run Portsmouth and Southampton. They stress the relatively uncontested nature of the PUSH process, allowing agreement across the local political elites of Hampshire County Council, the unitaries of Portsmouth and Southampton and the many district councils affected by expansion plans. They also make clear the importance of the dealing with central government, articulated in part regionally, with the partnership a lever to get growth-area resources. They admit that the consensus was a fairly narrow one, with civic and voluntary sectors only partially integrated and business in, at most, an advisory role.

Buser and Farthing do not probe underneath the more visible political relationships. The New Labour model in an area such as this was the controlled operation of largely public-driven partnerships in aid of 'growth' led by private sector agents, supplemented by strands of environmental sustainability and social inclusion, where local politics and national resources permitted this. It is reasonable to see this as the ideological foundation of the PUSH model in South Hampshire, the kind of governance partnership dissected by Davies (2011).

Phelps's study is a much fuller one of the sub-region going back to the middle of the 20th century. It demonstrates the very limited bases for agreeing about future spatial patterns during most planning periods, enshrined from 1974 in county Structure Plans which could not impose much order on the southern part of the county. The result was a fragmented and incremental approach to guiding urban development, meaning that the areas between the south Hampshire cities gradually filled up, often following the pressures generated by major road building, rather than benefiting from an integrated planning approach. The effect was a kind of sprawl affecting much of the area. So the book reveals the difficulties caused by both jurisdictional difficulties (competition between localities, despite the in-principle ring-holding powers of the county council up to the formation of the Portsmouth and Southampton unitary councils in 1996), and the underlying politics at work, of a broadly conservative and countryside protection kind. Phelps suggests that 'growth in South Hampshire has seen a broad shift from the last days of technocratic influence on planning decisions, through strong political influence, to a combination of politics and public participation' (2012, p 65). He puts the blame for the failures largely on politicians (not on planners). Politicians have been incapable of working across council boundaries, have pushed development to the boundaries of the jurisdictions, and so have failed to offer positive and strategic planning for growth (p 157–163).

It is not possible to attempt an extensive analysis of the ideological buttressing of such a complex process over several decades: Phelps did not do this, and so his picture of, as the book's sub-title says, 'Planning and politics in Britain' is only partial, documenting well many of the surface processes, but not probing very far into the succession of state and business models functioning in this relatively prosperous area of Britain. As always, it would be necessary to examine the intersecting of the successive national planning frameworks (including the presence and form of regional and national guidance), the nature of public investment and intervention by central government, with the party and pressure politics at county and district levels in Hampshire. In most periods these pointed to a light-touch type of planning, treating local sensibilities of suburban and rural electorates very carefully, as against taking a strong leadership role by governments at all levels. All that large framing was ideologically conditioned, as well as politically buttressed locally. The differences with Oxfordshire are significant, in that Oxfordshire had a somewhat more confident planning coherence during the Structure

Plan era, but there are also similarities: in the fear of large-scale public investment in public transport (compared to, say, the programmes in larger metropolitan areas) and the avoidance of strongly green politics, maintained over decades. In sum, both Oxfordshire and Hampshire demonstrate the dominance over long periods of broadly Conservative-style planning at the strategic level (differences may have been present in the cities, Oxford, Portsmouth and Southampton). Such planning arguably produced sub-optimal results for the populations as a whole, seeing the social and environmental forms over the long run, but used political modes of action acceptable to those governing these localities at all levels.

Neighbourhood planning

Planning at a local community or neighbourhood scale has been carried out extensively in Britain for several decades. This level of planning took different forms in different kinds of areas, with urban areas seeing community action or development or regeneration plans common in the 30 or more years from the 1970s, and rural areas being more characterised by parish appraisals and plans, with especially large numbers being prepared from the 1990s onwards (Parker 2008). A major change was marked by the Localism Act 2011, which made Neighbourhood Development Plans (normally Neighbourhood Plans, NPs) statutory, a part of the Development Plan, just as Local Plans are. This in itself was of course a decision full of political and ideological intent, as the earlier discussion on centralism and localism indicated. As the development of the new system progressed, it was then possible for observers to assess what was emerging. There has been a veritable avalanche of academic work on the topic, in marked contrast to so many other British planning issues, with 50 articles being categorised in Wargent and Parker's survey (2018, p 383). This has come from many angles, and from supporters of the new process as much as from sceptics (the fullest survey is in Brownill and Bradley 2017, also Juppenlatz 2016 for a broadly sympathetic study). Here the focus is on the political and ideological dimension of the plans and the planning process involved, rather than an attempt to assess the results, although inevitably some judgement on aspects of those will be relevant to the discussion.

From the extensive literature, I mainly use the survey articles, a few articles with a specifically political focus and the book edited by Brownill and Bradley (2017). This is valuable in giving a spread of types of analysis and of political positionings. Bradley's chapters are broadly supportive of the experience, finding some scope for progressive and radical democratisation, while being fully aware of the neoliberal colouring which the project has lived with and from which it emerged. Brownill insists on the importance of not dichotomising the experience, whether trying to condemn it as a neoliberal project pure and simple or praise it as a genuine example of local empowerment: it is, she argues, many things, and the task of analysts is to excavate this contradictory multiplicity. My own take, as will be clear, is largely on the critical or sceptical side of the spectrum of views. But I am aware that the experience is a very relevant living laboratory of how planning interacts with political change and how it lives within sometimes clashing ideological frames.

The innovation clearly aroused interest, from local activists as well as from academics. My interest is in seeing, in perhaps purer terms than normal, the combination of ideological grounding with the emerging political realities of this new planning activity. This is purer in the sense of there being fewer historically accumulated contingent factors around this kind of planning. Of course, other major institutional innovations have been present in UK planning in recent decades, such as the regional planning development of 1990 to 2010 and the infrastructure planning regime of post 2008. But it can be argued that neighbourhood planning has been more ideologically charged than these and more emergent from below, giving it a very special character. This also sets it off from the more continuous and, in a sense, hard-to-pin-down Local Plan making work, much more important though that work generally is.

The ideological foundation, while not that much commented on in this literature, surely conditions very powerfully what has emerged over these years, however large the variety may appear. Parvin (2008) identified some of this foundation in a perceptive article well before the system was invented, but when 'double devolution' and other brands of hyperlocalism were under intense discussion in both Conservative and Labour parties:

> In *Anarchy, State and Utopia*, Robert Nozick expressed the central libertarian dream of a society of autonomous, local communities, each self-regulated and co-existent with a wider society governed by a minimal state. It was, he said, the classic realisation of individual freedom: people would be free to create the local communities they wanted and if they found that they didn't like the community in which they lived, they would be able to leave and find a better one

elsewhere, one which was more in line with their views and more consistent with their aspirations and ideals. (p 356)

This of course underlies the Conservative version of hyper-localism more than any Labour one. Parvin was quite clear about the dangers that handing over power to small local majorities could constitute, and proposed better paths to take. 'Rather than devolve power down to local communities, then, more effective channels should be opened between the electorate and their central institutions' (p 360).

The removal of any higher-level regional or strategic planning, the effective weakening of the Local Plans system and the removal of most regeneration programmes and a large part of local government capacity: together these constituted a considered political project, with an explicit high-profile justification in terms of 'localism' and 'the big society'. Neighbourhood planning was the primary new output of this project, and could not help being utterly infused by this ideological foundation.

The detailing decided on as the Localism Bill was enacted and regulations were drawn up for the new regime reinforced this framing. One aspect discussed was the extent to which these new plans would have public legitimacy. Davoudi and Cowie (2013) expressed strong doubts whether the basis chosen, either parish councils or Neighbourhood Forums made up of a minimum of 21 people, met the criteria for being effective forms of democratic representation. A further legitimacy issue is that businesses can also prepare NPs, raising issues of a return to extra rights for businesses, as pre-democratic franchises allowed (and as still exists in the City of London Corporation). However, very few Business NPs have been prepared, and the most high-profile one, for the centre of Milton Keynes (Lock 2015, *Planning* magazine 2015), though controversial, did not appear to weaken the hand of the democratically elected council. It was noteworthy that the council stipulated that the Central Milton Keynes Neighbourhood Plan should be subject to an authority-wide referendum, giving it superior legitimacy. Evidently the council would have done this only if it had broadly supported the content of the Plan. The support for the Plan was strong, over 89,000 for as against 17,000 against, and 356 businesses voting for as against 47 against.

Other details reinforced the tensions in the new system, as NPs were required to fit in with Local Plans (prepared by elected local authorities with far more legitimacy, overall), and so very many of those involved in Plan making have felt that their powers have been minimal. Here we see the clash of the ideological rhetoric of taking local control coming up against alternative political demands, such as finding housing sites and keeping the development industry linked to the Conservative political interest.

In other ways the political working out of the new institution has pushed in fairly predictable directions. Surveys (such as Parker and Salter 2017) showed that most NPs had been in villages or small towns, and with few in the three northern English regions. Few were made in areas of multiple deprivation. No such definitive idea is yet clear of the substantive content of plans, but it is generally thought that NPs have not been the vehicle for producing more housing, and specifically much more affordable housing. It is still too early to say what substantive difference the NPs have made or will make, but the prospects appear to be largely as strong support for the local status quo. Politically, it can be considered that this was a likely outcome, as the NPs were emerging from the middle classes with the time and capacity to take on these very demanding processes, based in the great majority of cases in Conservative-controlled rural or semi-rural authorities. As Brownill and Bradley state: 'it would be surprising if, as chapters in this book suggest, the majority of neighbourhood planning policies were not quietly conservative' (p 262). Given that parish councils have been in charge in most cases, it is not surprising that neighbourhood planning exercises have reflected in style and content the composition of such councillors – overwhelmingly elderly white males (Vigar et al 2017, p 430).

Researchers studying middle-class activism and the effect on attitudes to development concluded that: 'Neighbourhood Plans may act as a vehicle for legitimisation of activist, influential opposition, driven by socio-cultural identity, as a spoiling tactic in debates about how much housing gets built where' (Matthews, Bramley and Hastings 2015, p 69). Hastings and Matthews (2015) used Bourdieu's social theory to illuminate the way in which those with most cultural capital could guide the new localism to their own advantage, with a middle-class informed habitus fitting snugly into the relevant bureaucratic field. They included some reference to how such cultural capital operated in very local planning, noting for example the capacity of parish councils to use retired planners to promote their conversations with the planning system (Hastings and Matthews 2015, p 552).

Sturzaker's work has consistently pointed in the same direction (Sturzaker 2010, Sturzaker and Shucksmith 2012), using his pre-2010 research to show how housing allocations were pushed to those communities least equipped to oppose them. Sturzaker and Gordon (2017) also illuminate how post-2010 localism was full of tensions, such as the democratic or participatory elements in planning at the local level competing against each other, as in parish councils against district councils. They also discuss the role of the law in arbitrating on the complexities of the system, showing that early judicial interpretations were 'generous' to NPs, as had been examiners of plans, possibly showing sensitivities to government power – which would support an interpretation of planning law's partially political nature.

The process of making NPs was widely reported to come down to a few (at most four or five) active individuals, very often led by councillors and with either essential local council planner support or the contracting of planning consultants to carry through the process (Vigar, Gunn and Brooks 2017, p 431, Wargent and Parker 2018, pp 384–386). The fear expressed by some planners (Lord et al 2017), that this was the start of the deprofessionalisation of planning, seems unlikely to be realised, given these realities. Exhaustion of the activists, disillusion at limited gains and a handing over to professionals seem more likely outcomes, as recorded by several researchers (Lord et al 2017, Vigar et al 2017). Looking at an earlier case, Parker and Street (2015, p 798) showed how the best efforts of community activists were consistently 'modulated' by the governing authorities of different kinds (by means of delay, deflection, rebuttal, withholding information and so on). While this may be seen as simply the normal situation of the greater power held by governing bodies, it may be that statutory neighbourhood planning has this risk even more strongly inbuilt than any normal community pressuring, whatever the rhetoric of its inventors. This is, perhaps paradoxically, precisely because of NPs being within the statutory Development Plan. Planners, examiners, interpreters have therefore an inbuilt obligation to constrain and monitor NP content.

Another important dimension is the impact of neighbourhood planning on local planning authorities and the progressing of Local Plans. It has always been clear that there is the potential for councils' support for NPs to divert their declining resources from other matters, including Local Plan making. Equally clear has been the potential for NPs to disrupt such Plan making, given the temporal disjunctions between the two systems: it is almost inevitable that in areas with a lot of neighbourhood planning underway, they will risk prejudging what should go in a Local Plan which is being revised, whatever efforts may be made to stop this. Of course, those working on NPs will be delighted if they do have such an impact, and many activists have given this as a prime reason for all the effort involved. Salter (2018) studied the tensions which NPs generated for local planning authorities, examining their varied strategies (deflective, reactive and integrative) and admitting that there was a need for much more analysis of the impact on local planning as a whole. Neighbourhood planning certainly presents yet more difficulties in the path of district councillors, already generally trying to navigate the survival of their councils on disappearing budgets. So we can judge that there will have been significant political effects on the wider planning projects underway in localities.

One further interesting issue is how far involvement in neighbourhood planning might lead to more activity in relation to wider planning, particularly Local Plan making or strategic planning. One master's dissertation researched a NP process in Oxfordshire with this question in mind, and found no evidence at all of such spin-off effects (Joyce 2014). This seems logical to me, as neighbourhood planning is surely a quite different activity from higher-level planning. It is essentially inward facing, self-concerned, not about any sort of wider common good, as at least in principle wider-scale planning is supposed to be. The purposes of those involved are of another nature, for better or worse.

So, on the one hand there has been a very extensive take-up of neighbourhood planning in certain kinds of areas and parts of England (with over 750 NP referendums having been held by February 2019, according to government in May 2019), but also an often downbeat assessment so far of what has been achieved. Here the issue is not the extent of that achievement. More interesting are the political impact and realities. There are those who have seen a highly positive side to neighbourhood planning, such as Bradley (2014). He saw the process as one that can lead to a renewal of civic engagement, awakening a new generation of community action. He thought the system gave a statutory framework 'around which a sense of collective local identity and revitalised community activism can develop' (p 383). However, as indicated earlier, there is no consensus that such a democratic renaissance has been underway, and the examples Bradley gives of cases where great conflict has been generated over the setting of boundaries of NP areas do not give confidence that positive political effects are as present as he argues.

Brownill and Bradley's analysis provides a nuanced description of what this new level of the planning polity is doing to the dynamics of activity in varied places: 'localism constructs the neighbourhood but it also changes the power relations of the neighbourhood' (2017, p 253). Bradley in the theoretically framed chapter 3 uses the ideas of Mouffe on radical democracy and argues that, post 2010, localism has allowed the emergence of antagonism, and that this can potentially promote social use value over development industry logics.

Brownill and Bradley also consider that neighbourhood planning has 'significantly reconfigured the power relations between citizens, state and the development industry' (2017, p 263) – a claim which I would have doubts about, but evidently one based on extensive research. But they also suggest that the book's case studies infer that 'neighbourhood planning has reinforced planning's arcane privilege', referring to the 'coded language of planning policy' (p 261).

So, this listing of actual experiences shows the real political layering on top of the ideological foundation, which has resulted in the present uneven landscape. The layering has perhaps complicated and diluted the ideological intentions of the regime, but the overall direction was quite strongly set, and I have presented the political outworking as flowing from the ideological starting point quite strongly, or at least without giving large surprises. This makes neighbourhood planning very different from Local Plan making, which is to a degree more ideologically and politically neutral, in the sense that it might be pointed in various directions politically. There are several reasons for this: neighbourhood planning is voluntary and therefore geographically highly uneven in practice; its micro scale gives it a different relationship to big societal issues; it is not steered by electoral (party) politics of a more programmatic kind; and, because of the class geography of England, it happens that the pressures in most NP areas (so far at any rate) are very likely to point to status quo plan making.

There has been very able academic discussion of how the process might be improved, we may say rescued from what many see as a quite limited achievement. Wargent and Parker (2018, pp 390–391) lay out six measures for improvement, to reimagine neighbourhood governance, although they admit that they are not optimistic about political will being present to progress these – it is indeed a very demanding package. While several of these may well be desirable if neighbourhood planning is to continue to exist, there is at least one, 'reconciliation of hyper-localism and strategic concerns', for which it is particularly hard to see any plausible resolution, even given political will. But the fundamental problem with this approach, coming from the 'sceptical friends' of neighbourhood planning, is that it addresses neither the fundamental ideological driving of the innovation, nor the real politics which almost inevitably flows from the system, in such a geographically and class divided society as England, with property, status and fraught local imaginaries at the core. Communities in general, but perhaps especially the kinds of areas where neighbourhood planning has flourished, are fractured, deeply imbued with class differences and protectionist of what they regard as their territory (Matthews,

Bramley and Hastings 2015). If the community studies tradition of British sociology had been alive and well in 2010 (Allan and Phillipson 2008), it would have had little difficulty in analysing the likely impacts of such an innovative state instrument.

Conclusion

This chapter has explored quite varied dimensions of the politics and ideology involved in planning government, from the constitution of the planning polity itself, through the way that planning's political and now partially commercialised character affects its nature as a public administration or bureaucracy, to the intersecting political and ideological dynamics involved in planning at the local authority and neighbourhood scales. As is inevitable in almost any planning system, the account is multilevelled, and the political and ideological interplay add to the need to keep many features in mind at the same time, so as to understand the real nature of the situations facing planning and planners in recent times in England.

We might mention here, if briefly, the case of the political and ideological nature of strategic and regional planning, even though this ceased to exist in England (except in London) in 2010. It could be argued that this also carries some degree of ideological steering with it, institutionally, but in the opposite direction from neighbourhood planning. It is, to some extent, a more interventionist tool, hence naturally more popular with Left politics, as its mode of thinking is rather rationalist, and with regulatory purpose, rather than leaving as much as possible to the market or to other hyper-localist forces. This is not to deny that such planning can also be very popular with some development interests, such as the Home Builders Federation, who had come to rely on it for a steady delivery of consented housing land. But, since 2010 at least, this scaling of planning difference between Labour and Conservative has been clear enough.

We may conclude that there are different kinds of politicalness and ideologicalness in these different kinds of planning, although all are ideological and political in their own ways. It was argued in Chapter 1 that scaling is a key mediating force in the degree of ideological intensity within planning. This is, in part, what we have been analysing in this chapter. Because of its foundations in a relatively 'safe' institutional form, the English district or unitary councils, the Local Plan is the more malleable, able to be pushed politically in more status quo or more interventionist directions, although in the absence of higher-level strategic, regional or even national steering, it has significant limitations in terms of really effective spatial transformation (hence, perhaps, its non-abolition to date by Conservative governments). Neighbourhood planning and strategic/regional planning may be both more ideologically 'primed', with lesser chances of being used for varied political purposes: the first being naturally conservative in its most likely incarnations, the second potentially at least giving scope for more effective approaches to guiding future change.

7

Ideology and politics in professions, lobbying, consultancies and pressure groups

We have examined the central importance of government institutions for planning, and presented their heavily ideological as well as evidently political structuring. That is government seen from the inside. This chapter looks at the pressures brought to bear on government from outside, from the forces active in societies seeking to influence the actions of governments – of all kinds, but here of course keeping the main focus on planning actions. Again, this is a core area of the subject of political science, as well as a matter of great practical interest to political activists. Both academic observers and involved actors have written on how pressure-group politics work in Britain, and we can draw on strands of both writing. The media are in many respects part of the complex studied here, but their importance makes it easier to deal with them in a dedicated chapter. But the intertwining of pressure and mediation should be borne in mind.

The position of pressure groups in politics

As in the field of politics as a whole (touched on in Chapter 1), we can start with two camps of opinion on how pressure politics works. The broadly pluralist view is that pressure groups are essential to give some balance to a democratic polity, allowing a more informed and balanced debate to develop on any issue. This is seen as complementing electoral politics of all kinds and the roles of political parties, both of which are often seen as severely limited on their own. It is assumed that views will emerge which cover a wide range of positions and that this will give at least a platform for discussion.

A less optimistic view of the likely situation of pressure politics is that certain interests will always come to be stronger in expressing viewpoints and developing the knowledge base on any topic – the elitist or sometimes Marxist position. This will tend to mean that, far from balancing the political system as it functions through elections and political parties, pressure politics will reinforce the already present tendency for the best-resourced societal forces to dominate the politics of a country – normally through wealthy interests controlling media and other means of policy development.

We will want to reach a conclusion on which position matches reality better in the current political and ideological creation of planning trajectories. To do this, the first steps will be to look at two zones of actors, equally important for planning: professionals (planners and related areas), and then those more conventionally distinguished as pressure or interest groups. After that, we will survey what evidence there is for the impact of these zones of action (which are naturally partly related) on what happens in planning, both in agenda setting and in decisions by the different elements of government. It will be necessary to use various proxy or indirect measures to try to judge these impacts.

Part of this examination will use the work on lobbying which has raised major concerns in Britain about the modes of functioning of pressure politics. The question of lobbying and planning is one that has not been studied in any great depth. It is a subset of the wider topic of this chapter, but one which may have some importance. One might, for example, imagine that the pluralists had a broadly valid position, but that this was being upset by the tendency of emerging lobby methods to unbalance what might otherwise have some characteristics of the fair play of political pressure in planning.

Professions and consultancies

Planning deals with development of land and property, and it is evident that several professions, not just the planning profession, deal with this field. So, while we will start with the planning profession and how it is changing, it is important to touch also on the nature and roles of the main associated professions of architecture, surveying and civil engineering. Others could be added, but these three no doubt have the most importance, alongside lawyers, already discussed. Of course, in other countries the survey would need to be very different, given that in many European countries much or most planning is done by architects and engineers, working from an educational base within these two professions with some planning specialisation. But Australasian and North American systems have a split broadly similar to that in Britain, so there may be more read-across to those contexts.

My position on planning professionalism is less critical than that of quite a few leading planning thinkers. For example, Patsy Healey (1985) found the professionalisation of planning to be negative for the opening up of planning, and proposed that the RTPI transform itself into a 'specialist knowledge society', without a remit to control professional standards. Huw Thomas (1999) found the profession's drive for occupational closure to be unhelpful, fostering a conservative and self-limiting approach to planning's social potential, and creating a self-image of neutral non-political actors. While I accept that these arguments have a considerable base in how the RTPI has normally behaved over most of its history, there are other sides to the value of planning's having a professional core, and I think it helpful to take a somewhat analytical rather than initially critical approach.

The professions have always differed in Britain, especially by the degree to which they are primarily located in the public or private sectors. Only planning has had a long tradition of a dominant base in the public sector. This was less the case in the earliest years as it gradually separated from the architectural profession, but by the interwar years a local government base was developing, and from the 1950s this base has always had major importance. Architects, surveyors and engineers have all been employed by councils, and to a lesser extent within other arms of government, but they have all had their dominant position within private consultancy or within large construction and development companies. Reliable data to back up these assertions is not easy to come by, but planning has certainly seen a gradual movement since the 1980s, with a growing private consultancy sector, so becoming more like the other professions.

The professions are different from other actors in planning in several ways, even if this is a matter of degree, not absolute. One is that they make their living through their involvement in planning. This evidently means a different relationship to the activity. They carry a responsibility, to their employer or client, to act in such a way as to continue gaining some form of material support (salary, bonus, pension and so on). This generates both pressures and opportunities, and in variable ways depending on the situation. For example, a public sector planner has a primary responsibility to the local authority (in most cases) to represent the interests of that authority, generally considered as encapsulated in some idea of the public interest. A planning consultant is primarily responsible to a client, not to any conception of the public interest, although this may not stop consultants arguing that the public interest is equally served.

A second aspect is professionals' greater degree of knowledge about planning. Clearly, others such as those in pressure groups can become very knowledgeable about planning laws and processes, but professional planners and those who work on planning matters in related professions will tend to have a far greater depth of experience and information about what they are doing, certainly those who have been working for some years. Planning often has the character of an activity where knowledge claims are argued out, but between actors with varying grasp of the technical knowledge needed. This is quite distinct from, say, a discussion about diagnosis of an illness by a doctor, or the judgement of stresses by an engineer in a project, where it would be normally regarded as highly risky for a non-professional to argue strongly a technical opinion (as against, say, on an ethical dimension of principle in relation to the illness or project).

An examination of reporting in the planning press (I use generally *Planning* magazine, a fortnightly publication accepted as the source for up-to-date information and discussion for planners) shows the domination of the consultancy sector in commenting on planning issues. Occasionally public sector planners may comment, but this is increasingly a rarity. This is likely to be the result not only of the rising proportion of planners privately employed, but also of the greater time available to consultants to keep up to date and respond to media queries. Local authority planners, especially since 2010, are likely to be unable to spare the time to read all government pronouncements and give considered views. Political sensitivities will also play a part, as planners may feel the need to get political backing for any comment, delaying response. The effect is to skew the comment in *Planning* magazine to a pro-development agenda, generally (certainly not always) sympathetic to the deregulating reform agendas of recent governments. To some extent this is balanced by comment from NGOs or possibly community groups, but this is also more and more limited, with only a few groups (notably CPRE) able to consistently respond to the emerging agendas.

This developing shift in the planning profession has been noted by academics tracking planning changes. This has been articulated in different ways. A recent book proposed seeing planning and wider urban development work as evolving a 'new technocracy' (Raco and Savini 2019). The authors see this as 'an ideological project that also aligns closely with neoliberal political projects and critiques of central planning in the 1980s and 1990s' (Savini and Raco 2019, p 262). The tendencies are managerialist, to insulate against popular control or opposition, generating a fragmented landscape of technical fixers, of privatised expertise. The book traces these tendencies across a range of planning fields – as well as in some related fields (accountancy, engineering, law, smart city managers), some of which are taking over previously planning roles. One area is that of neighbourhood planning, where consultants have arguably often transformed locally led inspiration into a technocratic process, a project to be managed (Brownill 2019), with one consultancy referring to their 61st NP. Another perspective considered the impact on professionalism of such distancing of control into primarily profit-seeking consultancies (Gunn 2019). Gunn's view is that the many new blends of public-private partnership (she tabulates nine variants) threatens fundamentally professional ethical standards, creating ubiquitous potential conflicts of interest. Hebbert takes a long view of the waves of use of technical expertise in planning, giving a moderate defence of technocracy, seeing it as having its pathologies but also being 'an essential component of an effective public service' (2019, p 30). The new technocracy lens is illuminating, with connections to the debate in Chapter 5 on the nature of planning technique.

Parker, Street and Wargent (2018) echo Gunn's perspective by describing what they find to be the emergence of fragmentary planning in England, which then gives numerous niches for a burgeoning planning consultancy sector, but also generates an 'extensification' of planning, in that many of those now taking up the new niches are not trained planners, but are from a range of backgrounds across the built and natural environment, the surveying and architecture professions, and economic development and regeneration experts. They highlight several concerns about these trends, seeing a disempowerment of local government as council planners become ever more dependent on private sector input to meet the targets imposed on them. They suggest that central government maintains some control at a distance by this means of private sector disciplining, where that sector has particular values and kinds of knowledge, in part different from those of the public sector. In other words, the now present 'mixed economy' of planning work cannot be relied upon to produce public interest outcomes, and government needs to wake up to the need for a re-regulation of planning activity, though the authors here do not point to what this might entail.

Raco (2018) has analysed a kind of co-evolution of the processes of cuts and deregulation affecting planning since especially 2010 and the growth and consolidation of the planning consultancy sector, with the larger companies buying up smaller ones and growing on the back of the expertise no longer existing in councils and other public agencies, but still required by the complexity of remaining regulation and the confusion generated by much deregulation. This entrepreneurialisation of planning is, in his view, changing fundamentally the nature of planning, which can in many cases no longer be seen as driven by public interest goals, as against making the maximum return for councils and agencies in dire fiscal stress.

Also significant is the varied resourcing available to the peak bodies of the professions. Those representing architects, engineers and surveyors are a great deal richer than the RTPI, as any visit to the headquarters of the organisations immediately shows. They can devote much more time to research, communication, lobbying. This reflects the much larger membership (RTPI 25,000, Royal Institute of British Architects 44,000, Institution of Civil Engineers (ICE) 92,000, Royal Institute of Chartered Surveyors (RICS) 125,000), which is also likely to be more highly paid, as well as a longer history, no doubt allowing earlier investment in property. An example is the ICE, founded in 1818, with magnificent offices a few yards from the Houses of Parliament. The ICE produces 'State of the Nation' summary documents at least every year, giving authoritative assessments of the current situation on transport or some other engineering sector. These have done much since the early 2000s to build up the head of steam on infrastructure policy. It is hardly a coincidence that it was the leadership of a senior ICE member, Sir John Armitt, which eventually led to the creation of the National Infrastructure Commission (NIC). Engineering thinking has in part shaped the way the NIC operates, as well as how the leading research programmes have framed their tasks.

The same applies to some degree to lawyers. Barristers and solicitors are widely regarded now as a dominant force in planning, both in the everyday management of planning appeals and the examination of Local Plans, and in advising on major infrastructure projects or sometimes on how to organise judicial review for opponents of development. A figure like the Cambridge-based lawyer Richard Buxton is hardly a typical one, but he is seen as having had a major role in stopping the spread of onshore wind farms in England, by taking on many cases from the mid-1990s onwards, putting scheme after scheme under intense pressure by the experienced use of legal knowledge and tactics (*Observer* 3 May 2009). More normally, every local authority planner is aware of the experience of arriving at a local inquiry where the one or two local council planners are outnumbered heavily by teams of top lawyers representing developers. QCs are highly paid for these activities, showing the very high stakes being played for in the granting of planning consents, or the allocation of sites within the Local Plan process. Again, it is a matter of knowledge, as the increasing legalisation of planning since the 1990s puts a premium on the specialised knowledge of the detail of Planning Acts and case law. So, professional knowledge, of varied kinds, is used as a resource within the planning process. This may be presented as largely technical, but here it is seen as also structured ideologically, and played out politically. It is important to remember that legal power is carried by identifiable actors, all with material as well as ideological interests.

So, I will try to sum up on the current role of the planning profession, although this is somewhat hard to pin down, having elements of ambiguity and transitionality. It is possible that a profession that had struggled for many decades to maintain a broadly public-interest ideological stance, mixed with a degree of support for public participation (to use McAuslan's terms), is now moving to another position in relation to planning's purpose, putting it nearer the development industry pressure groups, and further from many of the environmental and social lobbies, which will be examined next. However, this possibly transitional direction is in my view by no means determined, and may well be subject to changes in the near and medium term.

Pressure groups and lobbies

Typically, politics textbooks divide up pressure groups into 'interest' and 'cause' types. The interest or sectional groups are seen as primarily acting in their self-interest, for example the classic employers or trade union federations, the Confederation of British Industry (CBI) and Trades Union Congress. The cause or promotional groups are seen as more altruistic, for example with social or environmental aims, normally placed under the heading of NGOs, such as Oxfam or Greenpeace. This division clearly has limitations – some groups may be a bit of both, some may not fit too well under either heading. But it can help as a starting point to categorise the important pressure groups for the planning field.

When we have presented in overall terms the shape of the planning pressure world using this frame, we will then need to look more deeply at how the 'dark side' of pressure has been developing, and probably affecting planning as well as the rest of UK politics. This will need to confront the thorny issue of corruption and how this is defined, and so enter the murky world of contemporary corporate lobbying. But first we can look at the more apparently easy-to-grasp world of quite visible interest groups.

Development interest groups

Most obviously there are the development interest groups. To an extent, all of these will be supported by the weight of the overall business federation, the CBI. This has often had very close relationships with government, most noticeably under New Labour governments, when observers often noted the immediate access for and the direct impacts of CBI pressures. The CBI has plenty of research backing and also a regional structure. The Federation of Small Businesses is another generalist body with significant weight and local organisation.

Within the development industry, the most prominent body is the Home Builders Federation (HBF), which is well resourced, with considerable planning expertise, used to comment on all relevant government consultations and intervene in debates up and down the country, with a significant regional staffing. Clearly this grouping is about housing, and represents most the big housebuilders, as against the Federation of Master Builders, representing smaller builders. Other development interests are likely to have their own representative structures – for example Renewable UK, representing those building wind farms, and potentially wave and tidal power schemes, or the British Retail Consortium (BRC), representing especially larger retail interests. All these groups have interests wider than just development, including lobbying on fiscal policy and regulatory policy, but all will have a continuing interest in planning issues, and this is at the centre of the action of several, certainly of the most well-known, the HBF.

All these groupings (there would be hundreds, if one included all sectors) will be broadly pro-development, although this will vary on the case and detail. Clearly, a wind energy group may have interests to some extent opposed to some other energy sectors (coal, gas, nuclear, solar, all have their associations). And the Association of Convenience Stores may have partially distinct interests from the BRC. Many are likely to favour a deregulatory agenda and an anti-planning stance, but this will depend very much on what is within the current governmental planning policy spectrum. The HBF has often been said to favour quite firm planning guidance at all levels (including some support of regional planning during the 1990s and 2000s), because this can help housing developers plan forward more effectively. However, this is favoured if it gives the right results, which might typically be a 'flexible' attitude to green belt boundaries and greenfield release generally. The same would apply to an energy sector grouping, which will support planning (for example, clear designation of onshore or offshore wind farm sites) as long as this meets their growth agendas. Both the form and content of policy are critical, and this is what constitutes the core of lobbying, both generally on wider policy and, where necessary, on specific local plans and schemes.

Cause interest groups (often anti-development interests)

Some groups would probably accept the title of anti-development without complaint. The CPRE, or at least some county branches within that to an extent federal organisation, see their role as primarily to protect the countryside from development. While this does not mean resisting development everywhere, and certainly not on brownfield sites within urban areas, their initial stance is broadly to oppose development beyond the minimum which has normally been long allocated in a locality. Many local groupings exist too, not connected to CPRE or any other national body, often springing up to resist particular plan allocations, of big housing sites or some other large development (a warehousing complex, a nuclear power station, a road or rail scheme, particularly on new alignments).

Other cause groups have more complicated agendas, like Friends of the Earth, which campaigns for a long-term shift to greener ways of living, including in terms of development. This has meant strong prioritisation of action to limit climate change, seen as needing responses on energy, transport and building insulation. Housing pressure groups like Shelter, or Generation Rent, have a major focus on affordable housing, and so will direct their generally more limited pressure capacity at housing policy as against planning policy in the more limited sense.

One largely planning focused group, the Town and Country Planning Association (TCPA), combines roles of supporting the planning system as it was developed after 1945, with a strong social and environmental emphasis. It is less tied to a professional agenda than the RTPI, and can be more agile, and no doubt creative, in campaigning for long-term change, as well as responding very actively to government initiatives. As it grew from the Garden City Association originally set up by Ebenezer Howard in 1899, it retains a support for garden cities or new towns, but this necessarily forms only one block of its work. The TCPA and RTPI form the core parts of what pro-planning lobbying force there is in Britain, but this is frequently reinforced by collaboration on specific issues where interests overlap with, for example, environmental or social pressure groups which support planning approaches. The CPRE in particular can maintain more of an insider role, at least under Conservative governments, and will argue strongly for planning approaches to its own agenda, especially on green belt and countryside protection. It is often less interested in other fields of planning, leaving these to others to lead on.

The dark side of pressure politics: the restructuring of lobbying

As discussed in Chapters 1 and 2, there is a general understanding in writing on planning and urban change that the whole policy landscape has been 'neoliberalised' over several decades, in the UK as in all developed states (to varying degrees). As part of that complex of changes, a new political economy of influence on the state has been erected. This has been structured and framed by the privatisation and deregulation of key parts of the capitalist economies, especially of finance and utilities (core elements of capitalist functioning, as explored long ago by David Harvey 1981). Especially in a country like the UK, which is a core cog in the global financial system, this generates a mass of wealth dependent on the maintenance of the deregulated regime, able to continuously make super profits out of the financialisation of almost everything (now fully understood across a swathe of academic work, if not in the wider public – , Massey 2007, Lapavitsas 2013). Property is a core part of this system, and so planning equally becomes critical to the functioning of the financialised form of capitalism. The 2008 financial crash showed how easily capitalist crises can develop under this system, and so how important it is to have the right sort of governments to dig the economy out of these inevitably occurring crises.

So, in urban affairs, we have seen the remaking of urban development processes, exposed in the work of Mike Raco (2013, 2015a). Urban projects are now typically handed over to autonomous complexes of corporations, partially freed of democratic governmental oversight, as in the fully analysed case of the London Olympics 2012. The phenomenon of breaking up of contracts into enormous numbers of parts runs alongside the related out-contracting of many previously publicly run services to companies like Capita, Carillion, G4S and Serco (Bowman et al 2015, Johal, Moran and Williams 2016). This is held to require confidentiality about how all these contracts are run, meaning that the public no longer knows the basis of the delivery of services or of construction projects.

This process of privatisation, confidentialisation and generation of non-transparent structures is accompanied by a rhetoric of consultation by state bodies, and of supposed commitment to transparency, in an Orwellian dance generating ever increasing cynicism among citizens. It is this world in which pressure politics now has to work. And it is accompanied by a reforming of the lobbying landscape which has been underway since the 1980s. Reports like that of Transparency

International UK (2015) describe the numerous modes of damage being done to the UK polity by the failure of successive governments to regulate corporate lobbying and wider practices such as the absolute normalisation of the 'revolving door' in British central government, whereby politicians and senior civil servants move back and forth continuously between government and private corporations, with heavy implications for the confidentiality of governmental decision making and the personal gains to be made by the abuse of personal experience and information. Beetham (2011) and Wilks-Heeg (2015) also analyse the revolving door phenomenon in detail.

Cave and Rowell (2014) detail the rise of the new kind of lobbying industry in Britain from the 1980s onwards. But this emergence was placed within a longer historical and geographical frame by the excellent historical analysis of Miller and Dinan (2008). They show how the business of public relations (PR) had become critical for the functioning and, they argue, possibly the survival of US capitalism from very early in the 20th century, and how this had then become embedded in Britain from the 1950s onwards. As globalisation progressed, so the global PR industry went from strength to strength. Gradually the techniques developed in selling products were extended to selling politicians and political programmes. Each time capitalism was threatened by movements of political ideas and action (democracy in the early 20th century, welfare and distributive programmes in the second half of the century), conservative and business forces mobilised to fight against these challenges to corporate domination, and to seek to return to an unconstrained capitalist global order.

Miller and Dinan (2008) discuss how important lobbying is, concluding that

> lobbying is at the centre of, and can make a significant difference to, decision making. This happens in two ways: first, as is commonly understood, lobbyists attempt to affect particular legislation and can be successful in various ways at this micro-level. But the most important influence lobbyists have is in constructing the political rules of the game under which corporations operate. (p 82)

This means that business has to be connected to and essentially integrated into the political class, in order to drive the core agenda of deregulation, freedom of business from state influence. In their final chapter, on 'Corporate propaganda and power: the manufacture of compliance?', Miller and Dinan argue the need to understand the present system as one infused with propaganda, ideas deliberately activated to achieve changed actions by states, in whatever way is appropriate (using misinformation, emotionally based strategies, anti-democratic movements). They stress that, in their conception, ideas are critical, but only attached to interests and in practical movement and action. In that sense, their approach is similar to that used in this book, examining the continuous interplay of ideas, ideologies, political actors and everyday policy making.

Miller and Dinan then show how this was taken to new levels by PR firms working for the success of Thatcherism in the UK. This was led by firms like Saatchi & Saatchi, founded by Tim Bell, with others, in 1970 – Bell was later to set up important PR firms like Bell Pottinger, and was a key advisor in Conservative elections from the late 1970s. By the 1990s this powerful lobbying industry was becoming ever more important, with corporations ready to pay large amounts to promote or protect their reputations, and the links between political parties and the PR industry becoming ever closer, through all sorts of revolving-door career patterns criss-crossing parties, think-tanks, lobbying firms and other kinds of business. New Labour is shown in Miller and Dinan's analysis to be in significant part the creation of the PR industry (2008, Chapter 8, 'Pulling Labour's teeth').

Grant (2018) surveys the 'public affairs' parts of the bigger commercial lobbyists in Britain, and his table is revealing of the number of companies with some links with the development and infrastructure sectors (Table 7.1). He notes some specialisation, with Curtin & Co working much in land, property and housing, Westbourne in rail, Newington Communications on housing, having been hired by Barratt Homes to help secure political buy-in for future Barratt developments (p 24). The situation is in fact more complex than this listing might suggest. Data collected by Miller and Dinan (2008, pp 111–117) showed that there was an intense concentration in the global lobbying industry, such that four mega corporations controlled a large number of these apparently independent companies. Thus Hill and Knowlton (H+K Strategies) and Burson-Marstellar are part of WPP, which is (or was) one of the few UK-based large PR corporations, the great majority of the rest being based in the US.

The dark side of pressure politics: corruption

Another theme follows on from this discussion of lobbying, that of potential corruption within planning. It is essential to discuss how broadly corruption should be defined. An emerging academic literature

Table 7.1: Leading political consultants, December 2016–February 2017

Name of firm	Number of public affairs staff	Examples of clients
Newington Communications (formerly Bellenden)	46	Barratt, British Land, Church Commissioners
Weber Shandwick	45	Asda, Barclays, Volvo
Apco Worldwide	41	Mars, Microsoft, Reckitt Benckiser
Hanover Communications	41	GSK, Goldman Sachs, John Lewis
GK Strategy	33	Babcock, Leeds University, Travis Perkins
Remarkable	33	Anglian Water, Bovis Homes, National Grid
Edelman	31	Crossrail, Gatwick Airport, Sainsburys
Grayling	28	Lloyds Bank, National Grid, Virgin Trains
H+K Strategies	27	Shell, Tata Steel, Total
Burson-Marsteller	25	Aldi, Addison Lee, British Sugar

Source: Grant 2018, p 23 (derived from Public Relations Consultants Association register)

has resituated this question in recent years (Beetham 2015, Whyte 2015, Grant 2018). The standard understanding of corruption starts from bribery, normally offering money to someone in government, or in some other position of influence, in exchange for doing something they would not have otherwise done. The World Bank definition is widely used: 'the abuse of public office for private gain'. David Beetham (2015) shows why this is far too limited, especially in current political circumstances. He recommends this definition: 'the distortion and subversion of the public realm in the service of private interests' (Beetham 2015, p 42).

So, the new approach is to propose that a *system* can be corrupt, in causing results which are desired by those with most existing power and money. This, it is argued, is needed so as to include the manner in which changes have shifted the way things work in most developed societies. Economies and polities have been restructured away from public decision making and steering towards control by private corporations. The processes of privatisation and of the accompanying reduction of government capacity to tackle most of society's problems affect many sectors, including the media, utilities and much of the housing and social sectors, and this generates a new sort of playing field in politics and, particularly, lobbying.

The strongest statements on corruption in Britain are by David Whyte, professor of socio-legal studies at Liverpool University, and David Miller, professor of sociology at Bath University. Whyte's edited book points to 'corruption scandals which now straddle all sectors of the public sector and the privatised economy' (Whyte 2015, p 16). The book aimed to map 'a political economy of neoliberal corruption' (p 25), and to show that 'corruption is a systematic power-mongering strategy' (p 27). Policing, the judiciary, prisons, PFI, the secret service, the big four accountancy firms and financial services regulation are some of the elements of the British system examined.

Miller's chapter in the same book argues that corruption should be understood not as pathological (generating petty corruption, bribery or similar actions) but as institutional, infusing the whole operation of spheres of policy and governing. He sees this as having grown up with a clear ideological backing from public choice theory, which provided the intellectual foundation for much of neoliberal innovation, particularly in the New Public Management. He then describes the opening up of government occurring from the 1980s in Britain, which 'required the influx of new ideas and practical ways of putting them into practice. As a result the neoliberal period saw the rise of a whole range of new policy intermediaries, including management consultants, lobbyists, public relations advisers and think tanks. The PR industry grew, initially on the back of privatisation contracts' (Miller 2015, p 65). He concludes that 'we live in an advanced "post democratic" capitalist society in which corruption is endemic for perfectly understandable and not accidental reasons' (p 67).

The analyses of Miller and Whyte give a flavour of what at least some well-placed academic thinkers have been concluding in recent years. They lay down a challenge to those in and observing planning, to understand the extent to which these developments are present in planning, in advanced or perhaps only early stages.

The dark side of pressure politics (in part): think-tanks

Some useful research has been carried out on the role of think-tanks. Some has taken a 'naïve' approach to studying think-tanks and their influence, assuming that they are essentially what they say they are, openly promoting ideological and political understandings of what governments or other agents should do. This has generated knowledge about the think-tank panorama (Jackson 2012, Pautz 2014). There are a good number of think-tanks in Britain, the great majority based in London: a Wikipedia listing in 2018 had about 140 for the UK. Some do not of course have explicit political or ideological agendas. Many of those that do have been on the Right and free market side of politics, with significantly fewer which have centre Left (Institute for Public Policy Research (IPPR), Smith Institute) or green (New Economics Foundation) tendencies. For most of these, planning is not at the centre of their agenda. But for some of the free market ones, such as the venerable Adam Smith Institute and Institute of Economic Affairs, or Policy Exchange (founded in 2002 as part of a new wave of Far Right think-tanks with, it appears, a lot of US funding, detailed in Miller and Dinan), planning is regarded as an ideological threat to be disposed of, alongside the rest of the post-war settlement. So, these think-tanks have taken a continuing interest in planning, and although their work may not, from a planning perspective, be very well researched or informed, their interventions have in some cases been influential.

It is noteworthy that this has not, by and large, been matched by an equivalent interest in the Left or centre Left or green think-tanks, which may be one reason for the weak policy development on planning by Labour, Liberal Democrat and Green parties. So, for slightly different reasons, we see the pluralist balancing act not actually working, again. In this case one reason is the material control of think-tanks described above. But a further critical underlying reason for this imbalance is that the ideological playing out of understandings of planning is distinct. The free market Right sees planning as important, and so directs some of its firepower against it, based on an understanding of Hayek, or at least some idea of the value of economic freedoms. The social democratic ideological position from around the turn of the century does not see planning as much more than a necessary but boring feature of local governing, complicating policies on, for example, housing. As IPPR, Demos and similar think-tanks founded since the late 1980s are analysed (at least by Miller and Dinan) as committed to the New Labour agenda of converting Labour to a centre and business-friendly party, the very moderate stance and weak interest in planning is not surprising. The centrist ideological stance suggests, no doubt, to think-tank directors and funders that other issues (housing itself in particular) are better focuses for work. In some areas like infrastructure, which has a complex ideological positioning, some think-tanks have made more effort to research the issues; the Institute for Government is an example in the the late 2010s.

Examples of the work by the free market Right are the reports by Policy Exchange from 2005 onwards, particularly by Alex Morton, who eventually became a policy advisor to Prime Minister Cameron from 2013 to 2015. Former director of CPRE director Shaun Spiers saw Policy Exchange as the most influential think-tank of the period (Spiers 2018, p 11). In *Cities for Growth* (Morton 2011), Morton took a classic free market right-wing position on planning, blaming it for almost every possible urban and rural problem. With a long historical view, he characterised planning as 'a dysfunctional ... system created by the post war Labour government as part of a new and socialist command economy' (Morton 2011, p 11). He attacked the basis of the system in local authorities, with the normal right-wing dislike of democratic politics. He considered unnecessary the making of local plans, and proposed private-led new towns, allied to a 'presumption against interference' (with the 'free market'), councils losing their role in planning, and removing or radically cutting green belts. The drive was to incorporate prices in all development, by companies compensating individuals affected by development – the classic call for dependence on contracts between individuals as promoted by Pennington (2002).

It is not surprising that Prime Minister Cameron should make attacks on planners one of his staples, with this kind of work emerging from what was described as his 'favourite think tank'. The work clearly grew from a small school of planning-critical economists at Reading University and the London School of Economics (LSE), and Morton thanked Henry Overman of LSE for help. Though not in academic terms that sophisticated, this work set the terms in which radical Conservatives thought about planning reforms. Already an earlier report (Morton 2010) had had immediate impact on policy, with the 2011 budget picking up the idea of making conversion of commercial buildings to residential use easier. Soon after, this was to become the fully fledged extension of permitted development rights, responsible for generating what many observers saw as many thousands of substandard and poorly located units during the coming years, and the loss of large numbers of potential Section 106 contributions (Clifford et al 2018). It is clear, by describing this example, that the extension of permitted development rights was ideologically driven, not a response to a perceived social or planning problem. However, it also naturally possessed accompanying political features which recommended it more widely to certain politicians, including the potential to produce more housing units, and the gains to be made by developers of certain kinds – either actual or potential Conservative supporters. So, as almost always with an implemented proposal, ideology went hand in hand with politics, even if in this case with ideology very much in the lead.

As in all of the think-tank world, there is differentiation to some degree within the right-wing bodies. The Adam Smith Institute has tended to take an even more radical approach than Policy Exchange in its occasional interventions – for example, proposing total abolition of green belts (Papworth 2015).

A significant part of the role of think-tanks is what Cave and Rowell call 'third party lobbying' (pp 130–131). 'The value to politicians bent on radical reform in having a privately funded media and research organisation, like a think-tank, should not be underestimated. "Think tanks are places where politicians put people to work" says one lobbying insider. "It's outsourcing with plausible deniability"' (Cave and Rowell 2014, p 254).

There has been at least one valuable study on think-tanks and planning, particularly their role in pushing governments in deregulatory directions (Haughton and Allmendinger 2016). The authors discovered how think-tanks especially like to make radical interventions, 'thinking the unthinkable', because this gets publicity, and may shift the terms of debate. The authors explore one example in 2012, when an old idea of giving compensation (or bribes) for those 'suffering' from nearby development schemes was resuscitated by two think-tanks, the Institute of Economic Affairs and Policy Exchange. Within a year, government proposals emerged to give financial incentives to communities and local authorities ready to accept new development. Although this did not progress in its strongest form of trying to buy consent from individuals (based on free market views that anything can be put within markets), it can be argued that the overall drive of 'deal making' between the Ministry of Housing, Communities and Local Government (MHCLG) and local authorities has had essentially that core, with money offered to those authorities prepared to commit to higher housing numbers (as in Oxfordshire). The founding director of Policy Exchange, Nick Boles, became planning minister and tried to progress strongly deregulatory policies, though with difficulties, given the varying agendas within government. Haughton and Allmendinger argue that such study of think-tank effects 'raises important issues about how national planning systems are shaped by external interests' (p 1688).

Impacts on government: national

So, we have surveyed some important developments in the world of pressure politics. But how does all this more or less visible pressure activity impact on planning? We will divide into national and local impacts, however much these drift into each other.

Most of the emphasis here has been on the national landscape of pressure groups relevant to planning. This is clearly a critical sphere, given the central direction of planning policy for England, at least: to some extent parallel structures now exist within Wales, Scotland and Northern Ireland, with, for example, separate RTPI structures and in some cases separate development industry organisations. A great deal of the lobbying activity for planning will take place in London, in or close to Westminster and Whitehall. In this sphere (at least for the UK, that is, for England) the power of pro-development interests is considerable and may generally have the upper hand.

A study tried to track the effectiveness of interest group lobbying in the 2010–15 government (Dommett, Hindmoor and Wood 2017), with revealing if uncertain results. It used the publicly available listing of meetings of senior ministers with outside groupings, to see who met most with whom during the 2010–15 government. Attendance by business bodies was much the highest, 45% of meetings, followed by 18% by 'third sector' organisations (for example, 25 with the National Trust) and 12% with media bodies. Local government formed only 3% of the total (a third of this by the Local Government Association). More interesting would be the make-up by department, which is given only in certain cases, for example, that local government did make up 32% of those attending Department of Communities and Local Government (DCLG) meetings. But ultimately one gets from this essentially the headline finding of massive business access at the highest levels. However, this has to be treated with care, as many very important meetings may well be with junior ministers and civil servants, not covered by this source.

One limited 'opening of the doors' occurred with the episode in 2011–12 of the making of the NPPF, the short document drawn up to sweep away the lengthy set of Planning Policy Statements developed by successive governments over the previous 20 years. The episode has been studied (Rutter 2012, Allmendinger 2016, Spiers 2018), but especially by Shepherd (2017a) and Slade (2018a), who were both able to interview many of the key participants. What happened was that the consultation draft contained some aggressively pro-development policy phrasing, including the central one regarding a 'presumption in favour of sustainable development', with no clear definition of sustainability. Apparently the Treasury had made significant changes to the draft emerging from DCLG, including insertion of the phrase: 'decision takers at every level should assume that the default answer to development proposals is yes' (DCLG 2011, p 5). There was a quick and organised response by heritage and countryside protection groups (most effectively, the National Trust), and this was coordinated in part by a campaign by the *Daily Telegraph*, the strongly Conservative daily newspaper, called 'Hands off our Land'. A pro-development campaign launched by *Property Week* magazine, called 'Campaign for Sustainable Development', supported by the British Property Federation, had far less impact publicly. Shepherd identifies three distinct lobbies in the debate, being those for the countryside and environmental protection, for development and for spatial planning, all tussling with the government positions. Slade analyses the impact on changing relationships within government, with civil servants and DCLG losing ground to other actors, overall.

What made this particularly difficult for the Conservatives was that the *Daily Telegraph* proceeded to reveal the extent of donations by the property sector to Conservative Party funds, setting this at £3.3 million over the previous three years. Another article on the same day exposed the work of the Conservative Planning Forum, which raised about £150,000 a year, charging members £2,500 to discuss policy and planning issues with senior MPs (*Daily Telegraph* 10 September 2011). Other articles explored high-level government links to the property industry (*Daily Telegraph* 24 September 2011, 26 September 2011, 23 February 2012). Those familiar with the scale of the lobbying business in Britain would hardly have been surprised at such revelations, but the extent of hidden influence on the Conservative Party's policy making probably shocked even many within the planning and development sectors.

The effect of this months-long campaigning (July 2011 to March 2012) within the Conservative pressure and media heartlands was that certain interests like the National Trust (as against the normal planning actors, who had generally opposed the new draft on even more fundamental grounds) met with the prime minister and a compromise was hammered out, the draft apparently being discussed line by line. In my view this changed the basic drive of the NPPF remarkably little, but the *Daily Telegraph* proclaimed a great victory for its campaign (28 March 2012), and the National Trust and other countryside protectionist groups endorsed the satisfactory nature of the changes. Shepherd notes that there was no consensus among his interviewees as to whether the final version really was a significant improvement on the draft, while Slade also shows that this was very much a matter of interpretation. At any rate, the final NPPF certainly did remove some of the more problematic phrasings, and, probably much more importantly, put the government temporarily on the defensive about making a too-aggressive attack on the core of planning. What happened subsequently was that the planning system suffered a trickle of reforms, continuing to the time of writing, which together amounted to a powerful attack on the system, going well beyond what was discussed in 2011–12. But there has been no repeat of the conflict within the Conservative camp since 2012. The Hands off our Land campaign was quietly closed down and only very occasional criticism of government planning policy emerged from the *Daily Telegraph* after this. The operation of industry lobbying will have continued as it was doing in 2011–12, we can be sure, but now hidden again.

A fair conclusion on the NPPF episode would be, I think, that it reveals very well the imbalance in lobbying and ideological power of the property sector, which can wield powerful continuing influence on governments, while the opposite lobbying and pressuring force can, even under the best (and very unusual) circumstances, make only marginal gains. And simply by showing the hidden side of the Conservative–property industry embrace, it reminded observers, if briefly, how much is unknown to even knowledgeable planning sector actors.

Cave and Rowell (2014) cover several areas of recent planning, from mega projects to local schemes. There was the sustained effort to rehabilitate nuclear power, after its fall from grace in Britain and most other states in the 1980s and 1990s. British Nuclear Fuels paid the PR and lobbying giant Weber Shandwick to create a communications plan to convince the public and politicians of the value of nuclear new build. This convinced the New Labour government, which made a dramatic about turn on the issue, from opposition in the 2003 Energy White Paper, to embracing a new generation of nuclear power stations in the 2006 White Paper. Similar work was underway to rehabilitate gas a few years later, culminating in the contracts to another big lobbying firm, Bell Pottinger, to persuade public and politicians of the value of shale gas fracking. In these cases, and for HS2 (taken on by Westbourne Communications), the key was to emphasise job gains, the likely 'growth' to be induced. In the case of HS2 this followed what had been some 'bad selling' of the project by government in the early days (Cave and Rowell 2014, pp 100–106, 159–161).

Grant takes the green belt as one of his case studies, and tracks through how this was argued out by the normal think-tanks and pressure groups. But he also noted several 'apparently independent reports' on the green belt, which turned out to be funded by or closely linked to the same group of housing industry consultants. He describes elsewhere how All Party Parliamentary Groups are used to front this kind of operation, and in this case this happened in 2016 with a report on London's green belt, co-authored by a director of planning at Colliers International, a planning consultancy used by many big housebuilders (Grant 2018, p 61–66). So, here we have (in his full study) a good example of the intertwining of 'normal' pressure group activity, think-tanks (like the Adam Smith Institute with its reports arguing for abolition of the green belt), planning consultancies and the commercial lobbying industry. The technique of getting more trusted or legitimate bodies to say what a lobbying operation wants to communicate is apparently normal industry practice, with think-tanks, fake local groups, MPs or councillors all being favoured vehicles for conveying messages.

Impacts on government: local

If we shift the focus to the panorama of pressure activity at local levels, the picture may be somewhat different. It is the local authorities which are then to a large extent the target of lobbying. Traditionally, they have had significant strength within their localities, whether at county, conurbation or district level. It is doubtful whether this strength is there to the same extent as it was a decade ago, or even more so 30 years ago in the early 1990s. It is at locality level that there may be considerable variation in the balance of forces. While development interests will tend to have the upper hand nationally, locally the resistance to development, expressed by myriad campaigns across England in recent decades, may be able to put development interests on the back foot. Local councils feel this pressure, and so, although many might wish to allocate more land for housing, and probably to develop more infrastructure, this is very hard outside existing urban envelopes.

Cave and Rowell (2014) also show that much 'community consultation' has been taken over by professional communications firms. They give the example of an incinerator scheme for Viridor (part of South West Water) in Devon. A communications firm, 3 Monkeys, was hired to 'consult', which in this case meant holding meetings. Despite the opposition expressed, the firm simply went ahead with the scheme. Sometimes there is use of a tactic entrenched in US politics since the 1980s, 'astroturfing', which means setting up a group in favour of the project, using various tactics to move into the community and find supporters: fake grassroots campaigning (pp 123–129). Another tactic was to put up candidates in local parish elections. Or more common was to hire local councillors to 'give advice' on planning applications, not something which is forbidden. Cave and Rowell report that

Westminster council contained at least 10 councillors in the lobbying business, while in Southwark council the number was 12 (pp 186–188).

Pressure group influence is very visible in the Oxfordshire case, where councils have been largely unable to promote significant areas of new urbanisation since the demise of structure planning in the early 2000s – and even in that era, allocation of urban extensions went quite gingerly. Since 2015, government has used several means to try to break what is seen centrally as a log jam, stopping development. This has involved the National Infrastructure Commission in the Cambridge to Oxford corridor study, which recommended in 2017 the promotion of road and rail infrastructure to support the building of large numbers of new homes (for 1 million more people up to 2050). In Oxfordshire this was backed by a deal signed by central government and the local authorities, who committed to allocate more housing land, in exchange for some funding of housing and infrastructure schemes (*Planning* magazine 9 February 2018). This included the making of a new strategic plan for Oxfordshire. However, the force of campaigning by local groups unhappy with the scale of development proposed makes it highly doubtful if any of this strategising promoted from above will result in the desired outcomes.

Another example of the scale and force of local group activity is the range of difficulties facing the new mayors of the combined authorities set up from 2015 onwards. Several, including Greater Manchester, West of England (greater Bristol) and Cambridge and Peterborough, are to complete new strategic plans. But all have found this very hard to progress (*Planning* magazine 16 June 2017, 1 June 2018, 26 October 2018). In Greater Manchester the Labour mayor had campaigned on a programme of a radical re-examination of the draft Strategic Plan produced by the shadow authority, meaning that less green belt land would be taken for development, with more stress on inner-city regeneration. This has meant repeated delays in the completion of a new draft Plan, with development interests resisting the cutting back of the Plan away from their prized sites on the edge of the conurbation, and anti-development interests equally opposed to the inclusion of countryside sites. The same dynamic is making the completion of a West of England Strategic Plan very hard (and here one of the four councils refused to join the process in any case, fearing imposition of development if it lost control of its local planning process). Even in Cambridgeshire and Peterborough, where Cambridgeshire has been held up as a good example of long-term planning of land release and infrastructure development since the late 1990s, the tensions arising with pressure politics appear to be delaying agreement of a new strategy. While it can be argued that the combined authority model is a very weak mechanism for progressing effective planning (compared with, for example, the use of proper elected metropolitan authorities, as exists in England only for London), the pressure politics would, it seems, be making strategic planning progress difficult under any institutional arrangement.

Some very strong corporations could indeed generally overcome local opposition, as is shown by an example from the now past era of massive supermarket expansion, in a study of Tesco's involvement in the planning system (Simms 2007). Andrew Simms worked for the New Economics Foundation, and was so struck by the capacity of Tesco to get permissions for new or extended stores across England that he wrote a book on that and other aspects of the company's strategy. He described the planning issues as a David and Goliath struggle, with Tesco normally winning, but the increasingly organised opposition of that period having occasional successes in stopping schemes (Simms 2007, especially pp 120–128). The range of tactics is described, and makes a textbook case of how a very large corporation, with good advisors, was able often to almost disregard planning controls. In one battle, finally lost by very organised opponents, in Sheringham, Norfolk, the ex-leader of the local council is quoted as saying: 'They [Tesco] are too big and powerful for us. If we try to deny them they will appeal, and we cannot afford to fight a planning appeal and lose. If they got costs it would bankrupt us' (Simms 2007, p 267). In this case the councillors had voted 20–0 against the application, but found that they could not stop the scheme because a secret deal had been done earlier to bind the council to Tesco.

These examples therefore point, if to varying extents, to a perhaps more pluralist realm of politics in action, with pressure being played onto the local political actors, who then convey this to the central governmental forces. But this may be painting the situation in rather more rosy colours than is appropriate. Partly the situation is the result of poorly structured governing institutions in recent years, with certainly the post-2010 years seeing the impossibility in many parts of England of making forward planning work effectively, within a Local Plan system not adeptly steered by central government. The result is that most local and strategic planning directions are set by bodies and processes largely unknown to most citizens (LEPs, groupings of district councils, combined authorities), within opaque and hardly democratic structures of deal making. Also, the evidence reported by Cave and Rowell (2014), and Minton (2013), on the trickling of the 'dark side' lobbying practices down to the local level, makes quite risky any judgement that the local level is working tolerably well. At most we can argue that two factors, the continuing existence of elected local government, and the presence of the forces most actively resisting development, at least prevent much movement at all on many issues, which may be seen by many as a positive outcome of planning politics. However, also relevant to this judgement is the issue of local-level corruption, if it exists at all widely.

Impacts on government: corruption?

There has been only limited discussion of corruption in planning. Historically there have been bursts of publicity, as in the Poulson affair of the 1970s, or a television film about dubious practices in a Cornwall district council in the early 1990s. In the latter case, the stir led to the formulation of new rules set by the Nolan Committee, particularly governing the need for councillors to declare personal interests when discussing planning applications. A *Guardian* newspaper report (21 February 2018) on the practices of the long-term chair of the Planning Committee of Westminster City Council raised again the issues about the extent to which locally elected politicians should be able to accept hospitality from developers. Robert Davis was Planning Chair from 2000 to 2017, and was recorded as having been entertained by various interests 514 times between 2015 and 2018. *Planning* magazine discussed the case (8 March 2018) and noted that although legislation requires councils to adopt codes of conducts on matters like the acceptance of gifts or hospitality, any council can choose the rules it wishes. While any normal view of the acceptance of such lavish and years-long hospitality from developers would be highly critical and likely to think that corruption could easily be present, this would evidently be very hard to prove. Many hundreds of planning applications will have been decided during these years, and proving that the councillor was influenced unduly would require special evidence.

Not long after its moment of NPPF activism the *Daily Telegraph* carried out an undercover operation to expose councillors who were claiming to deliver planning permissions, describing cases in Devon, Newcastle and Surrey, and explaining that this was common practice, as shown in the work of a lobbying company, Indigo Public Affairs. This company worked for companies like Tesco, Barratt Homes and Taylor Wimpey (*Daily Telegraph* 11 March 2013). A later survey explored the extent to which London councillors had moved on to jobs in planning lobbying work, detailing this for Southwark, and

Kensington and Chelsea, and describing the extensive hospitality received by councillors from the development industry. This added up to a culture of 'cronyism', which was weakly if at all regulated, which was not illegal but clearly raised major issues of accountability (Anna Minton and Tamasin Cave, *Guardian* 14 July 2017).

A curious *Sunday Times* newspaper article by an ex-advisor to Prime Minister Cameron claimed that corruption was 'endemic' in planning departments all over Britain (*Planning* magazine 12 January 2018). However, only limited evidence for this was given, with reference to a current case in Tower Hamlets council, and three other instances, including a notorious period of corruption in Doncaster council in the 1990s. Not surprisingly, the planners consulted by the magazine did not agree that corruption was at all common. The RTPI had found only eight cases of breaches of its code of conduct during the years 2014 to 2016, and these were about conflicts of interest, rather than evidence of actual corruption. So again, on this personal level, finding evidence of direct bribery is probably very difficult, under normal circumstances.

However, under the heading of systemic corruption, it could be argued that some features of recent planning reforms have raised the likelihood of unbalanced decision making resulting. One critical factor is the promotion of viability as a key factor for councils to include when judging schemes (Colenutt, Cochrane and Field 2015). The NPPF made viability a centrally important element of decision making, meaning that councils must include the profitability of a scheme in their assessments. The viability assessment is done generally in private, so only the most senior councillors or officers know the details, and the general public are excluded. Extensive community campaigning has been spurred by these changes, with the effect that by 2017 several London councils had committed to making all viability assessments public (*Planning* magazine 3 November 2017). Even in these circumstances, when at least the assumptions built into the assessment can be seen (and so the normally 20% profits expected on schemes is there to be judged), and with some changes to the NPPF in 2018, expert judgement is that the planning system remains distorted and corrupted by this process (Colenutt 2020). That is to say, decision making is being swung by dubious commercial practices built into a central government-mandated mechanism – nothing to do with individuals, but something made systemic to planning. The same can be said of the increasing dependence of councils on the revenue raising now built into planning processes – what developers pay for planning discussions and applications now matters a lot to poverty-stricken councils. This bends local planning practice, almost certainly sometimes in highly problematic ways.

A second example of the building of questionable practices into the planning process is that of neighbourhood planning. The present statutory form of NPs was introduced by the Localism Act 2011. The law allows any Neighbourhood Forum containing a minimum of 21 people to prepare a Plan. In addition, a Business Neighbourhood Plan (BNP) can be prepared, including businesses as well as residents within the decision making. The first BNP was approved in June 2015 (*Planning* magazine 5 June 2018), after three years' work, for the central area of Milton Keynes. While in this case the plan was voted on by the whole electorate of Milton Keynes, and fully endorsed, there must be strong doubts about the democratic legitimacy of such plans, which can alter the process of preparation of local plans for the council area as a whole. The greater resources of businesses to get involved in such planning immediately come into play, making this another example of the skewing of any potentially even playing field towards certain interests.

Conclusion

After a survey of this kind it is of course impossible to reach definitive conclusions on the modes, effectiveness, real arenas or fundamental value of all the varied kinds of pressure politics in planning. We can be sure that the great efforts made by the commercial PR industry are not done in vain, following the logic of the advertising industry: it must have effects, otherwise, after a century or more of high spending, advertising would not be so central to capitalism. But there are big methodological difficulties in tracing through precisely what (most) influences what in politics.

Here I think that one broad conclusion is plausible: that an effective and fair pluralist pressure politics is not generally present in the UK planning sphere. This certainly is not the case at the key national level, where the vital big policy issues are fought out. So, the pluralist dream is not being fulfilled, in that the overall positions of governments (New Labour, Coalition and Conservative) are all broadly reinforced by the national pressure landscape, not counteracted by it. At national level the lobbying industry in all its modes (think-tanks, entertaining policy makers, publishing, getting into political parties) and all its arenas (party conferences, invitation-only seminars, report launches, parliamentary select committee hearings, legislative amendments) makes the running.

Ideology and politics in professions, lobbying, consultancies and pressure groups

This is of course intertwined with a core theme of this book, the very general centrality of ideology, within and between all these processes, above all within the political parties and the lobbying leaders. Both the underlying grounding of ideas within planning and the creation of detailed approaches within these ideological envelopes, each of these is wrapped up in the evolving pressure politics one sees at national level. An understanding of the lobbying landscape and of forces of systemic corruption is core to seeing how planning works. These elements are in the middle of the political and ideological forces acting on and inside planning.

At the local level it is less easy to be so sure about the overall drive of lobbying success, whether development interests can in general rule the roost, or whether their path is in many localities and at many times balanced by competing narratives and groupings, which can sway local political decision making. It may be that this is the case in a good number of localities, even if overall development interests normally win out. Even if a relatively optimistic (pluralist toned) conclusion is reached for the local level, this is moderated by the centralisation built into much of the planning system, with the appeals process the most powerful weapon available to development interests and governments intent on helping them. Central control, in a very wide range of circumstances from major infrastructure projects to the smallest housing schemes, can sway the argument and results to development-driven interests.

More worryingly, there is a strong probability that much of the force of what I have called the dark side of pressure politics has been playing into British planning for some years, and, given the nature of recent reforms and the movement of politics as a whole, to an increasing extent. The corporate lobbying industry in particular is surely merging into some everyday planning processes and affecting planning reform directions, however difficult this is to analyse and describe. To go further than this now would go beyond any really solid evidence, as far as I can tell.

The planning profession has a big role in all this of course, and there has been limited research to unveil what the impact is of the now powerful and generalised process of the privatisation of the profession, to an extent merging with the already considerable private force of the other development professions. It is likely that this process carries Conservative ideological assumptions into the midst of everyday planning practice. This is not to embrace any assumption that 'traditional' corruption (bribery or similar) is a significant issue in British planning. This seems to me to be unlikely; at any rate, it remains unproven for recent years. But this leaves plenty of scope for the dark-side influences to be affecting professional practice, on all sides of the public, private and third sector divides, through less dramatic but perhaps nastier versions of systemic corruption, whereby bad practice becomes institutionally embedded because that is the way the planning process has become structured. Without a lot more (difficult to carry out) research, I do not think more can be said on this. But certainly this is a worrying trajectory and we will need to consider various responses in the later chapter on possible solutions.

8

Communication, the media and deliberation

We have now looked at the functioning of planning from a range of perspectives – historically, the significance of technical and legal perspectives, the forces acting inside and outside government at different levels. Next it is important to put the spotlight on processes of communication, mediation and deliberation. If we are trying to imagine a democratic process of good government, such as would give reasonable chances for beneficial planning, we would naturally put some stress on how citizens get to know what is going on. In the terms of Habermas, we are thinking about the quality of the public sphere, national as well as local. How well does this public sphere work for planning, so that citizens interested in any aspect of planning, general or very local, can know what is happening? The impression gained by the Raynsford Review in 2017–18 was that the answer was, not too well, given the discontent expressed by many outside the planning profession. So it is important to think about what the conditions may be for a better-functioning public sphere. In relation to the Chapter 1 framing, these issues of communication and deliberation are key 'political and ideological dimensions of planning', as should become clear in this chapter.

All public policy depends on communication in some kinds of public sphere, for the possibility of democratic or at least reasonably wide-scale debate to take place. But planning, due to its continuously evolving and variously scaled nature, and the strong and often obvious implications for the numerous and varied interests, may be even more dependent on forms of communication media than, say, are the health or education policy fields. If no one knows of a development scheme, or even if people know only unreliable rumours, the possibility of meaningful engagement by citizens is minimal.

These questions of open policy making form part of ideological strategies of those in power, in this case sometimes to limit available information and reduce participatory and deliberative spaces. This has been evident in many UK governmental instances in recent years, as in the Planning Act 2008 centralising of decision making on major infrastructure and the abolition of regional and strategic planning in 2011, effectively centralising what public control existed at these levels into central ministries and obscure deal-making processes in LEPs and similar business- and elite-led bodies. The Irish Republic case was mentioned in Chapter 1, on the same lines, cutting back public participation.

Approaches to democracy are bound up with ideology, although much democratic theory does not come at the question from this angle. Conservatism and some forms of liberalism have generally been opposed to, or at least had deep reservations about democracy during the two-centuries-or-more-long struggle for democratic government. Hayek's opposition to democracy has already been mentioned, with all the implications this has from the guru of neoliberalism. So, this chapter is also partly about the planning and democracy relationship.

Underlying planning-specific factors, there is a powerful shift underway within political communication, related to the now continuously discussed digital revolution, the power of the social media and data corporations and the rapid evolution of political practice since the early 2000s by use of systems like Facebook (Finlayson 2018, Moore 2018). As Finlayson emphasises, 'technologies of political communication do not simply reflect or transmit political ideas and opinions. They give shape to thinking ...' (p 77). In particular, the passionate case made many years ago for 'a single public sphere' (Garnham 1992, p 371) confronts enormous difficulties in the face of the fragmentation and individualisation of the political communication landscape which Finlayson describes. The impacts on planning are starting to be studied (for example, in the Digital Civics project in Newcastle upon Tyne), but it is too early to say how the matters discussed in this chapter are being affected by these momentous changes.

Here two main stages of process management are dealt with, first that of information and communication, including the roles of various media, and then the scope for participation and deliberation, on the basis of available information. Of course the division is in part artificial, as we get informed, communicate and deliberate to a significant extent in closely connected ways.

Information, communication, media and language

Local government

Two main elements of communication in planning are evident: one about the communication of tiers of government, the other about the role of wider media.

For local government, the key dimension here is how far councils, and especially local planning authorities, are communicating what they are doing to their publics and allowing them to make inputs to those activities, in whatever degree is seen as compatible with electoral democracy. Many councils do communicate what they are doing, not only because in certain areas like dealing with planning applications and making local plans they are required by law to do so, but because it is part of council and planning culture to be fairly open about what they are doing. Some readers may think this is being too kind to councils, and it may well be that in some cases, some degree of secrecy or holding back information in terms of timing or detail does occur. I am not aware of recent research on this informational role of planning authorities. But my impression is that, at least for those who have full access to the internet, it is not hard to find out about local planning, more or less continuously, in each part of the UK.

One way in which council communication has been impoverished has been in the Publicity Code imposed by government on councils in 2011, following minister Eric Pickles's attack on 'town hall pravdas' – in other words, Labour councils issuing newspapers or other communication critical of central government. Since then, only 'politically neutral' communication is allowed, with at most four editions of papers a year. While a few London councils (Hackney, Waltham Forest) have continued to publish more frequent editions, insisting that this is informative, not political, they have been put under ever more pressure by central government, and this form of communication has been dying, alongside the commercial local press which it was intended in part to counterbalance – while the 'national press pravdas', almost all presenting central government views, continue to flourish.

Communication by councils certainly has problems, which need to be considered in understanding how planning works and how it might be improved. One is the language which planners use. Weston and Weston (2013) examined the extent to which planning committee reports were written in clear language, accessible to the average citizen. They concluded that this was far from being the case, although practice varied considerably. Reports were often 'shrouded in the language of the rational professional expert' (p 186). Jargon and technical acronyms could exclude the wider public, as well as be a means to create social distance between planners and the public.

A further and in part newer feature of (non)-communication is the tendency for information on planning schemes to be limited due to the claimed need for commercial confidentiality. This has become more and more an issue as viability has been given a large role in planning decisions, after its prioritising in the 2012 NPPF. Sheppard et al (2015) explored the impact of this decline in public disclosure, and argued for more transparency than was happening in some of the cases they examined. Further campaigning on the viability area has increased the stress on the importance of communicating full scheme information to the public, not limiting this to top councillors, or even in some cases just to the council leader (Colenutt 2020).

Central government

The quality of information on planning in central government has almost certainly been lower than in most councils, even though here, too, there is at least a formal culture of consultation on changes of policy in the MHCLG. Slade (2018a pp 225–227) suggests that New Labour tended to broad if often shallow and managed consultation, while since 2010 the tendency has been to talk in depth with chosen groups or individuals – that is, a much more closed mode. The website of PINS in relation to large infrastructure policy adopted a policy of full exposure of all dealings on Nationally Significant Infrastructure Projects (NSIPs), though how far this commitment has endured since 2009 is unclear. The NSIPs regime is a good example of the critical link between information and real impact on results. While the regime is good at informing in a general sense, the information is often highly technical and difficult for laypeople to deal with (Natarajan et al 2018). Furthermore, the chance of effective influence is minimal, given that the vast proportion of NSIPs are approved (Marshall 2017b).

Non-governmental bodies and communication

The second main element is in the mediation and debating of planning issues outside or alongside the communication activities of governments. This is in the hands of various media actors. Some of these channels are managed by interest groups, those discussed in Chapter 7, and have all the features of that sector of planning activity, nationally and in each locality. Some websites may be very helpful to the less well-informed wishing to understand a national or local issue, some may be quite impenetrable and mysterious except to those in the know. These interest groups do not have as one of their core purposes to promote the quality of the planning public sphere. By their nature they can serve only partially to facilitate wider public discussion. Studies of the adequacy of digital news media as substitutes for traditional forms suggest that they have not so far evolved into forms which give a wide and balanced plurality of reporting (Mediatique 2018). A pluralist heaven may hope that their vigorous continuous interaction will generate such a comprehensible and open-to-citizens public sphere, but this is being optimistic. Is there a realm of independent, alternative but also authoritatively researched information in planning matters? Many bodies do what they can to form this realm, including the RTPI and TCPA, but against the weight of government and the development machines, this may not be enough.

At any rate, the explosion of web-based information, reports, opinion, podcasts and so on has certainly expanded what is available, and we may hope that the net effect on the growth of this public discussion space has been overall quite positive during the relatively short life of the internet (to 2020, at most two decades in any effective form). In this area, paper-based media must now have a very secondary role, in comparison.

The professional press is in many ways related to this field of pressure group and business communication. In the narrower definition of planning, it is dominated by one magazine, *Planning*, now appearing fortnightly, linked to a web service, Planning Resource. This relates more to a discussion of professional and expert communication than to the issues explored here. But certainly this magazine, alongside others in related professions (surveying, architecture, engineering), has an important role as part of the continuing conversation about matters understood by those trained in planning.

But there is of course a sector which does have a specific role to communicate or mediate with citizens, at least as one of its roles. This is constituted by the mass-media businesses in their current incarnations. These businesses are now examined, with an assessment of their contribution to planning.

Planning and the mass media

During the century-or-more life of the planning system, communication has occurred in various forms beyond word of mouth, but with newspapers dominant, at least until the early 2000s. Since around 2000 the internet in its many shapes has challenged or probably superseded print media as the main source for knowing about planning matters, for those outside the councils and consultancies especially, but even to an extent for those producing policies and decisions: planners and councillors. Here the situation at national and local levels is surveyed, in order to raise issues about the links to political and ideological dimensions of planning. Not for the first time, this survey cannot be based on any widespread research base, such a base being non-existent, to my knowledge. Reliance on my own knowledge of the issue over many years will have to suffice, in most areas. Nevertheless, it is hoped that a broadly recognisable account can be given, providing at least a springboard for further exploration of the implications.

There appears to have been limited treatment of the relationship of planning and the media. One exception is the article of Rydin and Pennington (2003), which suggested that the media play a larger and more positive part at local levels, acting as an autonomous force as well as having mediating roles in some policy areas. This may chime with a fuller treatment of a local media case, the analysis of the impact of the Cardiff newspaper the *South Wales Echo* on a redevelopment scheme in the Cardiff docks, called Atlantic Wharf, in the period 1983–85 (Thomas 1994). This critiques the assumption in the growth-machine literature that local media are automatically allied with political and economic elites promoting development schemes. It was true that in this case the local newspaper did give consistent support to the redevelopment scheme, but this needed to be understood in terms of the relationship between governing agents (councillors and officers) and the press, and the approach of newspaper editors to 'newsworthiness', especially the editors' understandings of the cultural assumptions of the readers of the press – in this case, of the value of blanking out some aspects of the 'Cardiff Bay' area, including the long-standing immigrant communities, in favour of a project to link the city centre with the waterfront, forgetting inconvenient elements of the city's history. Future studies of planning and the media can learn from this valuable study, although as will become clear, the present era is dramatically different from that period, when advertising revenue and circulation were buoyant for local papers of this kind.

A final exception to planning and the media desert is Ben Clifford's examination of the extent of positive and negative portrayals of planning in the British press (2006). He noted that the national press was generally highly critical of planning, while the local press focused more on what planning did locally. He described the ideological tone adopted in relation to planning, and how this deeply coloured media positions between the dominant right-wing press (virulently anti-planning normally) and the one or two Left or centre national papers, whose criticisms were much milder. 'Ideological issues were much less prominent in the local press' (Clifford 2006, p 435). Changes have occurred since that time, of course, as we will see.

National media

Planning does not have a continuously visible profile on the national-level media, whether daily newspapers, radio or television. Generally, large issues, such as efforts to reform the planning system, the incidents around large development projects or the occurrence of varying kinds of (perceived) scandal, will provide the hook on which either newspaper editors or (much more rarely) television or radio programme producers will choose to present some part of a planning matter. Mostly this will be confined to the 'quality press', in UK-wide terms this being primarily a very few daily newspapers (*Daily Telegraph*, *Guardian*, *The Times*). But this is extremely occasional. The most notable example has already been recounted, the campaign led by the *Daily Telegraph* in 2011–12 to change the draft NPPF. This gave a very unusual high profile to a planning reform, from a particular perspective, linked to a continuous web presence for the Hands off our Land campaign for the year or more of that campaign. I am not aware of any other newspaper in recent times dedicating this level of coverage, including several front-page banner headline articles, to planning matters. Possibly the coverage of controversial infrastructure projects since the early 2000s, such as the Heathrow expansion, Hinkley Point or HS2, has been the nearest competitor to such a profile. These, however, due to their atypicality, will convey less about the everyday core of planning than would coverage of more normal schemes or planning procedures.

In my experience of noting planning matters in national television and radio, the number of programmes cannot be at most more than a handful each year. There were, for example, three BBC series, each of eight episodes, called variously *Meet the Planners*, *The Planners* and *Permission Impossible: Britain's Planners*, screened in 2008, 2013 and 2014, which gave some kind of insight into a range of contentious developments in a number of UK localities. The title shifts may reflect the increasingly critical attitude of government to planning. These are the only programme sets I can remember in recent decades which might have served to some degree to expose the realities and complexities facing planning authorities and communities in various arenas. A BBC Radio 4 programme by author Will Self to mark 70 years of the Planning Act 1947, broadcast in March 2017, stood out as a rare broad view of planning questions, given an hour of radio time.

Despite this uneven coverage (in time and by theme), touching just the tip of the iceberg of planning issues at national level, my judgement would be that at least some degree of exposure of key issues is given, for those wishing to access information, in the 'quality' press or very occasionally on radio and television. The situation may be no worse than in many other 'non-dramatic' fields of public policy. However, as or more importantly, the political and ideological nature of the coverage of the issue will be skewed, in the case of the press, by the nature of the UK press, which is heavily tilted to ownership by those on the Right of the political spectrum. Among the quality press only the *Guardian* is likely to give a more positive picture of planning action (unless one includes the continuing online presence of the *Independent*, or the *Financial Times*, which, however, would have relatively limited coverage of the planning field). So, most reporting of planning in the rest of the press (including newspapers like the *Daily Mail* or *Daily Express* or *Sun*, which would have weak and limited coverage of directly planning matters) will take a broadly anti-planning and pro-market position. Of course the case of the Hands off our Land campaign of the *Daily Telegraph* shows the risks in such generalisation. As the earlier account made clear, the fault-lines here were not simply pro and anti planning, but more pro and anti (perceived) countryside and heritage protection. At any rate, the mediation of understandings of planning takes a particular colour, given the press ownership at national level in the UK, notwithstanding this somewhat exceptional case.

This press-led mediation may be balanced to a certain degree by some television and radio reporting. But, as this is limited, the effect of television may be rather to have an impact via programmes not directly related to planning, such as those celebrating nature, countryside, gardening, heritage or property matters, of which there are large numbers spread across many channels. All of these will, taken as a whole, support a protectionist and property-defending stance towards planning, rather than, say, stress the interests of those without property-owning prospects or of those with deep green ideological positions (although it may be argued that, say, a David Attenborough nature series can lead to deep green understandings). Though these programmes may not be intended to have such an effect, they will doubtless set agendas which will affect planning debates.

Local media

Given the locally variable impacts of development and local functioning of planning systems, the role of the media is no doubt even more critical at the level of regions, counties, cities and towns. It is here that there is some researched commentary (on trends as a whole, with little specifically on planning), and this tells a common story (Minton 2013, Media Reform Coalition 2015, 2017, 2018, Ramsay and Moore 2016,

Mediatique 2018, Cairncross 2019). This notes the gradual decline of localised newspapers (going back to the 1980s, and so predating the shift of advertising to digital), and also, to an extent, of local radio stations, and the concentration of those outlets remaining in a few corporate hands. Five companies owned 77.1% of the UK local press in 2017 (Media Reform Coalition 2017) and these companies have been cutting back staff rapidly, such that few local reporters remain in many of the surviving papers, with papers put together by combing of websites. The most recent surveys show the emergence of 'news deserts', where no local press remains. Only 80 of 406 UK local government areas in 2017 were directly served by a local daily newspaper, with another 53 covered by a daily in adjacent or nearby authorities (meaning 67% not so served). In nearly half the cases, there was only one newspaper serving the area. The collapsing advertising revenue is the result of the migration of advertising to digital/social media, leaving the local press with no secure revenue base. One conclusion of the government-commissioned Mediatique report is that newspapers matter even more at the local level, because alternative television, radio and internet sources are weaker there (2018, p 33).

The Cairncross Review (p 22) summarised key points from a Cardiff University doctoral thesis:

> Rachel Howells's research in Port Talbot, Wales, following the closure of *The Port Talbot Guardian* in 2009, provides both quantitative and qualitative evidence of a consequent democratic deficit. Dr Howells found a decline of almost 90% in reporting by journalists at Port Talbot local council meetings, public meetings or political party meetings over the period from 1970 and 2013. In addition, the proportion of stories based on sources local to the Port Talbot area declined from under 60% to 44% by 2013 – with voices from outside Port Talbot rising. In extensive interviews with local people, Dr Howells recorded that they felt frustration at their inability to influence decisions being made in institutions such as the local council and the Welsh Assembly. She discovered high levels of rumour and speculation. People felt it was difficult to find out what was going on in the town, to know where to complain, and to get answers to questions. She also found that voter turnout suffered.
>
> What is particularly noteworthy about Dr Howells's research is that she noticed a decline in measures of

democratic and civic engagement after journalists ceased to be based in the town and to cover it in the depth they once had, and before the local newspaper closed.'

Howells noted that planning was a particularly missed element among her focus groups' participants. In fact, planning in the broad sense dominated the issues raised spontaneously (Howells 2015 pp 247–248). Howells noted that there was a clear shift from planning stories coming from journalists attending council and other meetings, normal in the 1970s to 1990s, to full dependence on managed media sources, normally press releases by local or other authorities (pp 260–262). As a result, scrutiny by local people was much harder and there was a reduction in what she calls the local public sphere (echoing Habermas's conceptualisation of the public sphere, and transferring this to the local level). This suggests that a generally fruitful symbiosis of planning and the local press existed in Britain for many years, a situation which is now rapidly disappearing.

Two further examples can be given from widely differing contexts, London and Edinburgh.[1] London has a dominant, now free, daily paper, the *Evening Standard*, alongside other free news sheets. The *Standard* reports planning only very sporadically, never hunting out stories and relying only on developers or the mayor of London's press releases. A few borough-level newspapers survive, including the *Camden New Journal* and the *Southwark News*, with the Camden paper especially likely to undertake genuine investigative journalism. All other boroughs (so, 31 others) therefore have no or only weak coverage at borough level. Internet provision does go some way to fill the gap in some areas and on some topics, with sometimes local bloggers persisting in trying to keep localities informed. But this exists only thanks to the most dedicated work of a few activists, who run pressure groups, including Just Space, and the London Forum of Civic and Amenity Societies. This is clearly the description of a very poorly functioning public sphere for planning, whether at the London-wide or borough or neighbourhood level.

Edinburgh has a daily paper, the *Edinburgh Evening News*, as well as the national paper, *The Scotsman*. Planning is very much present in these papers, and they are backed up by lesser presences, the *Edinburgh Reporter*, monthly online, and the *Broughton Spurtle*, a local online paper but one picking up city-wide issues. My knowledgeable contact considered that Edinburgh was a very distinctive case, given its well-informed audience and its small networks where everyone tends to know everyone, at least all the key players. This can make lobbying very open, as the Scottish Parliament is local, and so can be easily contacted, as can local councils. This expert's view was that online elements would not replace paper presses effectively, as they remove the regular presence of journalists who are (in principle) acting to report change. On both the production and consumption of news, online practices generate, at most, sporadic functioning, possibly replacing traditional print forms at key crisis moments (big rows about terrible or controversial schemes), but otherwise unlikely to be effective replacements. However, there is the additional problem that those local papers still remaining do not have journalists knowledgeable about planning, so they will at best wake up at the mention of something they have heard of (green belt, big road scheme), but otherwise be poor at participating in or leading public debates. This puts an onus on those knowledgeable outside to provide copy and pressure.

The Oxford Times

Though giving almost certainly an atypical picture, a consideration of the situation in Oxfordshire will show what may be the best-case position for planning coverage in the local media. Most of Oxfordshire is served by a daily and weekly press produced in Oxford, with sister titles to the Oxford papers for all the main towns; just the north of Oxfordshire is to some extent separate, with Banbury having another weekly paper. The *Oxford Mail* is a daily paper, with some planning coverage if a dramatic issue can be headlined, but probably having lesser impact in affecting local knowledge and opinion. The weekly *Oxford Times*, on the other hand, is quite widely read by the sorts of people most likely to be involved in local planning debates, including by politicians, those active in pressure groups, as well as those simply interested in local affairs. However, in parallel with the *Oxford Mail*, its circulation has fallen rapidly in recent years, from around 26,000 in 2006 to an Audit Bureau of Circulations-reported 7,283 in 2017.

There are effectively four sections to the paper, the news part, a property supplement, an arts and events section and the sport and other advertisements pages. Disregarding the property supplement, the news part of the paper takes up normally around 34 of the 80 pages, although even many of these 34 pages are all or in part made up of advertisements.

Planning has a high profile in the news section. A short survey of content conducted in December 2018 and January 2019 (six weekly issues) showed a very heavy presence of planning and related issues. In related issues have been included matters about traffic and transport, something of apparently deep interest in the city and county, as well as some environmental and social issues which can be judged close to planning. Table 8.1 shows that on average 11 pages had such planning or planning-close matters each week. Moreover, on five out of the six weeks the front-page headline was on such a planning matter, and, reflecting the prominence thus given, the editorials were on the same issue these five times. While the salience of planning matters may have been especially high, due to certain issues at that moment (including the impending opening of the very controversial Local Plan examination of Cherwell local authority, north of Oxford), this is probably not an unusual result from such a survey.

It should also be noted that there is a highly knowledgeable quality to some of the planning coverage, due in part to the concentration of the letters page on planning or transport matters. In these weeks there were also two longer articles discussing long-term futures for Oxfordshire, one by the director of the Oxford Preservation Trust, one by an ex-director of planning of Oxfordshire County Council (which then sparked a letters exchange by equally experienced correspondents).

So, in the case of Oxfordshire, there is an area of continuous debating, for those wishing to find it, in the pages of a weekly newspaper. Clearly, only a relatively small minority will read this paper, but that minority will include many who are most involved in local affairs. In Oxfordshire's case, there is an attempt by the newspaper editors to provide 'balanced' coverage, probably reflecting the divided nature of local politics, Conservatives normally controlling four of the councils and Labour controlling Oxford city. A much fuller study would be needed to give these and any more judgements a solid foundation. In particular an analysis of the assumptions carried into the newspaper editorials and decisions about what to headline, and about what to include in articles, would reveal, I would guess, a broadly 'conservative' mindset, to some extent celebrating the past and preserving the status quo. As always, therefore, I would argue that the planning coverage is infused with political and ideological understandings, however little visible these may be to many readers.

The decline of the local press will tend to spread the areas of 'planning news deserts', unless it is stopped by determined government intervention, as recommended by the Media Reform Coalition (2018) in its evidence to the Cairncross Review on the press in 2018–19. This complicates considerably the effective functioning of planning of localities (let alone regions). The Cairncross Review reported in February 2019 and recommended urgent measures to inject resources into the local press, as well as to a lesser extent to take

Table 8.1: *Oxford Times* planning and related fields coverage, 2018–2019 (by page numbers)

Week date	Local plans	Housing sites	Transport issues, including road works	City centre and shops	Environment	Economy	Society, schools	Totals
6 Dec 2018	7, 27,	1–2, 5, 10	3, 7	5, 14, 17	55	4		13
13 Dec	3	9, 14	5, 7, 11, 63	15, 21	59		1–2	12
10 Jan 2019		12, 14, 16	4, 9, 12, 26, 53					8
17 Jan	3	23	1–2, 4, 8, 9, 10, 11	2	18, 53	12, 21, 55, 57		16
24 Jan	4, 23	7	5, 14, 16, 53 57	13	1–2, 8			12
31 Jan	1–2	5, 15, 53	9		6, 27			8
Total pages	8	14	24	7	9	5	2	69

Note: This does not include the letters pages, which always have many planning-related topics

measures to support high-quality, particularly investigative, journalism (Cairncross 2019). The local element was under the heading of a 'local democracy reporting service', and while there was no direct reference to planning, this was clearly in part about reporting the activities of local authorities. It remains to be seen if government action will be on a scale to save the British local press from slow disappearance from most of the country.

Planning, participation and deliberation

Once an issue is out in the open, there may be the chance to influence decisions in relation to the issue. This scope for participation can include opportunities for deliberation. Some of these matters have been touched on already, including the early advocacy of the ideology of participation by McAuslan in the 1970s. The debate on the role and effectiveness of participation in planning in Britain has never really stopped since the 1969 Skeffington Report (Brownill et al 2019). Practice has taken many different forms, with some governments being much keener on the idea as a whole than others, and with different councils and regimes of planning pursuing different approaches over the decades. The field of planning probably has more experience in the arena of public participation than any other area of public policy, though of course it is not alone, with, for example, schools policy also having many different dimensions of such public and particularly parental involvement over the years.

Participation and deliberation literature

Planners and planning theorists are very familiar with many decades of discussion of public participation, and, since at least the turn of the century, with the whole field of collaborative and communicative planning (Healey 1997, 2007, Innes and Booher 2004). In these areas there is both developed theory and a massive international swathe of empirical studies. There has been less engagement with the area of deliberative theory, a key field of advance in political science since about 1990 (Dryzek 1990, 2000, Goodin 2008, Chappell 2012). However, some examination of the wider possibilities of deliberation in planning has occurred, most fully in studies on experience in Australia (Maginn 2007, Hopkins 2010a, 2010b, Legacy 2012), especially the 'Dialogue with the city' in Perth in 2003–04. Hopkins in particular has demonstrated the considerable potential pitfalls involved if politicians, or planners, do not wish to genuinely open up decision making. French experience in using deliberation in major infrastructure projects could help the development of best practice (Marshall 2016). Vigar (2006) analysed the difficulties in attempts to widen discussion on regional transport planning in North East England.

There is a large political science literature on participation and deliberation, even though most planning academics, let alone planning practitioners, are hardly aware of the great majority of this set of discussions. The theme of democracy was a continuing thread from the late 1960s to the 1990s, with an oscillation between an interest in how to improve representative democracy (for example, to meet sustainability long-term needs) and work on 'micro deliberation', looking at the range of techniques or procedures that might be deployed – citizens juries, deliberative polling, planning cells. Experimentation ran alongside theorising. From the 1990s one push was to consider the scope to scale-up deliberation, so that macro deliberation could be seen as a practical option for countries or large regions or cities. This was stimulated in part by practice with participatory budgeting in the 1990s, developed by the Workers Party in Brazil, and extended to some other contexts, in that this was already a scaled-up activity, involving hundreds of thousands of people in decisions on parts of municipal budgets. Current circumstances are not so propitious for such novel practices, in that right-wing governments are in power in most European and American states, with a limited interest in democratic experimentation of this kind, but this has not stopped the ferment of discussion in political science circles.

The political use of participatory and other democratic devices

Decisions to allow participation, consultation and deliberation, in the many possible forms, are deeply political. (These terms to describe the spectrum of practices are by no means mutually exclusive or necessarily tightly defined). All such practice sits alongside electoral or representative democracy. Michael Saward paints a fluid and contingent picture of how democracy really works in concrete situations (2003). He sees democratic potentials as containing a repertoire of 'devices' on which it may be possible to draw in kaleidoscopically changing combinations. These devices, which may include any number of electoral, interest group or deliberative elements, are phased or sequenced to generate varying forms of responsiveness, in any particular case. It is the interlocking of devices in temporal and power relations which determines who has the larger say over what. A device is whatever part of a democratic system is put in motion over a particular issue, such as a council or parliamentary vote, a public debate, a referendum or an online discussion forum.

Timing and phasing have the effect of narrowing or widening the 'funnel' of possible influence for different interests. As is well known in planning, if one consults on an issue too late, this may well leave the real decision only in the hands of elected members or officials, while if one consults too early, this may have the same effect if an issue has not been defined clearly enough in terms of location or substance for the public to form a proper opinion. Different devices may fit at different stages of processes, if we conceive this in classical terms of agenda setting, debate and discussion, decision and implementation. The practical question is: 'which devices, singly and in combination, enact desired interpretations of democratic principles within and across the different stages of the decision making process?' (Saward 2003, p 168). Of course, in planning this question is much more easily asked than answered, given the systemically messy nature of planning processes, where decisions may not come in a neat order, with iterative or simply contradictory dynamics. Planning has been configured very variably. For example, in a Regional Plan certain decisions may be taken in years 1 to 3, which frame decisions in a Local Plan in years 4 to 6, and then individual planning application decisions in years 7 to 15. Publics may be involved in some way in all stages, but the sense among most citizens of influencing such a cascade over many years may be relatively limited.

Macro deliberation or deliberative systems

A collection edited by Parkinson and Mansbridge (2012) built especially on work by the two editors (Mansbridge 1999, Parkinson 2006). It tackled essentially the question of scale. It is broadly accepted that it may be useful to use micro deliberative approaches at certain times, even though the weight these should have is always likely to be contested, on the grounds above all of representativeness. What has been widely seen as less applicable in modern democracies, with millions of citizens, is how deliberation may help across a whole territory – city, region, country or even wider. The latest discussion has aimed to modify these doubts. This has been done by two moves. One argues that it is possible to 'reason together' at wide scales if we loosen the requirements for what 'reason' and 'together' mean. Claims can be made, narratives created and contested, by using contemporary forms of communication, even if the classic forms of debate, especially face-to-face debate, cannot be used. The second move is to see *systems* of deliberation. These systems bundle together or sequence sets of deliberative elements, some possibly small scale, some very large scale, so that, perhaps in a rather rough and ready way, the whole adds considerable value to the evolving of the public sphere around issues. Part of such deliberation may take place in conventional arenas, such as parliaments or local councils, or within constitutionally recognised processes, such as elections or referendums. But the distinctive element of deliberative systems thinking is to see these as part of a wider *package* or dynamic of political and public policy evolution, linked to other, more innovative ingredients. Those ingredients may include some of the micro deliberative devices, or scaled-up elements such as large-scale public debating exercises.

Deliberative theorists raise a whole range of issues on how far macro deliberation can really work (see particularly the first and last chapters in Parkinson and Mansbridge 2012). These include how well sequences of deliberative devices can be linked together (answer, get politicians and officials to be more conscious of the ordering of deliberative moments throughout a policy process), how to overcome the 'deliberative gap' between what citizens want and what governments can offer (answer, aim for 'richly representative' deliberative systems), how to ensure fair access in discussion (answer, set up systems with 'tribunes' or 'umpires' institutionally arranged to work for neutrality). Owen and Smith (2015) make a more fundamental criticism of the prospects for genuinely deliberative macro-systemic sets of practices. They prefer to press the case for exploring the value of the 'deliberative stance', wherever it may be found, as one part of a battery of democratic practices.

A further issue is the question of 'repeat deliberation', where reflection may be an option at different stages of the development of a project or strategy. This may be related to the separate stages of policy making: agenda setting (defining a problem), discussing, deciding and implementing (Catt 1999). The new twist from deliberation is to imagine how processes of deliberation may be brought in at various points of this sequence. This can overlap with the idea of the 'policy funnel', which has been used to suggest that different scope to frame problems exists at each of these moments. While the idea of a linear policy process has been challenged repeatedly (Barrett and Fudge 1981 on implementation theory for example), it is unlikely that such phased policy making can ever be completely removed. In simple terms, deliberative approaches in the public realm are likely to fit most straightforwardly in the first two stages (agenda setting and discussing). The classic complication for planners is that agreements made there may not stick later when individual projects come into view. That then gives scope for further deliberation at that stage, if the system allows such 're-opening' of matters of principle – as many systems do, in some degree or another, for a range of reasons – finance, power, changing contexts and so on. We will come back to the repeat deliberation issue at the end.

Evolving work on representation is very relevant to thinking on deliberation. Saward (2010) argues that representation should be thought about in a much broader manner, as a process of claim making and audience creation. While the standard machinery of electoral democracy can be analysed in these terms, there are, he suggests, many other actors who successfully claim to represent other people or other arguments. These people or groups may claim to 'speak for' interests, and if their claim is seen as valid by certain audiences or constituencies, this contributes to a panorama of representation which goes far beyond the classic discussion of how a member of a parliament represents electors. Saward uses examples such as western celebrities (e.g. Bono on Africa) claiming to speak for the poor of Africa. Macro deliberation can draw some support from this concept of representation, because it can fit in a landscape of continuous construction of the public sphere (Habermas 1996) without challenging the legitimacy of representative democracy. The wider concept of representation claims that there are multiple bases of legitimacy in a complex contemporary polity. Electorally based representation is still likely to be at the core of any democratic polity, but it fits in this wider landscape, so legitimacies are not in reality competing, but overlapping and complementary.

Experiences of participation and deliberation

Two valuable if now quite old surveys of public participation in Britain came to mixed views on the quality of public participation since the 1960s (Thomas 1996, Rydin 1999). They both suggested that the full range from genuine consultation to the purest tokenism could be found, with no especially clear trend up to the moments of writing in the 1990s, although Thomas detected a consistent diminution in the push to promote public involvement in policy formation, caused by the New Right philosophy of British governments. Recently Beebeejaun (2018) has argued that post-2010 governments especially bear responsibility for the diminution of participation within mainstream planning (as against the odd island of neighbourhood planning). Her case study of fracking certainly supports that view. My own judgement is that since the 1970s many planners and councils have made very serious attempts to manage discussion with the public as well as they can, that is, giving chances at the right time, if frequently under very difficult circumstances (caused very often, as Beebeejaun claims, by central government policies). For example, there was, certainly up to 2010, a long history of participative efforts on regional, structure and local plans, on regeneration schemes or conservation programmes or rural planning initiatives. One could document thousands of such participation efforts since the 1970s in Britain, based on the attachment of many planners and councillors to the value of open debate of future development options. No doubt Ines Newman's assessment (2014) that England had at best an 'elitist democracy' in its local government system was broadly correct, but in planning practice, I think that very many efforts had been made to widen beyond the elite, when this was not the case in many other policy fields. That judgement does not remove at all the need to make very big improvements, as will be discussed in the final chapter.

Nevertheless, the classic impediments to adequate participation, in any field, remain (Fraser 1992 and Garnham 1992 for the public sphere as a whole, Thomas 1996 and Rydin 1999 for planning). The most important is no doubt the result of social inequality and the extreme imbalances of economic power. This generates imbalances in the capacity to participate to strong effect, with prosperous and time-rich communities much more active and effectively active than poorer areas. Wider structuring forces are also important, as they can limit the range of dimensions on which decisions are being made. Anyone with a feminist or green standpoint will notice this nearly all the time. More generally, it is evident that on most issues our views are now not asked for – for example, we have been told since the 1980s that issues of unemployment are matters for market forces, not public involvement. Given the historic aspirations of planning to make better lives, this is evidently a massive hole in what can be open for discussion. At certain periods these gaps may have been filled by self activity from below. For planning, this was very obvious in the period of forceful community action in the 1970s and 1980s. In most areas and most places, such action from poorer communities has been far less evident since the late 1980s, in Britain at least. Neighbourhood planning, as we have seen, tends overall to tilt the political system's attention to the zones of the already more privileged.

Rydin (1999) concludes her survey of participation with a caution that aiming for wider participatory democracy may not necessarily be the correct goal. One reason is the social bias, the skewing of the capacity to participate. The second is that there may well be necessary roles for elected representatives who can take a wider and more considered view than that which may sometimes emerge from public participation processes. Her conclusion is that the 'new urban governance of planning should involve different roles for planners, groups *and* the public' (1999, p 197). In my terms, this is about restructuring the politics and institutional forms of planning, from several directions, as discussed in the final chapter.

This cautioning may have been prescient, as there have emerged in recent years other grounds for doubting the value of promoting widespread deliberation across all or even most public policy fields. Promoters of the ideas of 'post-politics' tend to criticise consultation or participation as part of the governance mechanisms maintained by states who have no intention of allowing meaningful discussion of anything important. Meanwhile, the rise of right-wing populist movements also generates doubts about what should be open to deliberation and how. Such movements often argue for 'direct democracy', government by referendum, so that all issues are put to popular votes, with less reliance on electoral democracy. This clearly risks generating a 'tyranny of the majority', rather than more mature conversations about futures, taking into account the rights of minorities.

Nevertheless, at national level there has been a significant amount of well-meaning use of deliberative democratic devices, including, for example, the Irish Citizens assembly set up in 2016 (with a resulting success on the reform of abortion law soon following), and the French national debates on environmental sustainability and on energy under the Sarkozy and Hollande presidencies (Marshall 2012, 2014). Most recently a proposal has been made by German academics to promote public deliberation at the federal government level by instituting an independent office for a 'Federal Participatory Workshop', which would promote discussion of some of the most difficult issues facing the country, with a direct link to debates in the federal parliament (Rohr et al 2019). In my view this would be a valuable avenue for institutional innovation. At present in the English part of the UK the only body undertaking long-term and reasonably open examination of matters close to planning is the NIC, though its brief is limited. There is scope to hold full public national debates, in different forms, to deal with some of the underlying questions confronting the planning system, such as responding to climate change or addressing housing need.

Conclusion

We can now summarise how this dimension of theorising and practice relates to the ideology and politics of planning, directly. There is a clear relationship with the ideological landscape at any one moment. Some kinds of participation would be validated by Conservative and right-wing government periods – neighbourhood-level activity, most obviously, but also a few other kinds of non-threatening discussions on landscape, heritage or technical aspects of road or rail schemes. The current rise of Far Right politics may start to challenge the acceptance of participation more widely, as nationalist and right-leaning populist movements are unlikely to be sympathetic to the more pluralist and not necessarily traditionalist values embodied in many public participation exercises. A wider range of participation and deliberation forms, with more real chance to influence important decisions, could flourish with more Left ideological success at national level.

Any such assessments of the intersection of ideological positions and the scope for genuine participation and deliberation will also have to be conscious of the play of political processes, as they will continue to be present, bar major restructuring of such processes. In particular, the articulation of the relationship between electoral representative democracy, especially in local councils, and all kinds of deliberation and participation, will be critical. The scope for more effective sequencing of democratic elements, and for some use of macro deliberation techniques, will be always conditioned by such structuring and the everyday politics it generates. There is certainly scope to structure this relationship better, but this will meet some logical limits. Equally, the scope for well-informed public involvement will be narrowed or widened by any movement backwards or forwards on issues of informing and mediating, particularly on whether any local independent media survive in England in the coming years.

Note

[1] Thanks to Michael Edwards on London and Cliff Hague on Edinburgh for their kindness in sharing their considerable experience of interaction with their respective local presses.

9

Facets of planning action: heritage, local environment and design

The fundamental framework of how planning works in a country is set by the overall ideology of the country within the periods being examined. The difference between eras and places is clear enough, if one scans systems of planning from the late 19th century. This ideological conditioning also works more continuously, with the changing pressures for reform of planning being in part driven by ideology as well. However, we have also seen that 'everyday' politics has an important role in this month-to-month and year-to-year shifting of planning policies and systems. What we look at here in this and the next chapter is the way in which the duo also condition the way in which different facets or fields of planning are affected.

Here therefore I am examining varying ways in which one can 'carve up' planning as an activity. Often the most important distinctions may seem to be between the type of development which is being decided on – housing, industry, transport infrastructure, retail. Here these are called planning *fields*, given that the term 'sector' is often now used in a slightly different way to refer to 'the planning sector'. But often it may be interesting to put the spotlight on the distinctions flowing from the *facets* of consideration which are most salient in any development, for example heritage, design or environmental impacts of many kinds. Another division which brings out other important features is that between the dominant *forms* of planning activity, certainly within most local authorities: those of development control or management (of planning applications), of plan making and of implementation work, often promotion of schemes for renewal or development by the council in partnership with the private sector.

We will find that some fields, facets or forms have a more pronounced ideological character, which makes the play of shorter-term political change less vigorous, while others can be more subject to such pressures, both nationally and locally. It was suggested in Chapter 1 that some planning matters will be ideologically hotter, if they are nearer the core issues of maintaining the system (the form of capitalism being one key element of that), and that this was mediated by fields of planning and scalar issues. In this and the next chapter, we will see scalar differences between fields, facets and forms as to the extent of impact, between the overall national policy making and the play in localities. Table 9.1 is a demonstration of how this examination can be done across a variety of fields, facets and forms of planning work.

Three facets of planning work (heritage, local natural environment and design) are examined in this chapter, to exemplify how such an approach can be developed. It may help to stress (in case the tone may appear too critical) that there is no intention to dispute the value enshrined in the three facets explored in this chapter; the assessment is analytical, though it does take a deliberately critical approach. These are core facets of planning. The concern here is to excavate what conditions their general nature and to highlight how political and ideological factors are important to this conditioning.

Heritage and historic conservation

Before legislation in the 1960s, the fate of older buildings or landscapes was not primarily a matter affected by the planning system. Property owners were able to do more or less what they wanted with buildings or land they owned. The limits to this were largely set by the ancient monuments legislation developed since the late 19th century, which affected famous sites or buildings, not the vast majority of places or spaces. These laws were implemented by a small-scale part of central government, the Ancient Monuments Department (Thurley 2013), with local authorities only gradually building a role through the 20th century by acquiring threatened buildings or landscapes, and often opening them to the public. So, this is another area of planning where the first understanding of the role of the state has to be set within the ideological struggle over the right of property owners to act independently, or not. To a large extent that struggle was lost by those wishing to maintain absolute property rights, and despite the turning back of the state's role in many fields since the 1950s, in this area the high valuation of preserving signs of the past has generally trumped such pressures in Britain.

The limited role for councils changed dramatically from the 1960s, as the listing of buildings, the declaration of Conservation Areas and the general heightening of consciousness of all things more than a generation or two old made 'heritage' into a significant part of every local authority's planning work, as well as empowering central government agencies in this field. There is therefore a partially separate regime for heritage, with a distinct policy community and, to a large

Table 9.1: Impinging of ideology and politics on different fields, facets or forms of planning

Field, facet or form of planning	Play of ideology	Play of politics
Field		
Housing	Ownership, tenure, cost, locational arrangements, city and country, class.	Local pressures against development of sites, especially greenfield, but also local and national lobbying force from housing industry as an economic sector.
Economy, including industry, retail, warehousing	Role of state and market forces, planning economic futures as against non-intervention, including spatially.	Pressure of business interests in localities, and especially nationally strong lobbies across all economic sectors.
Transport	Public versus private transport.	Force of private transport interests, car lobbies – greater than public transport lobbies – or cycling pressure groups.
Facet		
Environment	Collective action on range of environmental issues, from climate change across to landscape and green spaces. Left and Right ideological issues affect this profoundly.	Varying force of environmental pressure politics.
Land	Private versus public control.	Probably no direct political effect will be derived from each of the sectors involved in land. But specific large landowners like Duke of Westminster or Duke of Northumberland may have impact (Hetherington).
Design	Issues of demand and of control by the public over changes in appearance. Variable by class and 'cultural' dimensions.	Organised public pressures tend to be towards traditional forms.
Historic conservation	Class issues central to control and public action. Also attitudes to styles, such as modernism and other ideologically loaded movements. Power of nostalgia forces in media and in British culture, against ideas of the modern and the future. Betjeman-type attitudes promoted over several generations, valuing the old over the current and useful.	Numerous local groups in many places, mainly on preservation-at-all-costs side.

(continued)

Table 9.1: Impinging of ideology and politics on different fields, facets or forms of planning (continued)

Field, facet or form of planning	Play of ideology	Play of politics
Form		
Development control or management (DM)	Based on socialist idea of the nationalisation of development rights. Deregulation by right-wing governments has been reducing the force of this system. DM is at centre of battles over power of public sector and of democratic decision making, and relationship to highly resourced private actors. Different property relations and potentials for profit (direct or indirect, including owner occupation).	Fragmentation effect, with specific lobbies and very local groupings having strong force, but also power of property and development interests promoting schemes. These two forces may squeeze out ideas of wider public interests in good developments.
Plan making	Key remaining area of public sector-led planning, supported by Labour more than right-wing governments, at all levels. Often heavily diluted by collaborative and business partnership-based approaches to planning. Mixed economy of plan making, promotion of private sector as key and potentially veto actor.	Limited forces beyond profession and some local political leaderships behind the value of resourcing and prioritising plan making. Then within plan-making processes, quite uneven attention of different groups, with many of the above forces coming into play during public consultation phases of plan making. QCs at Examinations in Public for development interests versus enthusiasm of local groups.

extent, distinct professional training. With this goes, I would argue, a different mindset among most actors involved.

One valuable historical study illuminates the evolving relationship of conservation in the Thatcher period (Pendlebury 2000). Pendlebury chronicles 'a consolidation and strengthening of conservation policy to a previously unprecedented level' (p 31). 'Not only was conservation not the subject of the neo-liberal agenda but positive measures were taken ... conservation largely escaped even the rhetoric of liberalization' (p 41). Pendlebury argues that the Conservatives consciously used the past for political purposes, constructing a heritage model, partly via commodification. He explicitly inserts this within a consideration of the 'dominant ideology thesis' and of Bourdieu's ideas on the collaboration of the dominated in their own domination (country house visiting, the National Trust's ideological approach). 'Thus, in the context of Conservative governments, sustaining support and value on the protection and retention of heritage could be considered part of a strategy of maintaining existing power structures and social relations or indeed reasserting a set of social relations perceived to have been eroded by modernism and the welfare state' (Pendlebury 2000, p 47). This constructed consensus was, at the time of writing, seen as continuing under New Labour, as indeed it has since. Pendlebury and Veldpaus (2018) discussed the possible challenge to heritage consensus posed by Brexit, suggesting that the very different imaginaries embedded in some nativist and nationalist thinking could threaten at least the liberal assumptions within heritage ideologies, if not neoliberal strands (as they distinguish these).

With the cutting back of all public planning activities underway, it is hard to say how well the local authority heritage effort is surviving at the present. But it would be surprising if this sector of planning activity has suffered quite such serious cuts as some other areas. Heritage protection is almost certainly now a highly valued activity by some key actors in the planning polity, locally and nationally, including many councillors, ministers of all the main political parties and very influential pressure groups nationally and in most cities, towns and villages. From a relatively 'Cinderella' theme half a century ago, it can be argued that this now has strong cross-elite support, so that in many places the fate of any older building or any plot of land, small or large, is watched with intense interest by groups of enthusiasts.

A partially distinct sub-sector of heritage is archaeology and its linking to planning. Development, and excavation for archaeological purposes, have naturally always had much to do with each other, but since the instigation of developer-funded archaeology under the Planning Policy Guidance Note 16 of 1994 they have been fully chained together. The date of the policy is a clue to the ideological drive behind this policy shift. Before 1990 any archaeology was most commonly funded by the state in one form or another, but, with government wishing to cut funding, the route of imposing obligations on developers for this purpose (as in other fields like housing or local infrastructure) became attractive. What this has done has been to place the archaeological project in the hands of developers, to the advantage of the excavators by and large, as some sort of investigation and where appropriate excavation has, since 1990, remained mandatory. So, the archaeological contractors who sprang up to run this new business are now parasitic on the development industry, in all its guises. There is plenty of detailed politics in this, as the requirements are negotiated by publicly funded archaeologists in each local authority area with each developer, but by and large a kind of custom and practice has grown up about what is paid for and what not (the latter including very often long-term storage of finds and publication).

As someone with a lifelong archaeological interest I have noted the varied outcomes of this archaeology–developer–planning embrace. Since the early 2000s, the most striking phenomena have been the impacts of the big infrastructure projects in England funded largely by the government. This has included big road projects like the A14 scheme near Huntingdon, or the new London Crossrail station sites, producing vast numbers of finds and run by contractor consortia on military lines, requiring the importing of skilled excavators from around the world. The preparations for HS2 are dwarfing even those projects, as will the proposed (and, in the view of many, very misguided) Stonehenge tunnel project (on the A303). In the case of Stonehenge both the National Trust and Historic England favour the potentially highly damaging roads project, possibly because they both expect to gain more visitors to the monument and the district as a result. This is reinforced by the partial privatisation of English Heritage in 2015 (split from the regulatory arm, Historic England, which remains a public agency). It appears that the archaeological interest is now in favour of such projects, as it delivers the contractors work, continuing on a large scale over the years. So, from 1995 onwards, the ideological framing has created a particular dynamic in this sub-sector, with a political strand also visible in a more minor key, with local planning authorities as part of the machine.

This protectionist regime and culture has surely a strong ideological basis, which has been tracked by a series of writers, from the work of David Lowenthal (1985) and Robert Hewison (1987) onwards, sceptical of the ever continuing rise of the heritage industry. Hewison (2014) noted the fit of Thatcherism and heritage as commerce, and later charted the governmental shifts through the period, including the renaming of the relevant ministry from Department of National Heritage in the Major government to the modernising New Labour Department of Culture, Media and Sport. Though New Labour took a slightly different approach to heritage, its apparent role as a handmaiden to regeneration meant that in practice little changed. The continuing ideological basis connects to the strong valuation of the past and its manifestations, something which finds a natural support in Conservative thinking (for example, in the writing of the Conservative intellectual Roger Scruton, as in on the importance of 'home', Scruton 2017). But it also runs across as easily to modern liberal or socialist thinking, if with some differences of tone and emphasis – sometimes more stress on working or industrial heritage or progressive movements of various kinds. Thinkers like William Morris can connect to such leftist currents very naturally, and even be admired by Conservative thinkers, with the excision of his revolutionary socialism. While the post-2010 Conservative governments have wished to cut back the state, both financially and in regulatory terms, the resistance to such measures in the heritage field has been strong enough to limit this. The risk of some slight weakening of the protection of buildings within national planning guidance in 2011 was immediately stopped by a wall of opposition, so that most heritage specialists felt that the resultant 2012 NPPF (with some adjacent documents, rarely allowed in other sectors, including Historic Environment Practice Advice 2015), gave as much support as the previous heavily detailed Planning Policy Statement 5 finalised in 2010.

I would argue therefore that this field of planning is heavily conditioned by a seamlessly operating merger of strong ideological foundations (the British love affair with the past and fear of modernity and, possibly, foreignness) and permanent political mobilisation. The politics runs with the grain of Conservative deregulatory reforms, as the protection of landscapes and buildings lends itself very well to action at neighbourhood or town level, as against the bigger challenges of social justice, major development schemes or meeting long-term environmental goals. While deregulatory measures could in principle threaten heritage interests, in general the areas most important to these interests retain high protection, effectively policed by armies of voluntary effort at many governing levels, and sympathetic support from local councils, however hard pressed. It is interesting to imagine how such a seamless combination of felicitous ideological positioning (built up by decades of pressing and organising, from the days of John Betjeman or Ian Nairn onwards) and efficient politics could help other fields of planning activity, which rarely benefit from such a force field blending public concern and public authorities.

It would be possible to press this argument more strongly, to say that heritage thinking is a core part of working Conservative ideology related to the built environment, able to stop development in most areas of importance to rich elites and enable development in the zones of the country seen as less important. This may be pushing the coherence of ideological and political amalgams rather too far, in that there may well be significant areas where heritage is now, from a development industry perspective, 'going too far': protecting objects that get in the way of making money out of property. Accepting that there are at least some of these contradictory pressures in action does not mean abandoning the idea of an often very tidy fit between Conservatism and contemporary heritage thinking.

One sign of this was in a series of lectures in 2016–17 by Simon Thurley, chief executive of English Heritage from 2003 to 2015 (Thurley 2016, 2017). Thurley launched a strong attack on much of the planning ethos and the inability of parts at least of the planning system to support heritage goals. The point is not to present Thurley as a card-carrying Conservative, but the arguments he used in relation to the importance of the individual and local community as against the state, backed with references to Edmund Burke and a particular interpretation of 'the Commons' of Elinor Ostrom suggest a strongly conservative orientation, as well as a dislike of planning as a whole. He judged the NPPF to be a great step forward, as it 'had succeeded in getting heritage taken seriously as one of the key determinants of planning policy' (Thurley 2016, p 1). There was no sign of any interest in other social or environmental aspects of planning, or of public policy generally. In part this may have reflected the relative protection of heritage from the financial cuts experienced by most fields of planning, in that factors like funding of the Royal Palaces, the functioning of the National Trust, the buoyancy of the private sector-owned country house market and the availability of Heritage Lottery Fund moneys will have all helped to cushion cuts in general state funding.

Green spaces and the natural environment

It is now difficult to find an overarching term to describe the complex of overlapping and partially conflicting concerns for preserving the countryside, increasing biodiversity, creating 'green infrastructure' and improving environmental conditions in terms of open spaces within urban areas (Sinnett, Smith and Burgess 2016). However, here I consider this swathe of concerns, which constitutes another zone of strong enthusiasm and organisation in pressing the work of planning to give these matters a very high priority, both in Local Plan making and in decisions on individual planning applications. Some of the same historical movement is evident in this field as in the heritage area, in that at least the more environmentally coloured aspects of green area protection have gained some force in government policy and guidance since the 1960s, as well as in the action of local authorities. As well as historic conservation officers, many councils in Britain will employ some kind of ecological or natural environment specialists. These local staff may be backed by the central agencies like Natural England and the Environment Agency, though as government cuts spread, this support is less evident.

I would argue that this zone of 'light green' activity in planning is well backed by the ideological drives. The environmental and green ideologies described in Chapter 3 have concentrated some of their firepower on this area, and that has blended with the much wider educational and mass media support for 'nature'. Conservatism has much of its core electoral base in the countryside and small towns, and almost certainly even more of its ideological imaginary, in a partially invisible way linked to conceptions of preserving the countryside, the green and pleasant land of television dramas and National Trust imagery and ordinary practice (however much the National Trust may at times wish to change its image and trajectory). The idea of 'natural capital' has been invented to attempt to turn biodiversity and countryside protection into monetarised values. The Natural Capital Committee (NCC) was set up in 2012 under the chairmanship of Dieter Helm, an Oxford economist specialised in energy economics and long in touch with Conservative interests, publishing at times with think-tanks like Policy Exchange. The application of mainstream economic concepts has been controversial, but is now at the core of Conservative government policy in this area, with the NCC promoting a 25-year Natural Capital Plan. This suggests the way in which ideological compatibility between zones can be built, with two values close to the heart of contemporary Conservatism – neoclassical and monetarising economics and protecting the countryside – brought into some sort of policy synchrony.

But socialist and liberal ideological amalgams of the 20th century had just as much of their values and appeal linked to the idea of urban dwellers able to enjoy the countryside and nature to the full, hence the centrality of national parks, countryside access and green belts in the planning foundational period of the 1940s. The role of the Ramblers Association is a good example of this link of countryside campaigning and the Labour Party. Tom Stephenson, the long-serving secretary of this association after its national founding – from being a loose federation – in 1935, was also press officer in the Ministry of Town and Country Planning, working with minister Lewis Silkin to write the key national parks and rights of way legislation of 1949. These ideological drives on the Left and centre were strongly affected by green thinking from the 1970s onwards, so raising the profile of at least a light green agenda in the Labour and Liberal programmes from that period onwards.

As with heritage, there is some strong linking with local political pressure systems, taking general form in bodies like the CPRE and the Wildlife Trusts, active throughout England and backed by many other local or specialist organisational foci, ready to come to the defence of particular species, spaces or media and senses (odours, noise, air, water). Often there is a clear overlap with heritage interests, so that a boost to the structure of feeling for one may at times help the surge of support in some locality for the other. It is doubtful, though, whether the merging of general ideological support with political activity works quite as effectively in this area as for heritage. As implied above, this area has more fuzzy boundaries and the threats are arguably significantly greater. For example, it is taken as read in the great majority of cases that 'heritage objects' (however widely or narrowly defined at a particular moment) should be avoided by new developments. Massive efforts will be made to ensure that a housing scheme or ring road will avoid ancient buildings or historic landscapes. In extreme cases like Heathrow third runway or HS2, demolitions may be allowed, but this becomes intensely controversial. But building on green fields or putting a road or rail line across the countryside is less easy for light green lobbies to mobilise against. The standard balancing arguments in planning come into play. The cumulative impacts on biodiversity are less calculated in the majority of local plans or development decisions, given weaker guidance and more spatial dispersion and invisibility than in most heritage cases. This does not mean that the 'nature lobby' in planning is by any means weak, but it has overall a less strong position, one that no doubt has to be continuously fought for. Localness is still a strong card in this field, and it can be argued that the post-2010 reforms have at least not damaged too much the countryside zone of planning, as much can be done locally. But the dismantling of planning capacity, in local and strategic planning and nationally, has almost certainly weakened the ability of wildlife and ecology interests to promote effectively their wider goals.

One example can be given from the campaigning underway at the time of writing against the Oxford–Cambridge Expressway scheme being promoted by the UK government, with a large new stretch of motorway (this is what expressways are, effectively) proposed in Oxfordshire. The local wildlife trust, Berkshire, Buckinghamshire and Oxfordshire Wildlife Trust, almost certainly wishes to oppose this scheme, but has found it hard to deal with the various 'consultations' underway since 2017. This is in part because it finds it hard to fit the road scheme to its core interests (as it sees them) of protecting particular valued nature sites within its area. Other countryside pressure groups like the CPRE have had some of the same difficulty, in this case probably because their core membership, being village- or small town-based, is necessarily car oriented and so may sympathise with the building of extra road capacity, as against extra housing provision. Light green facets of planning may be pushed aside by determined development forces, unlike in the heritage sector, which has a significantly stronger position.

Design

Design is an area which is no doubt caught in a more complex force field than the two cases explored above. It has certainly had the attention of important thinkers in planning, urban design and architecture (Punter and Carmona 1997, on to Carmona 2018). It may be argued that no one can be against good design of the built environment, that it is a cross-class issue which affects everyone relatively equally. It has gone through various reincarnations in British planning since the 1980s, with neoliberal thought sometimes imagining that planning should have nothing to do with appearance or design (this sometimes gaining support from architects fed up with interfering planners), but with the view that this was a significant field for planning gaining the upper hand in the 1990s. This led to the creation in 1999 of a state agency with significant resources, the Commission for Architecture and the Built Environment (CABE). Although CABE was abolished in 2011, its legacy has continued in the promotion of design considerations in a range of fields, including within Design Council CABE. One argument, for example pressed by Conservative think-tanks like Policy Exchange, has been that if housing was better designed, even beautiful, there would be less nimby opposition to new development (Airey, Scruton and Wales 2018). Other initiatives include the drive within the NIC to improve design in big projects. This reflects the existing institutionalisation of design panels within various spheres, such as in the planning of Crossrail and of HS2, and in localities, as in Oxford, where a special panel now oversees all new development, following a much-criticised development of student housing next to a popular open space, Port Meadow.

I would argue (again) that this zone of planning thinking resonates very easily with Conservative ideological positions, including on heritage. This is not to say that there is the same kind of rather hegemonic force as in the heritage case, as different views no doubt compete in the design field, with modernist and contemporary approaches to material use and other design facets competing with precisely the heritage default position of trying to 'blend in with' whatever is existing nearby. But there are similarities with the heritage case, in that a very local and micro approach to design can be ideologically unthreatening. It does not necessarily bring in 'difficult' areas of often bigger-scale thinking, like meeting low carbon goals or being sensitive to gender issues. Of course such goals can be imported into design thinking and, given the make-up of the design professions, there is perhaps a good likelihood that they will come in, even though government planning guidance since 2010 has given little encouragement to such intrusion.

It has been noticeable in the world of planning education that design considerations have raised their profile in most planning teaching, as against earlier tendencies to prioritise matter from the social sciences, including on social and economic issues. I think this can be traced in part to the more bland and ideologically non-threatening nature of most (not all) design thinking, fitting the rise of market-dominated approaches in Britain since the 1980s. Urban design skills may have smoothed the way for many graduates into private consultancy planning, where such skills can be attractive in working up development industry schemes. There are other reasons, including the demand of students to be given practice-close answers which they can apply (or they think they can apply) in the jobs they expect to get on graduation, answers which some design teaching approaches offer to supply, as against the more difficult territory of directly political and economic dimensions of planning.

In this case the blending with the political forces at play in localities has been less tending to seal a strong alliance than in the heritage case. It is true that many civic society-type local associations will take an interest in design matters, and so raise the profile of these considerations in public discussion of schemes. But this will be cut across by the need to make speedy decisions with limited public planning resources, increasing the power and protagonism of developers and their professional advisors. This applies at any rate to private sector schemes. Where the fully public realm is in play, the design push should and often does have more scope for having a major role, as mentioned in the major infrastructure cases (Highways England is now also a great supporter of design panel techniques). This can apply in the design of public areas like streets and squares.

Is the design field therefore more ideologically indeterminate, and more politically subject to pressures arising mainly from the provision structure of the sub-sector or scheme in question? My judgement is that it is indeed more subject to the buffeting of competing arguments from development and other interests (the play of ideological contention in action), and open to the swaying of decisions by the personal predilections of influential individuals such as key councillors and leaders of very active local pressure groups. It is equally open to the play of the secondary or lesser ideologies described in Chapter 3. There is real scope for feminist, green and even nationalist influence in this field, perhaps even more so than in the heritage and natural environment fields. This may be because the dominant ideologies do not necessarily have such clearly set coordinates in their positions on design, meaning that the design arguments can be touched more easily by positions outside the core dividing arguments. However, as in all sectors, the provision structures are critical to what can in practice happen, as are the planning activity forms allowed by government. If there is no way for public voices to have real influence over, say, a design of an airport or a shopping centre, as funding is private, and the locality is set on getting the investment, planning activity is likely to have limited real influence (token consultation), and different ideologically based calls – prioritising feminist agendas, calling for low carbon forms, pressing nationalist or anti-nationalist agendas – may get very little chance to have effect.

Conclusion

Here three facets of planning work or considerations have been examined, as against the treatment of varying fields in the next chapter. This reflects the numerous cuts one can take across the range of planning activities and concerns. I have argued that the facets selected here all come in the 'non-threatening to Conservatism' category, if to varying degrees. They are generally also issues which liberal and Left ideologies have been comfortable to promote in recent decades. There have been differences in the ideological approaches, for example New Labour trying to shift the heritage orientation slightly and being rather more interventionist on design matters, and with more tolerance of modernist aesthetics. But this has still left large areas of consensus on heritage, local natural environment and design facets of planning.

These are all zones of strong enthusiasts and at the core of powerfully localised attachments, in tune with the *zeitgeist* of middle-class interests since the 1970s. If I had examined another set of facets (say, deep green or gender or race concerns), I would obviously have found other pictures. However, none of these has institutionalised roles and regimes within the British planning system and processes as these three do. I would argue that the three chosen in this chapter are particularly central to the operation of planning in Britain, and have become more so since the 1970s, to the detriment of certain social or more fundamental environmental dimensions. So, their ideological and political functioning is of particular importance. Their prioritising 'blocks in' part of the overall planning attention zone, hence, no doubt without wishing to do so, 'blocking out' other potential occupiers of that zone. When it comes to classic 'planning balancing', some facets (like these three) come to weigh significantly more than others.

These three facets are not so close to core capitalist system forces or to the maintaining of the bases of ownership of property and of investment conditions. However, as I have suggested, there are other kinds of ideological conditioning, consisting of gradual 'cultural' changes, involving the evolution of sensibilities and mentalities. These relate to class-identity issues linked to 'post materialist' concerns, stimulated in part by the move of millions to small-town and village life facilitated by near universal automobilisation since the 1950s. It can be argued that it has been as much, or more, these cultural, slow-moving understandings about places, nature, historical change and so on which have been in play in these three facets, and which have driven planning in one direction or another, as the normally dominant 'growth' concerns.

Naturally, the cultural elements are not fully autonomous from growth concerns, being in part tied up with core material practices (property most obviously, also consumption practices, and global interactions and consciousnesses related to trade and investment trends). All these fuel the politics, so that the ideology and politics generate together a kind of systemic conservatism in these areas.

So this positioning – less key to growth concerns, more related to cultural tendencies – may have skewed the power of ideological conditioning within them, and offered more scope for a certain (constrained) play of political differences. As none is critical to the system overall, views can vary and policies can be adjusted, a bit more pro- or anti-heritage, a bit greener or less green (but certainly not too green), more of one design approach or another.

10

Fields of planning action: housing, economy and infrastructure

A further cut can be taken across the variation of dimensions and fields of planning, by incorporating to a greater extent the differences of the national and local operation which are naturally present in the planning system. Planning is of course distinctive in this way, much more so than in some other areas of public policy such as, say, health or policing (not that variation is not present to certain degrees in those areas, but it is not built into the basic functioning of the system as it is in planning). The three fields examined in this chapter, housing, economic sectors and infrastructure, give more attention to this scalar variation, although still proceeding by means of overviews, rather than detailed longer studies.

Table 10.1 shows schematically how national and local dimensions might be incorporated into analysis of fields. This then creates 'planning situations' in any locality. Through the kind of thinking in this table, we start to develop an approach to understanding how the 'political and ideological planning situation' of a locality is formed.

Housing

Housing is often the most conflictual planning issue at local level, in varying ways in different localities. Its political and ideological framing and manipulation have taken very different forms in different planning eras. The present era often sees battles between the construction of 'needed homes' and protected land areas and environments, as well as the protection of the position of the house building interests and landowners. This set of interactions generates a force field of planning particular to the current UK, which contrasts with the situations in some other international contexts, where very different balances of production interests, state policy positions and local interests and ideological colours are in play.

There is of course much academic writing related to politics and housing, some reviewed earlier. Adams and Watkins (2002) argued that local housing matters are not so much ideologically or party politically driven, but are about stakeholder interests and local interactive politics.

Table 10.1: Impinging of ideology and politics on three planning fields, distinguishing national and local processes

Planning field	Level	Ideological structuring	Political structuring	Resulting planning situation
Housing	Nationally	Centrality of property in capitalism	Relative powers of primary lobbies (HBF, CPRE and so on)	Fundamental tension nationally and often locally over the goals of housing planning and priorities. Many varieties of planning and housing contexts, but failure to achieve planning goals is the norm.
	Locally	Locality ideological orientation within each area over the long run. Specific patterns of ownership (farmers, housebuilders, colleges and so on).	Local pressure politics, parties controlling local government, cost balances in consumption (wages) and production.	
Economy	Nationally	Economy prioritised normally in capitalism. Conceptualisation of 'growth' imperative within dominant parties.	Organisation of employers and other pressure groups (unions, green lobbies), and interest in planning.	Powerful national framing favouring economic development, but this has intense variation by localities, due to different political controls and different economic pressures. Poorer areas likely to be more desperate for approval of all economic schemes. Less likely to be deep conflicts either nationally or locally than in housing case.
	Locally	Locality ideological orientation within each area over the long run – nature of locality, such as strong dependence on local economic activities, or the opposite as a dormitory town.	Local council control. Force of different pressure groups for 'growth' or for countryside protection.	

(continued)

Table 10.1: Impinging of ideology and politics on three planning fields, distinguishing national and local processes (continued)

Planning field	Level	Ideological structuring	Political structuring	Resulting planning situation
Infrastructure – transport	Nationally	Tendency to promote mobility as part of normal dynamic of capitalism, but with contested variety between modes, including socialist, neoliberal and green alternative pathways.	Strong car lobbies can impact on even governments who in principle favour more public transport.	Mobility promotion driven from state–capital nexus and strong lobbies, affecting national policies and most localities, but with variable resistances, by sub-field and by locality.
	Locally	Distinctive patterning from ideological colouring of political control.	Different pressure politics may be more balanced, depending on the locality, with strong variation between metropolitan areas which may be more pro public transport, and rural and suburban areas which have larger car-driven electorates.	

They are contrasting this with the setting of national housing politics. Certainly this is an important distinction, and there is certainly much going on locally that is the product of such interest turf wars, not of a 'deeper' kind. However, as will become apparent, I do not see the local level as insulated from strong ideological and party political pressures, even if the balance of these and the more simply interest-based politics can vary greatly.

It was suggested in Chapter 1 that there are framing factors which can be seen as influencing the extent to which ideological forces have a more or less powerful role in particular planning fields or circumstances. The nature of the dominant 'growth model' was a primary element, in that if a planning matter was seen as close to the core drivers of this model they would be more ideologically charged. A mediating factor, seen as partly aligned, was the field of planning involved, the subject of this chapter. We will see here that some differences between fields or sub-fields can be distinguished, although all three fields examined in this chapter have at least significant parts close to the recently dominant idea of what the UK growth model should be, so all three have, it is argued, significant ideological components. Another mediating factor was seen as related to the scaling of management of a field. There is a scalar politics in each field. Housing is managed by particular centrally determined processes, largely pushing action to the private sector, but then planning aspects are split between a complex machinery of local council (and increasingly some neighbourhood) determination, and central (PINS and secretary of state) steering and oversight. A large regional and sub-regional planning gap has been present in much of England since 2010, also affecting the political play around housing. The current scaling politicises and depoliticises planning for housing in complex ways, but certainly does not remove the effect of ideology at all levels, even if this effect may be relatively invisible most of the time. The scaling present in the last regional planning era of 1990 to 2010 produced a different politics, though this is not one detailed here (Swain, Marshall and Baden 2012).

Ideology

Planning is caught up in the intensely ideological nature of views on how housing should be best produced, distributed and consumed. Clearly, planning is only one part of the whole housing structure of making, regulating, consuming the buildings for living in. But it is a part which some actors prefer to focus on, for political and ideological reasons. It is widely understood that a myriad of factors affect housing production, access and use, but planning's role in the provision of land with planning permission is a highly visible one at certain times and in certain places. Housing certainly figures in election manifestos (much more than planning), as shown by the analysis of Adams and Watkins (2002) for the 2001 election and Lund (2015) for 2015.

Housing's heavily ideological characteristics relate in part to the classic debates about public and private ownership. In Britain in the 1950s the Conservative Party promoted its vision of a 'property owning democracy' as the counterpart to the strong Labour push at that time for council-owned and managed housing. This divided opinion strongly, within parties, as well as between all three main parties, with many Conservative- and Liberal-run local authorities building large numbers of council houses, supported in the 1950s by Conservative governments. Not till the victory of Thatcherism in the 1980s was the current more or less hegemonic position established, which holds that private delivery and ownership of housing is the best answer. It would be quite possible to have a generally capitalist economy with no public ownership of the means of production, but still have goods like houses (as well as schools, hospitals and other 'social infrastructure') provided by public sector methods. But Conservative political thinkers have been very aware of the symbolic and material importance of housing in people's lives. Promotion of private ownership ideals in this sphere can bolster ideological views more widely on the best way to run a society.

Since about 2008 the promotion of council housing has been making a slight comeback (Morphet and Clifford 2018), with councils across the political spectrum starting to build housing with this tenure. Such an ideological shift can still raise important issues for planning. The same question may arise as in previous engagements of the planning system, which is how far planning processes can designate land for particular tenure uses. When this arose in the 1980s, the view was that plans should not distinguish between tenures, as this was 'not a land use matter'. No doubt it was the relation between the planning system and the land market which was in part at stake. At any rate, the return of council house building, even if still on a relatively small scale, is likely to affect the debate about whether new housing is genuinely affordable. At present opponents of new housing development can reasonably point out that most new-build is for those with sizeable incomes, and so arguably not for those in real need – so the legitimacy of much housing land allocation is challenged. However, in the past housing schemes have been opposed precisely because they were social housing, feared as lowering the value of owner-occupied property, or the overall tone of the area. So there is clearly a need for some wide societal agreement about future needs and how these can be met, ideally on the lines of the consensus which lay behind the construction of the welfare state. Just putting it that way highlights the challenge in progressing socially just housing solutions.

Another core ideological feature is the extent of permitted development rights, as this dictates the reach of planning control. The extension of these rights has been a feature of neoliberalising governments since 2010, and this has very much focused on housing, seen as giving justification for removing planning controls, such as the control of the change of office or industrial buildings to residential use, or the redevelopment of brownfield land for housing (Clifford et al 2018). It is noticeable that these changes enacted since 2010 are likely to affect major urban areas, and are of less interest to core Conservative protectionist concerns (not small towns or the countryside), but of strong interest to Conservative developmental interests. Evidently, 'housing' is not an undifferentiated whole, and this affects the nature of controlling its change.

The hegemonic position (private provision is best) does not take away the difficulties embedded in any capitalist society about how goods are produced and accessed. Above all, for new housing, fresh sites are needed, and while in some societies this may be left to private actors and private contracts, this has not been acceptable in Britain since the early 1900s. Always a form of regulation has been applied to the permitting of new development, and this has affected above all the decisions on the extending of existing settlements or, at times, the forming of new ones.

Allied to this land need is the essential feature of access – the new homes must be affordable at the wages currently paid in the society. This is not always directly, or primarily, a planning matter. It relates to much bigger and again completely ideologically infused state policies on incomes, finance arrangements (mortgages, rental laws, tax provisions), inheritance and much else. But it can very often be a planning matter, with judgements on what sort of houses will be built, aimed at which income groups. Since the 1980s, with the general supersession of social or public housing, this has often involved deals between private developers and planning authorities, requiring developers to provide some cheaper housing of some kind as part of planning obligations. This framing was brought in because it was seen as moving away from the provision of housing by, in part, public taxation, which Conservative governments wished to remove. But it imported a heavily ideological component into the everyday negotiations of development control decisions, with deep potential conflict over the division of the gains from this capitalist sector, something in principle unattractive to the house-building industry. Several potentially opposed interests stood to lose or gain – landowners, housebuilders, house buyers or renters, local councils having to carry infrastructure costs. At times extremely large sums could be involved, in situations like the South East of England, where farming land worth £10,000–20,000 an acre became worth several millions of pounds per acre with planning permission for new houses, in many locations.

A further important ideological dimension, especially since the 1990s when climate change has become an important planning consideration, is the degree of regulation or incentivising through planning and building controls of green house building. This became an important part of the housing agenda during the end of the New Labour period, with a pathway set out to achieve zero carbon housing within a set period. This was, however, dismantled by the post-2010 governments, showing how easily an ambitious programme could be stopped by governments with limited ideological commitment to green issues. Policy on density also relates to green dimensions of policy, as pre-2010 governments sought to raise the density of housing schemes, partly in order to save open land, and to concentrate more development on brownfield sites. This was seen as too interventionist regulation and the guidance was removed by the post-2010 government. The brownfield versus greenfield divergence may be seen as partly related to ideological differences in this way, but it also reflects political pressures on all recent governments to reduce the need to build on green belts or open countryside. This pressure is no doubt behind the post-2015 Conservative governments starting to give at least rhetorical support to the previous guidance of using brownfield land first.

The disastrous fire at Grenfell Tower in Kensington, London in 2017 sharpened the issue of the extent to which standards for building construction and maintenance were being cut back. Discussion since then has highlighted the effects of the poor management of some social housing, with a significant gendered and ethnic dimension (Bulley, Edkins and El-Enany 2019). It is normally non-white ethnic groups who are most concentrated in social housing, with also many female-headed families, at least in many English cities. It can be argued that such run-down of social housing is indirectly driven by racist and patriarchal ideologies, which are dominant in recent governments and, some would consider, have been present throughout the 20th century (de Noronha 2019). Another example of the relevance of racist views in planning for housing was given in the statement of the housing minister Dominic Raab in April 2018 (shortly before local elections). He said that the high levels of immigration had increased house prices over the last 25 years and that if the government cut immigration, fewer homes would need to be built (*Planning* magazine 20 April 2018). As the debate following these comments showed, the relation between immigration and housing need and demand is highly contested. The support given for the claim came from an econometric model developed by Reading University in 2007, with conclusions heavily caveated as to the effect on house prices either of immigration or of raising housing supply.

Politics of housing nationally

So, the above emphasises the ideological structuring of the planning situations in the housing field. But there are several political layerings over this ideological substratum (the latter existing everywhere and at all times in a broadly capitalist society like the UK, and infusing national as much as locality planning contexts). These political layerings are in general well known to those observing planning episodes across the length and breadth of Britain, week by week, as well as the making of national government policy on planning for housing. The politics is fundamentally structured by the above ideological and political economic framing, but can play out in widely different ways, nationally and locally.

Many of the institutional features of governmental and pressure group politics were surveyed in Chapters 6 and 7. National policy in this area has mainly been concerned with the setting of the rules of the game for giving planning permissions for housing. The government department concerned with housing has generally pushed for councils to give such permissions at least in line with the expected demand for new housing, and on terms which cut public expenditure demands (by agreeing planning obligations). This has chimed with the interests of probably the most powerful lobby force in this sector, the house-building industry, represented in recent years mainly by the HBF. But governments of all colours have to be aware of possible criticisms from the countryside protection lobby, which is also relatively well organised nationally, with the CPRE (and sister bodies elsewhere in the UK) as the most consistently in touch with ministers and involved in lobbying politics. Both lead bodies cooperate with several other pressure groups, depending on the needs of the moment and the need to make slim resources (in the case of CPRE) go further. Other actors in the almost continually live politics of housing planning are professional bodies, especially the planning and architectural professions. The outputs of such political processes will be the guidance documents produced by governments (in different periods, circulars, Planning Policy Guidance or statements on housing, the current NPPF and Planning Practice Guidance). Ministerial statements will also be material in the decisions of PINS, which manages both the appeals process and the examination of Local and Neighbourhood Plan making.

Politics of housing locally

In each locality there will be a virtually continuous layering of politics in this sector, with councils making local plans, communities drawing up NPs with crucial debates on housing site allocations and the local authority taking decisions on planning permissions. Some of this politics is therefore naturally more strategic, looking years ahead and across a wide area, occasionally across places with populations in the millions (the London Plan, the Manchester Combined Authority Strategic Plan). The sharp end, though, is the politics of any planning application for housing. This, certainly where new housing development is concerned, will generate normally intense opposition to development, above all on farm land or other open space, but also very often on already developed land. Against this opposition will be ranged the developer likely to make significant profits, alongside the landowner, and the local authority, under intense pressure from most governments to deliver housing permissions, but equally under enormous pressure from ever better-organised opposition groups.

The fights over the Greater Manchester Plan are revealing the difficulties faced by policy makers in the present period. A paper by the Director for Cities of the HBF (Stevens 2019) narrates the way in which the direct election of a mayor for the combined authority in 2017 led to a cut in the housing numbers to be put in the revised Draft Plan, as against the numbers proposed by the less politicised first draft prepared before the mayoral election. In that election the Labour candidate had felt the need to promise less green belt loss and that he would revise the plan, which, once elected, he has done. Given that the Greater Manchester Combined Authority structure is a very weak system, requiring unanimity among all ten authority leaders as well as the mayor, it is not surprising that the HBF press for the strengthening of the system towards at least the position of the London mayor, who in principle is free to propose policies in the London Plan without support of London borough leaders (in practice, though, mayors hope for broad consensus).

Another interesting study of housing planning politics in action looked at three Local Plan making processes in southern England (Holly 2017). Holly's concern was to uncover how far politicisation might be opening up basic issues valuably for public debate, showing the value of agonistic or antagonistic conflict at the local level. His conclusions were that the reality was more tangled and perhaps less encouraging than this, with the force of national rules about technical soundness of plans able to override or blanket over any more interesting basic housing questions, often blunting (whether for good or ill) local political efforts at influence. Political struggle was directed on technically set paths, with argument focusing on housing calculations.

Brake (2016) also looked at Local Plan processes, in Buckinghamshire, an intensely fought-over territory with powerful protectionist planning policies installed for decades. She paints a nice picture of the interlocking of national policies and the local particularities of territory (some councils with nearly all their areas with protective designations), local political leadership and staff capacity, with, in the period studied, the national framing intensifying the difficulties in completing local plans, against the claimed priority of central government to cut local plan-making delays. The housing demand, unmediated by any regional planning structure, came down as a direct pressure on local political leaderships, placing them in almost impossible situations in pressing for the release of more housing sites as demanded by central guidance. Local party politics mattered, but it was the brute combination of national politics with local pressures which was most determinant.

This naturally has played into local electoral processes, with for some years opposition to new housing development having a powerful impact, at least in some areas. Surveys of the 2019 results (*Planning* magazine 2019a, 2019b) highlighted the heavy losses of Conservative councils against Liberal Democrats or Independents who had campaigned against loss of green belt land to development. One dramatic case was where Residents for Uttlesford ousted the Conservative group, taking control of the council with 17 of the 23 seats which the Conservatives were defending. The controversial local plan contained proposals for three new garden villages, which the opponents promised to abandon. Another was the long fought-over Local Plan for Guildford, finally passed just before the May 2019 election. This did not stop the independent group Residents for Guildford and Villages winning 15 seats, and the Liberal Democrats, also against the plan, gaining 9 seats. Six other council cases were described, all with Conservatives losing to no overall control or to Liberal Democrats. This anti-development grassroots phenomenon was similar to some of the dynamic behind the successes of UKIP (right-wing anti-EU party) in the 2010–16 period.

This politics in each locality will be mediated by the nature of the council in party political terms, as well as by the nature of local media reporting, including the presence of more or less 'responsible' newspapers, who, as we have seen in the Oxford case, even in the age of social media and the web can have some influence on the tone of evolving decision making on housing development in a locality. The nature of the 'public sphere' in each locality will vary a lot. In some areas and in some periods the ideological substratum conditioning of housing politics may become more visible as certain actors challenge some of the basic features of the process. More normally, though, each development case will be fought out within the framing of the day, in relatively predictable terms, and with the spectre of PINS resolving disputes over the heads of local political processes. This national PINS oversight is precisely intended to iron out some of the force of local political opinion, so that criteria, whether from the NPPF or from locally decided plans, have some consistency of application across localities and time.

Skills in housing planning

The housing planning field is one where any polite idea of technically steered professional processes is least plausible to the average observer. The issue of techniques was surveyed in Chapter 5. It was clear there that all is not political. A significant amount of national policy making does have a technical or specifically skilled component. This was made clear in an influential study of housing planning (Murdoch and Abram 2002), when the 'science' of making national population and household projections was tracked through at national level, before examining how this played out in a particular locality (Buckinghamshire). Though the tone of the study was critical, to some degree revealing how hard it was to find firm foundations for setting housing targets, whether nationally or locally, this process continues today. Since 2010 there has been an extraordinary, but not unprecedented, roller-coaster of such national projections, and their varying and conflict-ridden translation into numbers in each council area, with a number confidently presented in one year put up or down 20% or 30% a year or two later.

The same presence of skill exists in the everyday work of planners dealing with planning permissions for housing. Partly, these are harder skills, applying criteria to schemes, such as planning obligations, environmental standards, infrastructure features, but soft skills matter as much or more in negotiating in highly conflictual situations – in other words, in operating within local politics, in a manner generally presented as ideologically and politically neutral, but in reality necessarily affected by the viewpoints of the ruling politicians as well as by the perspectives of individual planners and the group ethos within planning teams. In other words, the technical skills of planners (and those they work closely with in associated professions and council agencies or beyond) are embroiled in the political contexts of their work, but are not consumed by that context totally. The skills, what may be called the unwritten lessons of long experience in any working situation, are not made any less by the intensity of planning's political and ideological impregnation – in fact the opposite may be seen to be the case. A more depoliticised context (say an engineer designing a bridge) may be in certain ways far easier to work in, calling on less wide capabilities, than the context typical of contemporary British planning. This is not to give a defence of such a context, which can be seen as highly dysfunctional for the majority of those involved, and especially and deeply stressful as a form of work for the core mediators, the planners employed in local authorities.

Of course, approaches to housing could be framed in quite other ways, in terms of social need and ecological futures. But the housing planning model is one embedded in deliberately framed 'growth', generally equated with bare housing numbers formulas, an ideological move invisible to many, given the blanking-out of alternatives by normal media and political approaches to the housing question.

Industrial, commercial and retail development

The various types of economic activity involving physical development of some kind, including, to various degrees, changes of use of existing buildings, are naturally key elements of planning and development policy. The forms and impacts of this grouping of development are more variable than those of housing, and this affects to some degree the ideological and political structuring of planning in this area. The variability is by type of resulting activity – industrial production, office uses, retail or wholesale sectors, leisure uses – and also by size. Clearly, a change of use of one shop has different implications from the construction of a superstore or an out-of-town shopping centre. However, some of the same tensions are present as in housing, in both ideological and political terms.

'Growth' and 'the economy' dominate some fields of planning discussion, but these are of course political and ideological constructions. Terms such as these are used variably by different interests, across the different sub-fields of economic development, including office building, industrial and high-technology fields, and retail development. Jobs, productivity, environmental impacts, all are exploited variably to argue for different outcomes, and enshrined in national and local planning policies to varying degrees. As gender-sensitive planning writers have emphasised, this does not necessarily meet the needs of many millions of people, especially women, for whom the nature and location of jobs can be critical in terms of even minimal well-being, not only the existence of jobs. This has been analysed in economic studies on the nature of job creation in recent years in Britain, which point to the low pay and high insecurity of very many of these new jobs (IPPR Commission on Economic Justice 2018). On the other hand, there are some parts of the country where 'growth' is not the dominant concern for many residents, as these areas have very large retired populations. 'Growth' may be seen as more of a threat – another indication of how problematic the term is in practice.

We can see the language used by government by a quote from the short chapter in the NPPF on 'Building a strong, competitive economy':

> 80. Planning policies and decisions should help create the conditions in which businesses can invest, expand and adapt. Significant weight should be placed on the need to support economic growth and productivity, taking into account both local business needs and wider opportunities for development. The approach taken should allow each area to build on its strengths, counter any weaknesses and address the challenges of the future. This is particularly important where Britain can be a global leader in driving innovation, and in areas with high levels of productivity, which should be able to capitalise on their performance and potential.
>
> 81. Planning policies should:
>
> a) set out a clear economic vision and strategy which positively and proactively encourages sustainable economic growth, having regard to Local Industrial Strategies and other local policies for economic development and regeneration. (MHCLG 2019, p 23)

Ideology

These sectors are firmly in the dominant ideology's list of 'good things'. They are in the midst of the core zones of capital accumulation, and so inevitably likely to be seen favourably. The private sector is almost universally in Britain the developer concerned in these sectors, both as constructor and end user, and so provision of services, goods and employment can be seen to depend on such development. The view expressed almost always by central government guidance will be positive towards such development. Too much opposition to such development generally will be presented as a threat to national competitiveness, or, if in locally oriented sectors like most retailing that is not very plausible, as a brake on the wheels of competition within localities, seen at least by Conservative ideologists as core to proper societal functioning. So, this kind of development would come very much within the 2012/ 2019 NPPF's 'presumption in favour of development', other things being equal.

Of course, things are not always equal. Partly this relates to scalar issues. Generally speaking, decision making is not centralised in these areas (we will see an exception later), but the guidance of central government and the desire – increasingly, with government financial support being removed – of councils to attract investment, tends to mean supportiveness. Nevertheless, different degrees of supportiveness can relate to the details of location and the moments of decision, which will vary significantly, so that the factors to be balanced in deciding a scheme or the allocation of sites in a Local Plan will vary in their force from place to place and time to time. There is mediation of ideological generalities by locally variable institutional processes. This would be so to some degree in any part of the country. The generally pro-development ideological steering is modified by other features within the planning system, expressed variably in different guidance documents produced by different governments. In particular, green ideology will at times provide significant impediments in the way of building a large factory or shopping centre in 'unsustainable' locations. In some contexts historic conservation and design considerations can prove even more powerful constraints on development, but because these are generally incorporated into the dominant ideological positions of recent decades they are likely to be factored into the planning of developers, and ways will often be found to allow the development to go ahead through careful management of these factors, rather than blocking the development.

One important factor in this field is likely to be the distinct role of different professionals. The zones of office, industrial and retail property are dominated by those with RICS qualifications. The training of RICS members, including the very large planning division, is more focused on commercial considerations than on the wider spectrum of social and environmental matters which at least traditionally have been at the forefront of the mindset of 'mainstream' town planners. Planning dealing with these areas is likely to be led by the powerful professional drive of those with most knowledge and resources to promote schemes. The areas examined later, retail and Strategic Rail Freight Interchanges, will be affected most by such surveyors and property industry specialists, with planners struggling to keep up.

Politics

Probably even more importantly, local political and planning cultures will have different approaches to such development, partly expressed within Local Plans (and higher-level plans where and when they have existed), and partly continually applied within development control practice, even if approved plans may not spell out policies very clearly. Typically those parts of the country which are in economic difficulties, particularly ex-industrial areas in the Midlands and North of England, but also other areas at a finer spatial scale, such as many southern coastal towns, may, either again explicitly within plans or by understood practice, welcome all kinds of job- or tax-generating investment. The opposite case can work in the high-income 'leafy' commuter belts of especially southern England, where many well-off residents, including many retired people, may see no gain in further development in the area. This then merges into the party political structuring of planning in such areas, with the ideological colouring of 'growth is good' (in general, nationally) negated by locality circumstances, despite the fact that the great majority of such areas are Conservative council-run.

Ideology and politics of industrial, commercial and retail development: case examples

Overall there is a difference from the way in which politics and ideology play out in this area as against with housing. The starting point both politically and ideologically, especially at the national level, will be pro development, and against the planning system being any sort of brake on development. This will be more 'pure' than in the housing case, where the complexities of distributive and other social factors will be clearer to more actors, and so the mobilisation of pro-development mentalities for housing may often be harder. In industrial and commercial sectors these pro-development stances will be moderated greatly across localities, by both ideological and political forces playing out differently. As indicated earlier, this is not necessarily or even mainly a difference between Conservative- or Labour-run council areas. The difference is likely to be more by both the degree of 'desperation for jobs', probably most characteristic of Labour areas in many periods, and the social make-up of electorates and related local pressure politics, with both Conservative- and Labour-run areas in some kinds of localities being more choosy about development options, even if Conservative councils may be more consistent in this stance.

Two case studies will show how very differently sub-fields can play out. That on retail examines the core roles of local councils, but within strongly ideologically and politically constrained framing. That on big logistics schemes shows how a specialist area can be strongly affected by institutional reframing, in this case by incorporation within the nationally controlled infrastructure planning regime.

Retailing and planning

Retailing is an area where traditionally planning has sought to have significant control of change, both at the macro scale of the regional, or at least sub-regional, shape of big new retail investments, and at the micro level of regulating the 'vitality and viability' of local shopping areas, or primary, secondary or tertiary retail frontages. Retail planning is a sub-field in its own right, with a body bringing together parts of the industry with planners (National Retail Planning Forum) and a solid academic literature (Guy 2007). The 2019 NPPF places retail management under the heading of 'Ensuring the vitality of town centres', and maintains the sequential test used since the 1990s to restrain out-of-town retail developments, against some attempts during the post-2010 governments to water-down this 'anti-market' element of the system, which is clearly unattractive ideologically for some Conservatives.

This apparently reasonably well-structured steering system for retail, however, comes up against practical challenges of a political kind, which are structured by the kind of overall political economy popular with recent British governments. To varying degrees, this creates a strongly competitive system at the local and sub-regional levels, and retail investment is a major piece in this competitive game. Research on various parts of England (Torrance 2020) shows that the pressures and outcomes are widespread, in fact probably in some forms universal. The major case studies by Torrance, of Exeter, High Wycombe and Wigan, show how these places were extremely keen to develop large new retail complexes within their centres, even at the risk of destroying some areas of their existing centres. The varied politics of these places resulted in different balances of strategy. Exeter's aim was to consolidate its place as the major retail centre in the South West, and particularly capture retail spend from centres within its immediate east Devon catchment. Its redevelopment of part of its centre in the early 2000s managed to blend quite successfully the existing and the new centres, in part because an early plan was heavily modified by effective civic opposition in a nice example of intelligent urban dialogue. High Wycombe was less successful, with the Eden centre, completed in 2008, almost wiping out the existing High Street shops, to which the new centre turned its back. The effect was compounded by the district council's also allowing the development on its own land of, effectively, an out-of-town centre next to the M40 motorway, competing with the in-town Eden centre. At any rate, the outcomes no doubt reflect a slightly fragmented approach to planning typical of many smaller Conservative-run authorities, with little guidance from the equally Conservative and non-interventionist Buckinghamshire county council. What has been achieved is the maintenance of High Wycombe as an important player in the retail rankings of the region, in spite of the difficulties caused to the town centre.

Wigan had some of the same difficulties as Wycombe in managing the development of a big new complex in its town centre in the early 2000s. This also turned its back on the existing centre, and caused the abandonment of parts of that centre as retail chains switched to the new centre. Torrance has shown how such switching is integral to the model of retail development created in Britain, with councils and smaller stores effectively subsidising the key anchor stores (John Lewis, Selfridges and so on), which are the effective leaders of all large new schemes. Very large national and international investors, particularly pension funds, are the core part of this model in addition to these anchor stores. So this model is founded on an ideological base and political economic reality which hands over primary control of urban change in this sector to private sector actors. Councils have the roles of valorising land they own, often used for car parks, and of orchestrating the whole process – roles which are not insignificant and which can be played well or less well, but which, given the political desire to keep up the retail rankings and maintain their town or city as a focus for retail spend, do not give a wide spectrum of options to political leaders, especially in a period of extreme financial pressures on these councils. A further significant development in the last three or four years is that councils with surplus reserves have been buying shopping centres as investments, but how that role may develop remains to be seen.

Oxford can also serve as a good example of the dynamics of this process, played out over decades. The city suffered the imposition of out-of-town retail development in the 1980s (by appeal, given the Thatcher government's support for market-led planning), meaning that much retail spend is concentrated in the large stores on or near the bypass encircling the city. Though this is in some ways acceptable to the normally Labour-run city council, whose electorate is in part concentrated in the outer districts, which are heavily car dependent and therefore no doubt very happy with the resulting out-of-town model, the city leaders have also been keen to maintain the city as a competitor with other centres with big retail investment like Milton Keynes, Reading and Swindon, to where apparently keen shoppers drive in preference to Oxford. So, a core part of council proactive planning since the 1990s was to attract a John Lewis-led retail development to the centre of Oxford, extending the Westgate centre built in the early 1970s. This was due to be developed when the 2008 financial crisis hit, but council persistence kept the scheme live, and the very large new centre was opened in 2018. This appears to be fairly successful in the goal of attracting shoppers from quite a wide area, but has had the predicted impact on the rest of the city centre, with large numbers of empty shop units in 2019. It is expected that in the case of Oxford, a heavily touristed city, many of these units will switch to tourist uses, while the rest are already being lined up for conversion to college use, given that some frontages are already owned by colleges and falling values may allow the acquisition of others. Oxford University is a rich and successful institution, in symbiosis with its independent colleges, and so the changes in ideological and political terms have a very particular colouring, giving a different range of options from those in more normal locations. The city's built and natural heritage also gives it a much stronger hand.

So, the retail changes in Oxford, and the planning strategies of which these form part, sit within a very different political and economic landscape from those of the three cases surveyed above. What is similar, though, is the way that the available options are structured by some fundamentally ideologically conditioned forces (how the retail and financial systems are structured nationally, how localities are pressured increasingly to compete by the cutting back of the state, how transport systems are structured by national government assumptions about transport modes and investments, among much else). What this then does is allow the political choices around these options to be mediated by the political colourings and cultures in each of these localities. Each of the four cases discussed here will be seen to have embedded assumptions about what is important for the future of the place. All were heavily pro consumption, with strong support for car-based modes of access, despite also public transport being very much available. In the Oxford case the only significant opposition to the Westgate scheme came from Green Party councillors, who argued firstly that the cathedral of consumerism that the new centre represented was not what Oxford residents needed, and secondly that at least the centre should not incorporate a massive new car park and should include state-of-the-art energy generation in its structure in every way. On all fronts, these arguments failed, suggesting the difficulty in pursuing deeper green objectives even in a city like Oxford with a strong Green Party presence.

Shopping is clearly a deeply embedded 'good' in contemporary globalised societies, wired into social psychological dimensions as well as materially. This contemporary consumptionism is ideological, but at an almost impossibly deep level for normal political discussion, as can be concluded from the above cases. In this field, planning is indeed harnessed to 'growth'.

Big logistics schemes and planning: Strategic Rail Freight Interchanges (SRFIs)

The planning treatment of big logistics schemes (if they can be presented as having a rail component) can highlight the importance of scaling of decision making. Here, as in the Planning Act 2008 regime generally, placing decision making with ministers and weakening the roles of local authorities and community groups changes the political weighting of interests. The issue is deliberately discussed here, not in the infrastructure section, as these vast schemes are predominantly warehouse developments, although with significant road and rail elements. Warehousing developments clustered around the motorway spine of Britain have grown inexorably since the 1980s, to accompany the centralisation of provisioning now common in advanced economies, whereby each major company has only a few massive warehouses, serving big regions or even whole countries. Servicing in Britain is almost totally road based.

The Planning Act 2008 was originally designed for infrastructure schemes of 'national significance'. As commentators said at the time, this phrase was wide open to interpretation. The 2007 White Paper had its sights essentially on big energy schemes, airports and big road schemes. At the last minute, rail schemes were added in, carrying on their back 'Strategic Rail Freight Interchanges', seen by some as key to shifting freight from road to rail. Perhaps work done by the Strategic Rail Authority promoting the idea of big Rail Freight Interchanges and the pressure of lobby groups like the Rail Freight Group convinced ministers that SRFIs deserved to join the fast track. This was a distinct oddity, allowing the approval of massive warehouse schemes, overwhelmingly road served, as being 'nationally significant'.

One pressure behind this change was doubtless the experience of the LIFE warehousing scheme at Colnbrook in Slough, next to Heathrow, in the early 2000s. This had been refused on green belt grounds (and an appeal lost in 2002), and a similar scheme (SIFE) promoted by Goodman was similarly turned down in 2016 (though further legal challenge may emerge). Developers and their advisors have struggled in the London region to understand whether their schemes will be judged as 'nationally significant enough' to override green belt considerations (Simon Ricketts blog, https://simonicity.wordpress.com/category/rail/). Up to now, one big London borders scheme (Radlett) has been approved, in 2014, one (Howbury Park) still awaited the decision of the secretary of state in April 2019. All these schemes have used the normal town and country planning route, and some observers have judged that if the 2008 Act route had been used, they would have all been home and dry, and with less uncertainty, delay and waste of time and resources on all sides (*Planning* magazine 29 July 2016, p 10).

The English Midlands is now full of such schemes being promoted by the big logistics and warehousing operators, all crowding in to use the 2008 Act procedures. Three schemes have been approved under this regime – DIRFT 3 (2014), the East Midlands Gateway Rail Interchange (2016), the latter against the examining inspector's recommendation, and the Northampton Gateway Rail Freight Interchange (2019). Three further schemes have been promoted of a similar kind. One was next to the approved Northampton scheme, but this scheme, Rail Central, was withdrawn immediately Northampton Gateway was approved – an enormous waste of resources and energy for promoter and opposing actors, generated by the lack of forward planning and guidance in this field. Two schemes in the West Midlands are in process, one near Hinckley, which was expected to be submitted in late 2019, and one, West Midlands Interchange, still awaiting ministerial decision at the time of writing, having been under examination in 2019. Each of these schemes is enormous, around 200–300 hectares, with 500,000–800,000 square metres of warehousing – numerous football pitches with cathedral-high buildings on them. All would be equipped with rail access, but, as opponents have noted, there are no conditions that force the large-scale use of these rail facilities, and the evidence of existing warehouse complexes is that rail use is a minor part of the freight systems serving them. An example is the Marks & Spencer (M&S) mega warehouse at Castle Donington, very close to the East Midlands Gateway scheme. This was built in 2011, with the rail siding, but no trains have used the rail facility, despite promises by M&S that the warehouse would be largely rail served by 2015.

Whose interests has this planning process served? The logistics industry in the Midlands is gaining profitable new sites, which by their motorway locations will no doubt deliver good results for the global investors behind these schemes. But for many other societal interests these processes have been much more problematic. In the South East the lack of clarity has probably been frustrating for almost everyone: schemes are emerging with juddering slowness – virtually nothing in 20 years – in what has been regarded (since the Strategic Rail

Authority 2004 report) as the key region for rail freight. Local groups like those objecting to the East Midlands Gateway and Northampton schemes have to work against the odds to get their arguments to have effect on decisions. Local authorities, in the absence of any regional (or national) steering, have often taken a resigned position in the face of the 2008 Act procedures, leaving local opposition groups on their own; though those in the South East, such as Slough and St Albans, have been much more combative and have tended to have support from their MPs. PINS has arguably been placed in some very invidious positions, trying to weigh up poorly framed guidance. Most centrally, from the perspective of society as a whole, the policy of modal shift is hardly any closer to being achieved; there is no prospect of creating an efficient rail freight system along this track.

Infrastructure

In the UK, the infrastructure planning nexus has been an especially active area of evolving policy since the early 2000s. The impact of ideological and political forces in this force field is analysed, using examples of changes in legislation since 2008, the creation of new institutions such as the NIC and sub-national transport bodies, and the implementation politics surrounding large projects, within these changing regimes.

Infrastructure itself can be taken to be an ideological category, which has become popular as state policies have become more strongly market oriented, leaving such elements as transport and energy systems as major ideologically acceptable intervention instruments. Clearly, such an artificial category contains very significantly varying elements, both materially and in relation to their political economic status – state owned or financed, state regulated in very varied ways, and so on. So, telecommunications, investment for broadband, for example, are very different from local transport systems, just as making sure that water supply is reliable can be quite different from major power generation projects. Here I use broadly the categories of the Planning Act 2008, when certain kinds of projects, over certain thresholds, were separated from the normal town and country planning process and put under direct central government decision making.

Ideology

Approaches to infrastructure policy are not exactly land use decisions in the sense of the housing and economy fields, but they are affected by broad ideological stances as well as political pressuring. The UK central government has a very powerful position in England in most sectors, certainly in relation to most transport investment (aviation, rail and major roads), but also through strong regulatory systems in the energy, water and telecommunications sectors. Public funding is much more critical, in relation to transport at least, than for housing and economy: despite ideological rhetoric, most investment in transport is by government. So, the investment and regulatory forms in each sector can be seen to make a difference in how ideological forces are mediated. This no doubt reflects that this field too is seen as critical to capital accumulation, and so is generally steered centrally, at least in its main outlines and biggest projects. It therefore again counts as a 'hot' field, ideologically speaking. In scalar terms, therefore, the most important struggles on infrastructure are played out nationally, even though locality forces are significant when it comes to the detailing and implementation of specific schemes. This national importance means that this section will not be split between national and local dimensions. There is a strong tendency here for all but the smaller schemes to drift up to higher scales of politics.

The basic ideological position in most infrastructure policy over many decades has been to support growth – more traffic, more use of energy, more digital activity. This does not necessarily mean more infrastructure, as it may be possible to squeeze more performance out of existing assets or, in rather restricted forms in the UK, to move to manage demand for movement and energy. The environmental movements have introduced green ideological thinking into infrastructure debates, meaning that while growth may be the systemic reflex, such growth strategies will be often contested if infrastructure is to be inserted in areas seen as inappropriate. The struggles in Britain over building of motorways (in the 1970s and 1990s), nuclear power stations (in the 1970s and 1980s), airport extensions (1990s and 2000s) and new railways (HS2 in the 2010s) are examples of this heavy contestation, working against the underlying drive of state policy.

This underlying drive fits the growth model in the widest sense – the addiction of advanced capitalist economies to high carbon forms. At times, most notably for a few years in the 1990s, this was interrupted in a period when green ideology reached into the core of government thinking. However, these periods have generally been quite short, though in some fields, such as decision making on London's airports or on motorway policy, the opposition to pure growth accommodation has also been significant.

The infrastructure field in Britain is distinctive in the institutional change which it has undergone with the passing of the Planning Act 2008 and the subsequent developments, most importantly the forming of the NIC in 2015 (Marshall 2012, 2017a, 2018). I argued at one stage that one should understand these changes within a wider process of 'infrastructuralism', in which infrastructure is configured as a new state formula and instrument, within evolving shapes of neoliberalising capitalism. While not intended as an ideological neologism (and its use has not been taken up by others), this does point to the role of ideas at underlying levels, and hints at the role of ideology in infrastructure policy, including in relation to planning. As mentioned earlier, scalar issues are prominent, with as many powers as possible ushered into the UK central government and within the control of each field's secretary of state, to keep tight control of key decisions.

The founding of the NIC can also be seen as centralising, but this time with a more benign aim of providing a much sounder evidence base for long-term infrastructure decision making. The outputs of the NIC in its early years have naturally in part reflected the politics of the Conservative governments appointing its commissioners and paying for its work. But it has an element of independence from this political control, meaning that not all that it does is ideologically or politically coloured. Naturally, its stances on some issues are very much affected by the views of its successive chairs, Lord Andrew Adonis and Sir John Armitt, both of whom are strong supporters of big projects like HS2 and the expansion of Heathrow airport. But they also seem to have been strong advocates of the move to a low carbon transition, unlike to some extent recent governments. The prominent support for electric and autonomous vehicles is related in part to this element, though the autonomous vehicles part may reflect the pragmatic wish to support the Industrial Strategy of the May government in power when the National Infrastructure Assessment was published in 2018.

Politics

These underlying ideological stances have been given continuing support by political lobby forces, which have in general been stronger than their growth management or greener opponents. This lobbying effect was in the classic *Wheels within Wheels* (Hamer 1987). But the same strength of pro-car and pro-private development lobbying has continued. This was helped during the New Labour years, when some threat of car hostile policies was detected, by the organising on three occasions (2000, 2005, 2007) of direct action protests by road hauliers and farmers against the raising of fuel tax. How far this was stimulated by motoring interests is unclear (globally, high oil prices were major triggers), but the protests did coincide conveniently with those interests and had much media and Conservative support (Doherty et al 2003). Since that episode, no government has challenged the road development and pro-growth pressures. In fact, Conservative transport ministers have adopted strongly pro-car policies, no doubt reflecting the role of these protests in building one strand of opposition to the Labour governments. The fuel tax protests provide a simple example of the overall balance of ideological forces being confirmed and embedded practically at all levels by political action.

Ideology and politics of infrastructure: case examples

This is expressed in planning policy variably as guidance changes to reflect government orientations on transport. For some years national planning guidance on transport pressed for the 'minimising of the need to travel' as a principle to be taken into account both in making plans and in deciding planning applications. This principle faded away, along with the retreat from sustainability principles within planning guidance, so that only residual elements were present after 2012. The policy from at least that time has been to accommodate growth, on the roads, in airport expansion and, to a very variable degree, on the railways. Policy supporting travel limitation has been at most rhetorical, with a nod at digital possibilities (never in practice impacting at all on reducing travel growth).

In this field, localities have been very much subservient to national directions, with much less variation than in the housing and economy spheres of planning. So, political differences have been equally limited locally. Only in the exceptional case of London, long with a different transport economy and structuring, is a partially different playing-out very noticeable. Elsewhere the following of central steering has been very general, even if some distinctions can be found between totally pro-car localities and those with some other prioritising – for example, in some metropolitan areas and outliers like Oxford and Cambridge. In these latter areas there is at times some contesting of national and dominant lobbying approaches, though, given national government control of most funding, this can go only so far.

The Oxford–Cambridge Arc: road and rail schemes

In this and the following cases we can contrast pairs of projects which are differently affected by core ideological and political approaches of governments.

In 2016 the government asked the NIC to undertake a study of the 'corridor' between Cambridge and Oxford. This was a heavily directed brief, set up around three elements seen as of critical national importance by the government. One was the perceived importance of this part of England for economic success, given the concentration of high-tech and other research and development strengths in the two premier universities and in other science and technology industrial zones (Science Vale in south Oxfordshire, Milton Keynes's economic strengths). The second element was the need to find areas for large, new housing developments, potentially for two or three new towns, a topic explored in previous years but remaining unresolved. Third and probably critical in giving the push to start the study was a proposal to build an Oxford to Cambridge Expressway, as part of the transport ministry's programme of large new road building, to go alongside the already planned East West Rail, which was to reinstate the railway linking Oxford to Cambridge, which had been closed in the 1960s. These, at least to ministers, were seen as forming a linked package, whereby the transport infrastructure would 'unlock' the growth in both economy and housing.

The NIC dutifully carried out the study, and found indeed in favour of the creation of a corridor or arc (the finally adopted spatial metaphor by 2019), with these goals and with these transport infrastructures (NIC 2016, 2017). It is doubtful whether this should have been fitted within the brief of the NIC, being very much a regional or even sub-regional strategy, but carrying out the study may have won it support with some ministers, showing its sympathy with government aims. The NIC did point out the governance difficulties in progressing the proposal, being perfectly aware of how little enthusiasm there was among many councils and pressure groups either for a new expressway or for large new towns along the route. The government took a step back from the expressway proposal early in 2020, and it remains to be seen if it will be progressed at some later stage. Nevertheless, the two ministries Ministry for Housing, Communities and Local Government and DfT have set up a unit to progress the finding of unlocked housing sites along the route, so a new kind of centrally orchestrated spatial planning is being created, separated from the local plans and other plan processes underway along the arc (such as the 2050 spatial strategy for Oxfordshire being prepared in 2018–20). In early 2020 government was proposing that three or four Development Corporations would be set up to progress implementation of development.

The East West Rail scheme continues to depend on a drip feed of funding, despite the arguments of the NIC that it should be progressed much faster than has been the case since it was adopted by government in 2011. It has been argued that the ongoing improvement of road links between Oxford and Cambridge (and really between Swindon and Ipswich and Norwich, as DfT planners have at times made clear) removes significant amounts of the market for the rail line, which may in any case have an uncertain demand. Overall, it can also be argued that this corridor is only in the mind of government. At present it is not an especially important route, with the three important city regions on the Arc (Cambridge, Milton Keynes and Oxford) functioning largely as independent city regions, with few evident synergies between them. The history of this initiative up to the time of writing reveals the heavily ideological driving of central government policy in this sub-region, in favour above all of road improvements and significant new development zones, which has, however, been restrained by the play of political pressures of a more immediate kind in several localities on this invented Arc.

Hinkley Point nuclear power station, and Swansea Bay tidal scheme

Energy policy since 2008 has had a strange character in Britain, with contradictory directions pursued by governments. The Climate Change Act 2008 committed governments to pursuing radical decarbonisation by 2050, and an institution, the Climate Change Committee, was set up to comment on this process. The Act has not been repealed, and is still apparently government policy. Energy policy has meanwhile been focused on above all promoting a new generation of nuclear power stations, with one of these having been progressed and now under construction, Hinkley Point. However, securing this project has required a massive governmental support package, and it is currently uncertain whether any more investors can be found to develop further power stations. The New Labour governments had by 2010 promoted an extensive programme of renewable energy projects, including wind turbines, on land and off shore, solar power, carbon capture and storage, and tidal and other marine power schemes. This programme was common to Scotland, Wales and England, although opposition to wind turbines was highest in England, and so that part of the programme had not been progressing as fast as in Wales or, above all, Scotland. The post-2010 governments gradually cut back these programmes, leaving by 2017 essentially off-shore wind to take nearly all the burden of future renewable investment. The Climate Change Committee started to point out that interim targets of 2022 or 2030 would therefore not be met on the trajectory to the 2050 radical decarbonisation.

The Swansea Bay Tidal barrage scheme was promoted by a private company as an innovative way to extend the range of renewable options available in Britain. It obtained planning consent under the Planning Act 2008 regime in 2015, but in 2018 was rejected by the government for support under the electricity generation subsidy system, which had been used in 2015 to give the green light for Hinkley Point. The scheme was therefore pronounced dead – despite having figured prominently in the Conservative Party election manifesto in the 2015 election as part of how it would boost the Welsh economy. Proponents of the scheme argued that this relatively small scheme would pave the way for many more tidal schemes around the British coast, eventually lowering the costs, which they argued were no higher than those for nuclear (if all long-term costs were included). The government's logic was that there was no prospect of the technology coming down significantly in cost. In 2019 the company claimed that it would strive to go ahead without subsidy, something which appears unlikely, but which was no doubt intended to keep the issue open. While the balance in either nuclear or tidal cases between 'hard economic' and ideological factors would be strongly contested by those on different sides of the argument, the role of basic ideological positions does appear to be significant. A fuller examination would need to consider the consistent refusal of British governments since the 1970s to support the much larger Severn Barrage scheme, which had been strongly promoted by the Sustainable Development Commission (2007). In other words, fundamental aspects of British energy policy are involved, alongside planning and financial matters.

So this contrast of Hinkley Point and Swansea Bay can be seen to reflect an ideologically driven combination of energy policy elements. Conservatives have rarely been keen on green policies, and where these clashed with their ideals of countryside protection it was not surprising that nuclear power and, where appropriate, continued dependence on fossil fuels (gas, mainly, and petrol and diesel for transport) would be seen as preferable parts of a fuel mix, however this might clash with the long-term goals of the Climate Change Act. There were certainly more specifically political factors driving this changed agenda. The

Planning Act 2008 had made it easier to manipulate approvals of energy schemes, and this was used to favour the approval of Hinkley Point (which might have been difficult under the old planning regime) and to exclude on-shore wind from the regime after 2015, as in this case the ease of approval could have damaged the political base of the Conservatives, which was heavily affected by anti-windfarm protest campaigns, led by the Conservative press since the 1990s and also very much part of the UKIP agenda. Political pressure from certain quarters therefore played a role in these changes.

Technical dimensions of infrastructure planning

Again, as in other fields, this does not remove the technical dimensions of infrastructure planning. This field is strongly affected by engineering mindsets and a culture of quantitative work, so that modelling and technical expertise is given a higher profile than in most other sub-fields of planning. This is especially so in times and places of more strategic or regional planning, where some kind of land use and transportation modelling can be undertaken, if not to the extent of the high point of such exercises in the 1970s. Large general engineering and specialist transport planning consultancy sectors can do this work, if paid by government, though bodies like Highways England, Network Rail and the Environment Agency still have some of their own expertise, as do government departments to varying degrees. So, in infrastructure sectors there may be more of a negotiation between the more technical and more political facets of planning work. This can also be seen in the work of the NIC: there, a further impact comes from location in the Treasury, with some culture of economics expertise in areas like cost-benefit analysis. None of this is negating the political nature of planning infrastructure, let alone removing the powerful ideological structuring of the field. But it does change the nature of work, with probably more sense of expert-led decision making than in much of planning, for good or ill.

Conclusion

I conclude that there is certainly some validity in the argument of Adams and Watkins that local-interest battles were important in housing development planning. But the ideological substratum sets a pro-growth and pro-development framing for this and the other two fields, as also does the scaling of the decision making for the field. In the case of big infrastructure (and some related big warehousing schemes) this has meant radical centralisation. In housing politics there is also an unremitting push from the centre to try to guide ever more approvals for housing schemes, even though this strains against the maintenance of some local control in this sector. Local control continues also in much of the economic field, but this is generally less politically contentious, because of the perceived attractiveness of investment in many areas, such as retail investment in town and city centres.

So, 'local political and ideological planning situations' can matter up to a point, as we have seen here and in Chapter 6. But strong central government control (in several fields) combines with the (ideologically encouraged) inter-locality competition for businesses, in many areas, to bias the effect of such local planning situations in certain directions, quite rarely progressive ones promoting social equity and long-term ecological criteria. More normally the local planning situations push to weaken councils in relation to private development pressures, which tend to prioritise only certain outcomes – expensive new houses, nationally led clone town-type retail projects, commercial schemes likely to boost local tax bases. As a whole, in these fields I would argue that ideological conditioning is harder edged, leaving in reality less room for political contestation than in the facets considered in Chapter 9.

Nevertheless, no simple generalisations have been made as to the forms of ideological and political inflections of one field as against another. Rather, all are to varying degrees (depending on sub-field, government era and locality variations) strongly determined by these inflections. Clearly, this chapter has only dipped into the fields covered here: there is a great deal more to say, awaiting full empirical studies and fuller analysis and theorisation.

11

Paths to improving the ideological and political dimensions of planning

Planning in the UK has a near-continuous debate on ways to redirect the activity so as to obtain better results, largely among the 'planning community', both practitioners and academics, but sporadically spilling over into some bigger public arenas, perhaps spurred by a report from a think-tank or an especially sharp current issue or problem (inner-city decline, climate change's effects, death of the high street, for example). Even more occasionally a major review may be undertaken of planning as a whole, not just of one or more of its component parts. Such reviews have in fact been exceptionally rare. The most recent, the TCPA-sponsored Raynsford Review, reported in November 2018 and is the most authoritative and fully considered assessment for decades, with only the Royal Commission on Environmental Pollution report of 2002 and the Nuffield Report of 1986 having to some degree similar broad perspectives. It is noteworthy that no government reviews of planning of a comparable breadth have been undertaken since the Planning Advisory Group reported in 1965. Government planning reform programmes since the 1970s have normally proceeded on the basis of sketchy evidence and political hunches. What follows in this chapter will lean partly on the Raynsford Review (2018a, 2018b), although that Review did not of course have the specific focus of this book, and so the suggestions here go beyond the Review.

This chapter will first provide a listing of the problems identified in Chapters 2–10, partly to give a convenient summary of matters treated in the book, and partly to be able to have at hand the connection of the suggested measures to some of those problems. There are then sections on what to do about ideology and planning, and what to do about politics and planning, attempting to keep these analytically distinct. These follow the Chapter 1 framework, looking at possible ideological amalgams for planning, and the institutional and pressure politics needed to support good planning. Then a sketch for a possible reformed planning system (levels and roles) is given, and final comments on combining ideology and political reforms as a whole.

Problems found in this book

Chapter 2

The review of literature revealed a limited treatment of political and ideological dimensions of planning, whether in textbooks or in other areas of literature, although articles are beginning to appear since the mid-2010s with more interest in this area, including a special issue of *Planning Theory* journal (Shepherd, Inch and Marshall 2020). Work on that journal issue showed the range of theoretical approaches to the area, and the relatively early stage of any process of making deeper theoretical sense of this field. This may be offered as some excuse for the limited theoretical advances made in this book. Later in this chapter, a few suggestions are made about possible paths to further work which could help future theorising.

Chapter 3

The review of ideologies and planning suggested the strong base of planning in progressive, broadly liberal and socialist ideologies of the early 20th century, but also the complex composites which have been evolving. These composites have brought together continuing strands of classic state interventionist approaches with neoliberal deregulation, elements of mild environmentalism and heritage and landscape protection ideals, and, to a slight degree, parts of feminist thinking. The resulting amalgam at the time of writing is not an effective ideas carrier for the future of planning, and the response will need to address what may move matters forward in this quite fundamental dimension.

Chapter 4

This historical chapter of two parts was more about giving a brief analysis of the long run of British planning history, and a case study of one government, than about identifying problems to be rectified.

Chapter 5

The discussions of planning expertise and of the role of law in planning pointed to how these were strengths for the activity of planning, in some respects, bound into beneficial use of expert knowledge and the values of equity and fairness. The discussion also showed how these were partially linked to the political and ideological nature of planning.

These features of planning as a regime of regulation have often been criticised for making the activity inaccessible for citizen involvement. Problems of very challenging legal and technical complexity are definitely present in planning. The Raynsford Review frequently met these complaints, among lay people as well as from professionals themselves. Excessive legalisation of planning, excessive technicalisation and the relations of these to tendencies to deideologise and depoliticise planning, all these need to be taken into account in thinking about directions for improving the system.

Chapter 6

The Raynsford Review, with evidence from many different perspectives, concluded that the governing of planning was not effective, generating a deeply problematic system for almost everyone involved. The survey in this chapter came to some similar conclusions, though drawing from a different spectrum of commentary. Central government planning, in varying locations and agencies, is strongly pared down, and often seen as chaotic and ineffective. The same applies in most areas of local government, with heavy cut-backs and a strong reorientation of incentive structures making the system far more difficult to operate than is needed, prioritising speed and closed decision making over quality of decisions. The still emerging neighbourhood planning regime is also riddled, in my analysis, with problems which make it far more frustrating and ineffective than it could be (assuming that it is retained in its current or any form). The major infrastructure planning regime is also, in my view (see Chapter 10), highly problematic for most less-well-resourced interests. The need for major reform of the governing of planning, driven by fresh ideological perspectives and tied in with a new idea of political democracy, is therefore in my view clear. The discussion of bureaucracy pointed to the fact that there is nothing wrong with bureaucratic structures and processes. These have been improved in some respects to make them more agile and citizen friendly, and much more can be done along these lines. Well-managed bureaucratic processes are essential to good planning, if market- and corruption-driven alternatives are to be avoided.

Chapter 7

This chapter took a double-sided approach to analysing the pressure group landscape, one exposing the unfair biases present in the far-from-level playing field of most planning management and policy making, one looking at the even less attractive 'dark side' of some actual or potential planning practices flowing from the ongoing commercialisation and potential corrupting of planning processes. Discussion of possible responses therefore needs to take a double track, one looking at how to level up influence on planning, one considering the worst-case scenario and what would have to be done to move to really clean up lobbying and make a more fairly democratic operation of planning.

Chapter 8

Here the need to create a new planning supportive media landscape emerged, given the escalating collapse of traditional modes of informing and discussing, especially in the local press. New national and local conversation forums are needed, as well as the bolstering of the existing forms. The knowledge gathered in relation to deliberation and public involvement should be one useful input to a new movement of open planning at all levels, supported by public resources and tied in to representative and participatory democracy, in new balances.

Chapter 9

This chapter on three facets of planning did not necessarily point to major problems, as in many ways these areas show very real strengths in English planning. The implication is, however, that there needs to be a levelling of the playing field of planning dimensions, so that the fields treated in Chapter 10 and the social aspects of planning, particularly the dimensions highlighted by feminist thinkers and practitioners, get much more adequate treatment. This would also level up the environmental field, so that matters of core deep green importance such as climate change have at least as much salience as the more easily tackled issues of landscape and biodiversity protection.

Chapter 10

This chapter pointed to fundamental weaknesses in planning for housing, the economy and infrastructure, resulting from both the underlying problematic ideological framing and from the political pressures playing especially at local levels. Neither lends itself to any easy responses, but much improvement could be secured by means of the reorientations proposed below, which would change both the imaginaries driving the whole sense of the system and the political parallelogram of forces acting at each level.

Time-scales of planning change and the present

Any response to the situation of planning starts from a particular place and time. The time of writing has not been an easy one, as the UK passed through Brexit turmoil (and, at the end, the COVID-19 pandemic). I deliberately avoided discussion of the effects of the leaving of the EU on the UK, and specifically on planning in England, given the uncertainty. I will continue to abstract from these impacts, even though the 2019 general election sealed some of the shape of the future. One extra reason is that an important element of what has been discussed here plays out over quite long time-scales. Very schematically we may refer to three time-scales, the longue durée, of a century and more, of the foundations of planning in Britain and its development within a gradually democratising country, a shorter run of around 40–45 years, more or less coinciding with the period of EU membership and the drives of neoliberalisation of Britain, and a 'continuing present' of the post-2010 period, marked by a sharp attack on much of the remaining force of planning, but with other features complicating that generalisation (neighbourhood planning, NIC). EU-leaving impacts do not map tidily onto any of these three time-scales. The sketching of three possible scenarios for the 2020s in Chapter 1 (roughly, even more state cut-back within stronger right-wing ideological compounds, a middle-of-the-road moderate and liberal Conservatism, or a socialist-led reforming of public sector interventionism) suggested a wide range of possible ideologies and politics in which planning may sit during the coming decades, and it is not helpful to discuss which of these, or which combinations, may be most likely. Rather, the aim here is to present some ideas on what might help to improve the ideological and political framing of planning over the coming years. This will need to respond to the variable time-scales, to see 'how far back' one has to go, or how deeply it is necessary to excavate, in order to have a chance of making improvements. There are different potential pathways on each of these time-scales.

The current state of English planning

The Raynsford Review summarised what it saw as the parlous state of planning in 2018, with the structure of the 1947-based planning system under extreme strain, and the operation as a whole resulting in weaker planning, partly based on a gradual privatisation of the profession and of much originally public sector planning practice, alongside deregulation and a change of the purposes of planning, largely just to support 'growth', subject to heritage and countryside protection measures (the 2018/2019 NPPF). Power over the planning that remains is centralised in the hands of the secretary of state, and also of related important ministries, including the Treasury, and those dealing with environment and countryside (Department for Environment, Food and Rural Affairs), transport and business and energy. The system is driven, above all, by larger private company interests, whether in housing, commercial or financial sectors. Ferm and Tomaney (2018) generally see planning in this kind of deep difficulties in Britain in their extensive and expert survey.

This downbeat picture, while I am sure broadly pointing in the right direction, may be a bit too pessimistic about the current outcomes of the system as it works day to day. My impression, and it is a view some practitioners gave to the Raynsford Review, is that still a remarkably large number of good decisions across many parts of the country and many sectors continue to come out of the planning system processes. This is a tribute in part to the resilience of a fundamentally sound structure within local elected authorities and a PINS doing its very best to cope with declining resources, both for the major infrastructure regime and for the management of appeals and Local and Neighbourhood Plan making. Public sector and public interest values hang on, preserved by generations of planners, councillors and inspectors who have been reared in the traditions of these values and cannot easily transfer their allegiance to a private sector-driven ethos and profession. If one wanted to show an outsider the quality of good British planning, one could point to the schemes awarded prizes by the RTPI and by *Planning* magazine each year, demonstrating planning's part in the collaborative efforts of many professions and agents in forming new built environments (Geraghty 2017).

Nevertheless, it is still almost certain that the number of poor decisions and weakly formed plans is rising. One aspect that critics have been able to point to without much doubt is the stream of poor-quality housing coming out of the removal of the need for permission for conversion from commercial to housing use (Clifford et al 2018). Proving conclusively such an overall judgement of worsening results would be hard and require a large research project. At any rate, I think it is useful to consider such a balancing judgement on the current planning system – one under very great pressure, but with some remaining strengths which allow it to continue to provide many good decisions in hundreds of English localities. Institutions, legal factors, expert technique, as well as political and ideological factors all contribute to the strengths, as well as in various ways being implicated in the stresses and failures.

At the same time, the challenges set by the ever-growing commercialisation and cutting-back of public sector planning, interacting with the worsening pressure politics landscape caused by escalating systemic corruption, need to be confronted. The task here is therefore to try to balance this assessment and appropriate responses. One response is to say that, yes, the planning system itself needs many radical reforms, but that probably even more important is a transformation of the ideological and political landscape in some quite fundamental ways. This clearly sets a very heavy agenda for the remaining sections of this chapter.

What to do about planning and ideology

It is important to stress that there is nothing wrong with the presence of politics and ideology in planning, and, as I have argued from the start, it would be better if these aspects could be brought out into the open, not be talked about only in confined professional or political circles. It is not about making planning 'less ideological' or 'less political', as very many lay people and commentators tend to say. Rather there should be a change to being differently ideological and letting politics play out properly in planning, not in a chaotic, disempowering fashion. It is about the right sort of politics and ideology, more beneficially arranged.

So, as I see it, the need is for a new ideological amalgam into which the politics of planning can fit and in which more beneficial and new sorts of planning can emerge. Many of the problems faced now by planning are due to an ideological mis-structuring, and if that can be addressed the politics will have a fair chance to give better results. If not, the current dysfunctionality for the majority of actors and interests and the intensely stressed system will continue.

Given the often slow movement of ideological reconfigurations, the three time-scales mentioned earlier blend into each other to some extent. However, for the century-or-more long view, the fate of planning seems to be bound up with the continuation in some form or other of the underlying conditions which helped to form the UK variant. Most importantly, these include ingredients of democracy and of structures which allow some achievement of public interest goals. These have been notably a welfare state in its evolving shapes, and some kind of public control of land and utilities, whether by public ownership or by other means. All that points to the importance of the ideological currents which did in fact enable the formation of planning, socialism or certain kinds of advanced liberalism.

It is then clear that for the 40 years time-scale, the overriding need is for a rolling-back of many parts of neoliberalisation, as the ideological amalgams of Conservatism have removed the above conditions progressively. This has become most intense since 2010, and so the urgency to at least reverse this most recent attack on the conditions of publicly beneficial planning is very evident. In principle, even a New Labour-type of ideological mix might allow this degree of reversing (of post-2010 damage), though it is clear that this would be insufficient for the deeper rolling-back of neoliberalisation, as New Labour generally accepted that degree of neoliberalising and in fact pressed it forward in some fields.

However, consideration of the scope for advancing beyond the achievements of post-war British planning points to the need for considerably more change than such 'reversing the damage' ideological packages. From the survey of ideologies in Chapter 3 and the consideration of species of democracy in Chapter 8, it is possible to suggest that a more adequate ideological composite, which could genuinely confront the issues facing contemporary British society, needs to contain two new elements: a new imaginary blending progressive ideological strands, and a new wave of democratisation.

So, *the first element is a radically new imaginary* incorporating the cores of green and feminist ideologies into a broadly socialist-led set of values and mechanisms. It is much easier to headline such a mix than say quite what it would contain. In part, this is the always-present difficulty in specifying something as live as a mix of ideas and actions, something which Freeden's work has brought out fully. He stresses that ideologies are instruments for doing politics, mobilising, evolving in each period, not neat, fully rationally constructed formulas. The enormous environmental challenges pose ever sharper sets of challenges which need ideological incorporation. Neither sustainability nor climate change issues have found solid places in the ideological mixes since the late 1980s, with a clear moving backwards since 2010. The critical kaleidoscope of gender issues, above all of the challenges of improving the work and livelihoods of women, are likely to lead to changed planning practices only by means of a lot of local experimentation as well as strong state leadership.

Another critical part of the new composite is something to confront the planning challenge of rising xenophobic nationalism, which is increasingly based on a 'nativist' myth of unsullied Englishness. This is even more tightly tied in to wider state policies, and can be seen as related to deep ideological currents, as discussed in Chapter 3, and to the imperial history which some argue is a key factor in the Brexit campaigning groups (Dorling and Tomlinson 2019). So, initiative will be needed across numerous fields making clear the equal rights of all citizens. Non-racialised and non-nationalistic planning would have to develop as part of a wider effort across areas such as justice, policing, housing and welfare support. Planning is a significant part of the range of policy fields, but far from decisive in comparison with many areas. But planning's imaginary will need to incorporate this dimension also into the core of practice, given the still emerging super-diversity of many British cities, something which will clearly depend in significant part on state leadership as well. Leaderships in local government can play major roles here, as in certain ways Ken Livingstone and Sadiq Khan have shown as London mayors.

Part of this new ideological package should be the kind of economic programme contained in the IPPR Commission on Economic Justice (2018). This featured a ten-year economic plan to be drawn up by a national economic council, new national and regional investment banks, green industrial strategies at several levels, the whole brought together under a Sustainable Economy Act. The proposals on housing were also radical, laying out a pathway to control the cost of housing, whether for purchase or rent, with most new housing to be genuinely affordable. John Boughton's book (2018) on council housing's history is a good reminder of how to carry out such initiatives. Such a programme would contribute to a reorientation of many policy areas towards green and feminist concerns, so raising the profiles of these ideologies within a broadly interventionist drive, but one still set within a predominantly capitalist economy. The links to planning, especially for positive planning, which helps to improve the well-being of people in localities, should be evident. The material (resources) component of any ideological amalgam is naturally quite critical.

Another important component which now has a good academic development is the promotion of the 'foundational economy', which means the obligation of governments at all levels to provide good living conditions for all, which in itself equals up the economic buoyancy of places (Foundational Economy Collective 2018, Heslop, Tomaney and Morgan 2019). The basic idea is that local economies consist of export elements – certainly important to countries as a whole – but also, vitally, locally consumed services, whether public or market organised, which depend on collective provision to a major extent, directly or indirectly. The link to effective planning is clear, in that proactive planning needs this foundation in order to promote any socially fair measures in all localities – even rich areas need people who will clean the streets and run so many local services, and these people themselves need to be able to live. A Local Plan built on a local programme to rebuild or protect the foundational economy would be much stronger than one which just had to watch and adapt to economic and social changes beyond its control. The foundational economy as a concept is clearly not part of a neoliberal ideological amalgam, having far more affinities with social democratic ideological variants.

Part of such programmes, necessarily going beyond what the Economic Justice Commission proposed, must be a rolling-back of the decades of privatisation of property. A good number of commentators have concluded – really echoing views which were extremely common in the first half of the 20th century – that planning struggles to be an active social and environmental force for good because so much property, and especially land, is in the hands of private owners. These dominate decisions on land use change, and extract vast quantities of public wealth when development does occur (to 'compensate' property and landowners). The land question will almost certainly need to be tackled, however ideologically and politically difficult this is, if some genuine progress to meeting overall social needs is to be made. This will need to be matched by an equal push on public ownership of utilities, as it has become clear that the loss of the levers provided by public control of the key utility services of transport, energy and water weakens the chances of securing a fundamental transition to low carbon living, in a socially fair form. Energy transitions are going to be extremely tough politically and socially, as shown by the problems even serious states like Germany and France have been finding. At the time of writing, none of this is likely to be on the agenda of the Johnson Conservative government.

The second element in a new ideological composite is the need to develop democratic dimensions of this amalgam. This relates to the components described earlier, but can be distinguished analytically. Recent discussions of 'Rethinking Democracy' (Gamble and Wright 2018) have pointed to the relatively stunted nature of British democracy since the breakthroughs of the early part of the 20th century (above all, votes for women). Planning is very tied up in these various deficits, which have been critical in a number of fields deeply affecting planning – the democratic deficit of the EU, which British Conservative opposition in particular prevented being tackled in the 1990s, and the deficit evident in regional planning in England up to 2010. The democratic deficit at neighbourhood planning level is equally evident, though that in turn was spurred in part by dissatisfaction with planning practice at higher levels.

It is important to understand how central the question of democracy is in a reformulation of an ideological formula which could underpin planning progress. This relates to the 'dark side' discussions in this book, where escalating anti-democratic practices have been seen as present or potentially present in the lobbying and political spheres. Democratisation of these spheres of politics could help to reduce the spaces for these many problematic practices. Democratisation is a long-term process, just like the de-democratisation since the 1980s, so it will be a matter of gradually moving forward on several levels, constitutionally as well as in more specific forms. Big structural changes will need to intersect with micro, local and specific democratic practising. One part of this would be what may be called 'ideological education'. In the second half of the 20th century in Britain, political and ideological education came both from people learning subjects like politics, sociology and economics with some ideological understanding built in, and from practising the 'implementation' of ideas in trade unions, local parties and pressure groups. This is needed in new forms to facilitate democratisation.

The development of new ideas and values in planning

The zones of principles, values, ideas and planning cultures can be also seen as part of the ideological changes needed for better planning. I have not stressed values as much as some others (for example, as Ines Newman in her 2014 call for a refoundation of local democracy). This could lead, as the Raynsford Review proposed, to the making of a cross-sector compact on planning values. I have also not referred much to principles, although the planning profession very much uses this language. For example PINS espouses the principles of openness, fairness and impartiality – essentially procedural principles rather than meant to relate to the substantive outcomes of the matters (plans, appeals) which they deal with, but very welcome nevertheless. My own focus is more on the formation of ideas. Here the need is to extend the processes of innovative ideas making, within planning and in connecting planning with other policy fields. A great deal is already done in this area, by the RTPI and TCPA in particular, but also by some other pressure groups or think-tanks with a broad remit (as against mainly pressing their own material interests). Planning academics also contribute to this process, but not as effectively as might be hoped in most fields. This is in part due to the extensive damage to university planning schools (as with most university departments) caused by neoliberalisation (business universities), as described in Chapter 5. Generally, most academic, and often policy, focus is on a few high-salience fields such as green belts, housing policy, neighbourhood planning and some kinds of big infrastructure, with much of the rest of the wide spectrum of issues and the connecting-up of policy fields less developed. There is a real and growing research and knowledge gap affecting planning, with governments long having ceased to commission research on planning (of the kind which the Department of the Environment used to carry out as a matter of course).

Something can of course be done outside government, by the action of academics and retired planners, as well as in certain forms by consultancies. One positive model would be the work of the Highbury Group convened by Duncan Bowie since 2010 in London, including academics and practitioners, to debate housing policy and contribute to government policy in this area. Another is the Futures Network West Midlands, which has continued to press the case for strategic and regional planning in this region, after the 2010 abolition of such a mechanism. These initiatives have certainly raised the level of discussion and understanding in their areas, but there are not that many such ongoing planning groupings acting as policy watchdogs and policy developers.

Political parties are generally poor at developing thinking on planning and related areas. There are exceptions like the Armitt review of major infrastructure policy and the Lyons review of housing policy, both set up when Ed Miliband was Labour Party leader, or the Letwin and Howell work on Conservative localism policy (Power Shift) before the 2010 general election, but generally both Conservative and Labour parties have avoided effective engagement with planning practitioners or academics in developing policy since the late 1990s. This is particularly problematic, given the key need to make ideological and policy narratives converge both generally and at the level of policy detail, something which conventionally political parties have had as one raison d'être. It has been somewhat depressing to observe or participate in the work by the Labour Party to develop its planning policy in the post-2010 period. There has been plenty of goodwill towards planning among many Labour MPs, but it has been noticeable that whenever serious reforms have been suggested by working groups, the party leadership (particularly in Treasury teams) have tended to remove these before anything is finally firmed up.

From my perspective, the last time there was a dynamic and fruitful interaction between parties and academic thinkers, including a good number of planners, was in the GLC era of 'local socialism' in 1980–86. The GLC pressed forward a great number of initiatives across many planning fields, incorporating them in a new London Plan and spawning a new ideological mix, even though, given the abolition of the GLC, this mix did not become strongly embedded in a great deal of continuing practice or within the Labour programmes of later years.

So, the ideal future would be one which saw a waking-up of ideas discussion on fundamental directions for planning. For the short and medium term this task has been facilitated by the Raynsford Review, but the escalating uncertainties of current UK politics mean that an ongoing engagement with ideas is essential. How this can emerge, given the slender resources and other priorities of the obvious actors (RTPI, TCPA, think-tanks, academics) is not at all clear. Ideally, the relevant government ministry should have some role in this, instead of promoting reforms which are at best half thought through. The model of the German federal government agency (BBSR, Federal Office for Building and Regional Planning) which carries out research and development of new approaches in the fields of urban development, planning and construction is one that could be valuably copied. Germany also has the benefit of another nation-wide body, the Academy for Spatial Research and Planning (ARL), which brings together academics and practitioners, with a small central staff. So, in Germany there are both government-led and independent sources of research and policy development for the planning fields, and other countries (France, Netherlands) have similar agencies. While I have been putting the emphasis on the big ideological picture, it is clear that it is equally important that planning-specific ideas and agendas are developed so that both the wider level and the planning specifics have, as it were, strengths from both sides.

Some suggestions for fresh academic work

This book has not been mainly about developing the theorisation of the field studied. But there follow some suggestions for areas where development may help.

- It would help to systematise the range of theoretical approaches which may be useful in looking at ideology and planning. Different social, political and planning theory traditions provide quite a spread of templates.
- Reflection would be useful on why planning academics and (differently) planning practitioners find thinking about ideological

dimensions so difficult. This could confront the very widespread non-engagement with most political and ideological dimensions of planning. There is scope for some international empirical research on this, to identify attitudes of planners and academics. This could include examining the varied approaches to the subject within planning education: is ideology a blind spot, and should it/does it have to remain that way?

- There is plenty of scope for empirical research on the relationship of contemporary (or past) planning with ideological forces or dimensions – 'ideology in action' as keywords here. It would be useful to periodise the relationship of ideology and planning in each planning context, for example, the extent to which a neoliberal planning era can be identified in each context. Conjunctural analysis may well be one element of this.
- It would help to develop comparative and spatial thinking about this relationship, whether within states or internationally, including the force of ideology in localities or regions – local or regional ideological dimensions.
- The status of neoliberalism remains in question – how does this ideology relate to others such as nationalism or ecologism? Is there an emerging 'as well as neoliberalism' world coming into shape? What are the current nodes for thinking about key issues like trade, globalisation and planetary climate and extinction challenges? Does ideological analysis help such thinking?
- This should relate to the current ideological turbulence, especially the threatening impact of extreme right ideological positions on planning in different countries, whether conceptualised within populism or other frames.
- There would be value in developing the ideological coordinates of progressive planning, however different analysts conceive that – planning for democratic majorities with radically feminist and ecological values? This might include analysis of past experiences of planning with some characteristics which would now be viewed as progressive, as well as reflection on the planning priorities for Left governments of the future.

What to do about planning and politics

If it were possible to improve the ideological structuring within which consideration of and action on planning sits, much of the basic politics of planning could work much better than it does. However, there are still many matters which need to be tackled on the more straightforward institutional and balancing political front, in order to make really effective progress with the massive issues which planning faces. Many of these were covered by the Raynsford Review and I will list these here rather briefly. But, as was acknowledged by the Review in several caveats, much of what needs to be done is not directly within the sphere of planning, even though it affects it deeply. Also there is scope to say more than the Review could do about some areas where I think further thinking and practising is needed.

If several of the key framing conditions and institutions of planning are changed, this will allow the politics, which must be a core part of planning, to work better. Given the vital role of local government, the most urgent change is to rehabilitate the capacity and legitimacy of councils to undertake effective planning, reversing the drastic cuts to their finances, the outsourcing of planning to the private sector and the removal of powers to central government and other agencies such as LEPs. All effective forward planning and a great deal of planning application decisions remain with councils, and, if this first step is not taken, the political performance of authorities will continue to cause problems, of the kind seen in Chapter 6 in the chaotic forward planning of Oxfordshire. Many of the Raynsford recommendations (see Table 11.1) simply could not be implemented without an effective vehicle at local level which can engage democratically in each locality.

Several of the other core Raynsford recommendations would combine with this first step, particularly Recommendation 12, the creation of a 'smart structure for planning', which means a well-articulated set of instruments from national to very local level, including, very importantly, strategic and, where practical, regional plans to deal with the real scale at which lives are lived. Without this new articulated structure, neither citizens nor politicians will have any basis either for understanding future choices or for guiding their implementation once decided on. The present massive holes in the planning system, with nothing between often weak neighbourhood and local plans, and a generalised criteria-based NPPF, do not allow any democratic steering of the real spatial forces at work, beyond ad hoc decision making by ministers or PINS or by some better-resourced councils in richer areas. Politically, this is almost an invitation for council control of planning to be abolished completely, because the system is not given the chance to set pathways democratically. Many of the other recommendations relate to giving councils the capacity to implement, without which local democratic control remains a very weak instrument – for example, the proposals to capture land value,

Table 11.1: The recommendations of the Raynsford Review (2018b)

1. A new legal duty to deliver sustainable development in England.
2. A cross-sector compact on the values of planning.
3. A new kind of positive and powerful Local Plan.
4. Local planning authorities that act as 'master developers' to ensure that Local Plans deliver real change.
5. Community powers to plan effectively.
6. Increasing accountability and community participation.
7. A new legal duty to promote the Aarhus Convention rights.
8. Transformed public awareness of planning.
9. Promotion of a national conversation on our development needs.
10. A duty to local planning authorities to plan for high-quality and affordable homes.
11. Consideration of a new building code.
12. A smart structure for planning.
13. The use of bespoke delivery bodies to deal with long-term planning problems.
14. A new Sustainable Development and Wellbeing Act.
15. A re-purposed National Infrastructure Commission.
16. An enhanced role for Homes England.
17. Effective land assembly and land value capture powers for public authorities.
18. A strengthened status for the development plan to enable it to capture betterment values.
19. Reforms to the Community Infrastructure Levy and Section 106 planning obligations.
20. Redistribution of national land tax revenues.
21. Increased professional standing for planners, particularly within local government.
22. Attracting, training, developing and supporting the necessary numbers of high-calibre planners.
23. A requirement for university planning schools to have a social mandate to support basic outcomes for people.
24. Introduction of a 'Do no harm' obligation in built environment professional codes of conduct.

the recrafting of a positive and powerful Local Plan, making councils the 'master developers' in their areas.

More broadly, and going in part beyond Raynsford, there is a need for concentrated efforts to be directed to the forming of thriving local public spheres. Conditions for this include the reconstruction of local media systems, probably involving some of the measures recommended by the Cairncross Review described in Chapter 8, such as subsidy of local presses, but going beyond this to resourcing digital deliberation and debate modes at local, strategic and, ideally, regional levels. It is wrong to imagine that public deliberation has to be confined to very local levels. Already in the regional planning experience of 1990 to 2010 progress was made in opening up discussion at regional levels, even though a great deal more needed to be done (Swain, Marshall and Baden 2012). The same is possible at city-regional levels, if proper local government systems are created – the current fashion for elected mayors and combined authorities does little more than further confuse the public about the real levels of political accountability, spreading what influence exists across more and more overlapping agencies. The proposal for a new 'economic constitution' (IPPR Economic Justice Commission 2018) would be one way to restructure big decision making away from centralised control. The proposal there was for four regional economic executives, governed by indirectly elected regional councils, with powers over regional infrastructure planning and regional industrial strategies. This would be complemented by giving more powers to counties and city regions, setting the framework for local plans. This was phrased by the 2070 Commission as the need for 'a new regional framework for England based on the emerging networks of pan-regional bodies, combined authorities and unitary rural counties' (2070 Commission 2020).

Raynsford in Recommendation 9 mentions the creation of a Commission for Public Engagement (see also Slade 2018b), which could develop participatory and deliberative practices in planning from local to national levels. Such a commission could build up experience on what works best, particularly in combining digital and other modes. It could help local authorities, sponsoring pilot projects, as is done in Germany, where five-year projects develop best practice in contrasting localities before schemes are launched across the country. Such a commission could also support the NIC in preparing its National Infrastructure Assessment – which is to be prepared about every five years, with major impacts on long-term infrastructure steering. All this could help to reduce the democratic deficits present now at all levels of the planning system.

How much scope is there to progress in the use of more macro and micro deliberative elements discussed in Chapter 8? Probably the answer can come only by means of persistent exploration and experimentation at all levels. As others have emphasised (Ellis and Henderson 2014), the relationship between representative and participatory democracies remains unresolved. The need is surely to reinforce all kinds of democracy, in varying ways, making the ground rules clear, including that in most circumstances the elected representatives (councillors, MPs) will have the final say. Thus an infinitely better functioning of Parliament is needed, giving less executive dominance and more genuine powers to the committee systems, as exists in more efficient legislatures, such as the German Bundestag (federal parliament) or the Scottish Parliament, both designed with current social practices in mind (particularly in gender terms), not those of the 18th century as at Westminster (Lucas 2015). Flinders et al (2018) and Cotter and Flinders (2019) note how a more intelligent consideration of the options for the restoration of the Palace of Westminster (including that of moving Parliament elsewhere) would give opportunities to make the UK legislature less dysfunctional. Clearly, this applies across all sectors of government, but planning and related areas could gain perhaps disproportionately from further public deliberative uses of the committee system and, potentially once reformed, of a new Second Chamber.

As discussed earlier, the same applies to council democracy – a modern municipal democracy and a reformed planning system at this level would be essential partners. There will always be tensions between different democratic forms, and planning, by its nature, is strongly affected by these (scales, interests weighting), but can also gain more than many other fields by working through these tensions. A lot of such working through has gone on since the 1970s and so there is a good foundation on which to develop new, sophisticated practices, especially incorporating digital possibilities.

One rich source of experience which should be mined afresh is the work of John Stewart from the years when he was director of the Institute of Local Government Studies at Birmingham University. Especially, his reflections on the attempts by New Labour to reform local government explore how to make a functioning local democracy (Stewart 2003). A key feature was the schema of community planning which he had developed and which was partially adopted, in the form of Community Strategies, by the Labour government. Something like this (much improved from the hamstrung New Labour version) would be essential to effective planning, even though Stewart rarely discusses (town) planning. He was very much focused on the big service delivery roles of councils, and so managed to forget that his idea of community planning (a municipality making its future with its electorate) was intimately related to decades of thinking within town planning circles.

Going back to the discussions of Chapter 5, I do not think that these big transformations in the political and ideological functioning will remove the importance and the validity of the legal and technical sides of planning. Nevertheless, they should in due course tip much of the balance of planning activity towards a range of activities which are more accessible to easier lay understanding, precisely because the political core of planning will be out in the open and this will necessitate the ability to express the most important aspects in clear language. It should be possible to implement considerable simplification of the planning system, directly by reform and changes in public practices, and indirectly by taking other paths to mitigate certain inevitable features of regulatory regimes. Macro and micro deliberative approaches could allow wider discussion and therefore wider understanding of the basics of long-term forward planning, as well as open up to some degree decision making on planning applications.

A sensible planning system can evolve towards lesser legalisation in many areas, through reduction of the extreme tangles of complexity in current systems. Over time, planning law should become less an instrument of depoliticisation and of the obscuring of ideological forces, even though it will retain its role as an important instrument in arbitrating in certain very difficult zones of policy. Technical aspects of many kinds and a degree of legal complexity will remain, as these are doubtless inherent in the major institutions in which planning is embroiled, especially property regimes, and the need to make balancing judgements of some complexity in time and space.

Overall, these measures would combine to open up a less frustrating form of planning politics, where involvement had a good chance of actually leading to real changes on the ground or to genuine policy improvement, not emotional exhaustion for most of those involved (Inch 2015). The new mode of governing would be encapsulated in Vigar's (2017) phrasing of 'engage, deliberate, decide', as against the tangled and opaque decision-making processes present now in most parts of England. It is worth remembering that London has a model which can in many features be drawn on. Since 2000 an articulated system of planning has been managed jointly by the London mayors and the 33 London boroughs. The regular revision of the London Plan is undertaken in open and reasonably democratic view, with serious attempts to involve the public, and with deliberation on the Draft Plan before independent examiners. The intermediary bodies representing the wide range of London interests, such as Just Space and the London Forum of Amenity Societies, are able to engage in the debates, even though this is hardly the ideal of a public deliberative conversation with equally weighted and resourced interests.

The London Plan Examination in Public conducted in 2019 ran from January to May, with a fairly full discussion of the issues in the Plan's very wide range of topics. Certainly some interests, above all those representing big developers like housebuilders and Heathrow Airport, were especially effectively represented, given their greater resources and ability to be present at numerous sessions. But at least the London planning process does have some accessibility for quite a wide range of voices. This naturally, in this recent case, rests within a Conservative ideological frame at national level, and in fact the secretary of state took the unusual step in March 2020 of blocking the Plan and ordering a review – revealing the extremely powerful position of central government even in the context of a legitimate and significant lower-tier authority.

Nevertheless, what this offers is the example of an articulation between democratically elected levels of government, each with some strength and legitimacy – something rare in the English planning polity, but something which ought to be possible across the country if the system of local government and plan making is made politically more responsive to democratic influence. It is at least a starting point, to be improved upon, for a better model throughout England.

One specific need flows from the emergence of deeply problematic forms of pressure politics, in kinds of commercialised lobbying and systemic corruption affecting governing processes in Britain. For this a fundamental reform of the laws and regulation of lobbying is needed, going far beyond the failed legislation of 2014 (Grant 2018 gives modest proposals). But a key associated set of measures is the bringing of many sectors into public ownership, or at least much more effectively regulated control. This in itself would reduce the headroom for the lobbying industry which has grown up largely on the back of the privatisations of Britain since the 1980s, leaving vast economic spaces where gains can be made by bending the awards of contracts and the decisions of regulatory processes like those of planning. Privatisations generated not only an unnecessary new business sector, but one which is bad for democratic practice. Associated also with this is a full move away from the culture of complex and non-transparent contract practices, as has been documented by Mike Raco and described in previous chapters. Here, therefore, we see the necessary interweaving of changes in the political pressure world and changes in the deep political economy of ownership and property. The two go hand in hand, and reforms similarly need to be combined. So, substantive change and planning process change are both needed – something the Raynsford Review, for no doubt political reasons, was able to address only very gingerly if at all, but which will be key to resolving some of the problems identified in this book.

Social movements will need to be part of the energy for driving through reforms of this kind, though the issue is too large to tackle in this book. These have often had an important role in planning, for example, in pressing for social justice in housing and urban problems and in tackling environmental problems. Equally they have been the carriers and developers of ideological elements important to planning, such as the campaigns in the early 20th century to open up access to the countryside, or currently to tackle the problems of the new private rented sector, now backed by considerable activism in London, so putting issues of inequality back into the forefront of the ideological mix. So it is very likely that boosts to the reforming of planning will come in part from such movements and activisms. It will be essential that planning practitioners and academics can meet such emerging pressures and help with their coalescence into ideas and programmes.

Suggestions for a new schema for public planning processes

So, for planning to achieve its potential, there is a need for radical change, facilitated by the large ideological and political shifts described earlier. I have given some pointers to what this would mean in substantive terms for some planning fields, but it is not necessary to try to be comprehensive on this. There are already good texts pointing the way to the necessary measures for the core areas of housing, transport and dealing with climate change. But it may help to sketch out some suggestions on what planning *process* changes might involve in the medium or longer term.

The essential task is, in my view, to introduce more effective deliberation into the system of planning decision making, both on forward planning via plans at all levels, and for decisions on individual development projects, of all sizes. The primary principle should be to empower local decision making in both of these areas, and disempower central and profit-seeking forces, so that the planning system starts to work in favour of the democratic majority of the country. This would mean removing most powers of intervention by central government, whether by secretary of state or PINS, subject to improved rights of public judicial overview, to protect the probity of local processes. Faith would therefore be placed in local electoral and participatory processes, at the appropriate level, including by regional and strategic elected authorities.

This should involve process techniques already developed to a significant extent in Britain, and to some extent in varying Western

European countries. So, the practice developed by PINS for dealing with major infrastructure projects could be one big input to the transferred decision making of all larger development projects to the relevant strategic planning authority. Watching an examination of an NSIP in recent years, it is impossible not to be struck by the build-up of experience by inspectors, within a quite constrained system, and by the appetite of the public to be involved, both in big issues (often unfortunately ruled out by the Planning Act 2008) and in every small detail of schemes. This process should become the norm for all large projects, so that officers and councillors of local authorities would themselves build up expertise in this process, with the support of a national Commission for Public Engagement (Slade 2018b).

The same process would be used at key moments of the preparation of strategic and local plans. The difficult decisions here are in the scaling of the system, what parameters are set nationally or regionally, which more locally. One key here is to make the deliberation on national (and regional) planning guidance much more transparent, with parliamentary select committees probably taking a core role in this, alongside civil servants and ministers. But, within whatever parameters were set at a higher level, it is essential that localities can openly debate long-term alternatives, rather than be subject, as in recent years, to the importing of big infrastructure schemes from above without discussion, or to the imposition of obscure and incomprehensible deals formed between central government and local business and political elites.

Then, within this plans system, even small and medium-sized developments should be open to fuller public deliberation than is now normal. Of course, if these are already set by a recent Local or Strategic Plan, they will need less debate on principles. The recreation within councils of neighbourhood governing structures, which were common in the 1980s and 1990s, would provide one formula for progressing this discussion of planning applications where appropriate (Burns, Hambleton and Hoggett 1994, Newman 2014, pp 113–114). There may be other effective modes using the wealth of digital communication means now available, but face-to-face meetings will almost certainly be still needed for efficiently sensitive debating of schemes. There are increasing numbers of examples in English councils of such experimenting, such as in Camden, where citizens' assemblies have been used to deliberate on climate change, health and well-being, and planning around Euston station (Gould and Florence-Braithwaite 2019). This would of course relate to the need to return to the planning system some kinds of development which have been removed from public decision making by deregulation. Without such return, the scope for democratic control of local change would simply remain too limited.

Given a well-designed system and a better-resourced set of public authorities, there is no reason why such a system of public planning should consume too much public effort and time. Certainly the average citizen might spend a little more time on such matters than is now common, but this would be matched by the loss of most of the absolute frustration suffered now by most interests who try to influence planning policy, whether at neighbourhood, urban or large project levels. The supersession of such dysfunctional and draining politics should be a primary aim of building a new system. Combining electoral and participatory politics can be made to work, if goodwill is used to set up the right framework. Not all the outlines of a new system will be formed overnight: no doubt some years of experimentation will be needed before a sound balance is developed. As implied here, the last 50 years can be seen as providing a training ground, from many different directions – public inquiries, regeneration and community politics, debate of major infrastructure schemes, development of neighbourhood planning approaches. So, a new system would not be starting from scratch by any means, especially when international experience is brought in. In the creation of a new system it might well be useful to bring in a panel of experts from those polities which have also experimented much in these ways, above all France and Germany in recent years.

Conclusion

Whether or not the above attempt at remaking the planning process is convincing, it is intended to point to the need for profound change in the way in which national and local planning is conducted. One could easily gauge how political and ideological such a suggestion is by getting reactions from people with different political positions. There is little doubt that those whose main concern is ease of business and development success would give little support. It would be seen as multiplying the already existing barriers which planning throws up. But the key issue would be how such process changes might combine with substantively progressive agendas. Democracy generally has as one of its justifications that it will promote better outcomes for societies, for the big majorities, in class, gender and international terms. The case of some thinkers that there is a need for trade-offs of degrees of democraticness with such substantive goals (famously, to save the planet), I find unconvincing, with the work of Michael Saward consistently arguing against such a trade-off approach (Saward 1998, 2003, 2010). But this does not mean that what he calls the 'terms of democracy' will not be affected by the nature of governing challenges in any particular context.

As argued here, the need is to shift both the ideological substratum and the macro and micro framing of politics. In some cases this may be done by actions, legislative and otherwise, over short time-scales of months or a few years. But much will depend on slow, underlying movement over decades or even generations, matching the slow creation of planning arrangements to meet the circumstances of the early 20th century, as against those needed for the present century, and, in this case, for the UK and, for this book, primarily England. I have suggested that the Raynsford Review's 2018 report points some of the way to go, and that this can be developed in many aspects by a more ambitious programme of shifting the ideological and political coordinates. But, as I have argued, in order to do this it is important to recognise how much British planning is tied in to and conditioned by its political and ideological framing, and not to shelter too much behind the technical and legal firewalls created by some forms of professionalism and excessive stress on specialist expertise.

References

Adams, D. and Watkins, C. (2002) *Greenfields, Brownfields and Housing Development*, Oxford: Blackwell.

Adams, D. and Watkins, C. (2014) *The Value of Planning*, RTPI Research Report No. 5, June.

Airey, J., Scruton, R. and Wales, R. (2018) *Building More, Building Beautiful*, London: Policy Exchange.

Allan, G. and Phillipson, C. (2008) 'Community studies today: urban perspectives', *International Journal of Social Research Methodology*, 11(2): 163–173.

Allmendinger, P. (2011) *New Labour and Planning*, Abingdon: Routledge.

Allmendinger, P. (2016) *Neoliberal Spatial Governance*, Abingdon: Routledge.

Allmendinger, P. and Haughton, G. (2013) 'The evolution and trajectories of English spatial governance: "neoliberal" episodes in planning', *Planning Practice and Research*, 28(1): 6–26.

Barkan, J. (2011) 'Law and the geographic analysis of economic globalization', *Progress in Human Geography*, 35(5): 589–607.

Barrett, S. and Fudge, C. (1981) *Policy and Action*, London: Methuen.

Beebeejaun, Y. (2004) 'What's in a nation? Constructing ethnicity in the British planning system', *Planning Theory and Practice*, 5(4): 437–451.

Beebeejaun, Y. (2012) 'Including the excluded? Changing the understandings of ethnicity in contemporary English planning', *Planning Theory and Practice*, 13(4): 529–548.

Beebeejaun, Y. (2018) 'Public participation and the declining significance of planning', in J. Ferm and J. Tomaney (eds) *Planning Practice*, Abingdon: Routledge, pp 85–100.

Beetham, D. (2011) *Unelected Oligarchy: Corporate and Financial Dominance in Britain's Democracy*, Liverpool: Democratic Audit.

Beetham, D. (2015) 'Moving beyond a narrow definition of corruption', in D. Whyte (ed) *How Corrupt Is Britain?* London: Pluto Press.

Beland, D. and Cox, R. (eds) (2011) *Ideas and Politics in Social Science*, Oxford: Oxford University Press.

Berry, C. (2011) *Globalisation and Ideology in Britain*, Manchester: Manchester University Press.

Berry, C. and Lavery, S. (2017) 'Towards a political economy of depoliticization strategies', in P. Fawcett, M. Flinders, C. Hay and M. Wood (eds) *Anti-Politics, Depoliticization, and Governance*, Oxford: Oxford University Press, pp 245–265.

Blackburn, D. (2017) 'Still the stranger at the feast? Ideology and the study of twentieth century British politics', *Journal of Political Ideologies*, 22(2): 116–130.

Blomley, N. (2004) *Unsettling the City: Urban Land and the Politics of Property*, New York: Routledge.

Blomley, N. (2017) 'Land use, planning and the "difficult character of property"', *Planning Theory and Practice*, 18(3): 351–364.

Blowers, A. (1980) *The Limits of Power: The Politics of Local Planning Policy*, Oxford: Pergamon.

Blowers, A. (1984) *Something in the Air: Corporate Power and the Environment*, London: Harper Row.

Booth, P. (2003) *Planning by Consent: The Origins and Nature of British Development Control*, London: Routledge.

Booth, P. (2016) 'Planning and the rule of law', *Planning Theory and Practice*, 17(3): 344–360.

Boughton, J. (2018) *Municipal Dreams. The Rise and Fall of Council Housing*, London: Verso.

Bourdieu, P. (1987) 'The force of law: toward a sociology of the juridical field', *The Hastings Law Journal*, 38: 814–853.

Bourdieu, P. (2000) *Pascalian Meditations*, Cambridge: Polity.

Bowie, D. (2010) *Politics, Planning and Homes in a World City*, London: Routledge.

Bowman, A., Erturk, I., Folkman, P., Froud, J., Haslam, C., Johal, S., Leaver, A., Moran, M., Tsitsianis, N. and Williams, K. (2015) *What a Waste: Outsourcing and How It Goes Wrong*, Manchester: Manchester University Press.

Bradley, Q. (2014) 'Can neighbourhood planning breathe new life into local democracy?' *Town and Country Planning*, 83(9): 380–383.

Brake, R. (2016) 'The structural origins of plan-making delay', *Town and Country Planning*, 85(8): 327–330.

Brindley, T., Rydin, Y. and Stoker, G. (1989) *Remaking Planning: The Politics of Urban Change in the Thatcher Years*, London: Routledge.

Brindley, T., Rydin, Y. and Stoker, G. (1996) *Remaking Planning: The Politics of Urban Change*, London: Routledge.

Brownill, S. (2019) 'Localism and the reconfiguration of planning's publics in the landscapes of technocracy', in M. Raco and F. Savini (eds) *Planning and Knowledge: How New Forms of Technocracy are Shaping Contemporary Cities*, Bristol: Policy Press, pp 169–180.

Brownill, S. and Bradley, Q. (eds) (2017) *Localism and Neighbourhood Planning: Power to the People?* Bristol: Policy Press.

Brownill, S., Ellis, G., Inch, A. and Sartorio, F. (2019) 'Older but no wiser – Skeffington 50 years on', *Town and Country Planning*, 88(3/4): 122–125.

Bulley, D., Edkins, J. and El-Enany, N. (eds) (2019) *After Grenfell: Violence, Resistance and Response*, London: Pluto.

Bullock, H. (2011) 'Legislative comment. Localism and growth', *Journal of Planning and Environmental Law*, 13 Supplement, Occasional Paper, 9–34.

Burns, D., Hambleton, R. and Hoggett, P. (1994) *The Politics of Decentralisation*, Basingstoke: Macmillan.

Buser M. and Farthing, S. (2011) 'Spatial planning as an integrative mechanism: a study of sub-regional planning in South Hampshire, England', *Planning Practice and Research*, 26(3): 307–324.

Cairncross, F. (2019) *The Cairncross Review. A Sustainable Future for Journalism*, London: Department of Digital, Culture, Media and Sport.

Campbell, T. (2012) 'Legal Studies', in R. Goodin, P. Pettit and T. Pogge (eds) *A Companion to Contemporary Political Philosophy*, Chichester: Wiley-Blackwell, pp 226–253.

Carmona, M. (2018) 'The design dimension of planning: making planning proactive again', in J. Ferm and J. Tomaney (eds) *Planning Practice*, Abingdon: Routledge, pp 101–119.

Catt, H. (1999) *Democracy in Practice*, London: Routledge.

Cave, T. and Rowell, A. (2014) *A Quiet Word*, London: Bodley Head.

Chappell, Z. (2012) *Deliberative Democracy*, Basingstoke: Palgrave Macmillan.

Cherry, G. (1982) *The Politics of Town Planning*, London: Longman.

Claret, J. (2017) *Pasqual Maragall: Pensament i Accio*, Barcelona: La Magrana.

Clifford, B. (2006) 'Only a planner would run a toxic-waste pipeline through a recreational area', *Town Planning Review*, 77(4): 423–454.

Clifford, B. (2018) 'Contemporary challenges in development management', in J. Ferm and J. Tomaney (eds) *Planning Practice*, Abingdon: Routledge, pp 55–69.

Clifford, B., Ferm, J., Livingstone, N. and Canelas, P. (2018) *Assessing the Impacts of Extending Permitted Development Rights to Office-to-Residential Change of Use in England*, London: RICS.

Colenutt, B. (2020) *The Property Lobby: The Hidden Reality behind the Housing Crisis*, Bristol: Policy Press.

Colenutt, B., Cochrane, A. and Field, M. (2015) 'The rise and rise of viability assessment', *Town and Country Planning*, 84(10): 453–458.

Cooke, P. (ed) (1989) *Localities: The Changing Face of Urban Britain*, London: Unwin Hyman.

Cotter, L. and Flinders, M. (2019) 'The Palace of Westminster: another window of opportunity?' *Parliamentary History*, 38(1): 149–165.

Cowell, R. (2017) 'Policy and practice: the EU referendum, planning and the environment: where now for the UK?', *Town Planning Review* 88(2): 153–171.

Craig, G. (ed) (2012) *Understanding 'Race' and Ethnicity: Theory, History, Policy Practice*, Bristol: Policy Press.

Crouch, C. (2004) *Post-Democracy*, Cambridge: Polity.

Crouch, C. (2016) 'The march towards post-democracy, ten years on', *Political Quarterly*, 87(1): 71–75.

Crouch, C. (2018) 'Post-democracy and populism', in A. Gamble and T. Wright (eds) *Rethinking Democracy*, London: Wiley (special issue of *Political Quarterly*), pp 124–136.

Cullingworth, B. and Nadin, V. (2015) *Town and Country Planning in the UK*, Abingdon: Routledge.

Daily Telegraph (2011) 'Conservatives given millions by property developers', 9 September.

Davies, J. (2011) *Challenging Governance Theory. From Networks to Hegemony*, Bristol: Policy Press.

Davison, S. and Harris, K. (eds) (2015) *The Neoliberal Crisis*, London: Lawrence and Wishart.

Davoudi, S. and Cowie, P. (2013) 'Are English neighbourhood forums democratically legitimate?', *Planning Theory and Practice*, 14(4): 562–566.

De Noronha, N. (2019) 'Housing policy in the shadow of Grenfell', in D. Bulley, J. Edkins and N. El-Enany (eds) *After Grenfell: Violence, Resistance and Response*, London: Pluto, pp 143–164.

De Vries, M. (2016) *Understanding Public Administration*, Basingstoke: Palgrave Macmillan.

Delaney, D. (2015) 'Legal geography 1: Constitutivities, complexities and contingencies', *Progress in Human Geography*, 39(1): 96–102.

Delaney, D. (2016) 'Legal geography 2: Discerning justice', *Progress in Human Geography*, 40(2): 267–274.

Department of Communities and Local Government (2011) *National Planning Policy Framework*, Consultation Draft, London: DCLG.

Doherty, B., Paterson, M., Plows, A. and Wall, D. (2003) 'Explaining the fuel protests', *British Journal of Politics and International Relations*, 5(1): 1–23.

Dommett, K., Hindmoor, A. and Wood, M. (2017) 'Who meets whom: access and lobbying during the coalition years', *British Journal of Politics and International Relations*, 19(2): 389–407.

References

Dorling, D. and Tomlinson, S. (2019) *Rule Britannia: Brexit and the End of Empire*, London: Biteback Publishing.

Dryzek, J. (1990) *Discursive Democracy: Politics, Policy and Political Science*, Cambridge: Cambridge University Press.

Dryzek, J. (2000) *Deliberative Democracy and Beyond: Liberals, Critics, Contestations*, Oxford: Oxford University Press.

Du Gay, P. (2000) *In Praise of Bureaucracy*, London: Sage.

Eagleton, T. (2007) *Ideology: An Introduction*, London: Verso.

Eatwell, R. and Goodwin, M. (2018) *National Populism. The Revolt against Liberal Democracy*, London: Penguin Books.

Ellis, H. and Henderson, K. (2014) *Rebuilding Britain*, Bristol: Policy Press.

Evans, B. (1993) 'Why Britain no longer needs a town planning profession', *Planning Practice and Research*, 8(1): 9–15.

Ferm, J. and Tomaney, J. (eds) (2018) *Planning Practice*, Abingdon: Routledge.

Finlayson, A. (2012) 'Rhetoric and the political theory of ideologies', *Political Studies*, 60: 751–767.

Finlayson, A. (2014) 'Proving, pleasing and persuading? Rhetoric in contemporary British politics', *The Political Quarterly*, 85(4): 428–436.

Finlayson, A. (2018) 'Rethinking political communication', in A. Gamble and T. Wright (eds) *Rethinking Democracy*, London: Wiley (special issue of *Political Quarterly*), pp 77–91.

Flew, A. (1979) *Philosophy: An Introduction*, Sevenoaks: Hodder and Stoughton.

Flinders, M. (2012) *Defending Politics*, Oxford: Oxford University Press.

Flinders, M., Cotter, L., Kelso, A. and Meakin, A. (2018) 'The politics of parliamentary restoration and renewal: decisions, discretion, democracy', *Parliamentary Affairs*, 71(1): 144–168.

Flyvbjerg, B. (2001) *Making Social Science Matter*, Cambridge: Cambridge University Press.

Foley, D. (1960) 'British town planning: one ideology or three?', *British Journal of Sociology*, 11(3): 211–231.

Foundational Economy Collective (2018) *Foundational Economy: The Infrastructure of Everyday Life*, Manchester: Manchester University Press.

Fox-Rogers, L., Murphy, E. and Grist, B. (2011) 'Legislative change in Ireland: a Marxist political economy critique of planning law', *Town Planning Review*, 82(6): 639–668.

Fraser, N. (1992) 'Rethinking the public sphere: a contribution to the critique of actually existing democracy', in C. Calhoun (ed) *Habermas and the Public Sphere*, Cambridge: MIT Press, pp 109–142.

Freeden, M. (1990) 'The stranger at the feast: ideology and public policy in twentieth century Britain', *Twentieth Century British History*, 1(1): 9–34.
Freeden, M. (1996) *Ideologies and Political Theory: A Conceptual Approach*, Oxford: Clarendon Press.
Freeden, M. (1998) 'Is nationalism a distinct ideology?', *Political Studies*, 46(4): 748–765.
Freeden, M. (1999) 'The ideology of New Labour', *The Political Quarterly*, 70(1): 42–51.
Freeden, M. (2003) *Ideology: A Very Short Introduction*, Oxford: Oxford University Press.
Freeden, M. (2017) 'After the Brexit referendum: revisiting populism as an ideology', *Journal of Political Ideologies*, 22(1): 1–11.
Freeden, M., Sargent, L. and Sears, M. (eds) (2013) *The Oxford Handbook of Political Ideologies*, Oxford: Oxford University Press.
Fryer, P. (1984) *Staying Power: A History of Black People in Britain*, London: Pluto.
Gale, R. and Thomas, H. (2018) 'Race at the margins: a Critical Race Theory perspective on race equality in UK planning', *Environment and Planning C*, 36(3): 460–478.
Gamble, A. and Wright, T. (eds) (2018) *Rethinking Democracy*, London: Wiley (special issue of *Political Quarterly*).
Garnham, N. (1992) 'The media and the public sphere', in C. Calhoun (ed) *Habermas and the Public Sphere*, Cambridge: MIT Press, pp 359–376.
Geraghty, P. (2017) 'Why are planning awards important?', *Planning Theory and Practice*, 18(1), 168–172.
Giddens, A. (1998) *The Third Way and the Renewal of Social Democracy*, Cambridge: Polity.
Gilg, A. (2005) *Planning in Britain*, London: Sage.
Goodchild, B. (2010) 'Conservative Party policy for planning: caught between the market and local communities', *People, Place & Policy Online* 4(1): 19–23.
Goodin, R. (2008) *Innovating Democracy*, Oxford: Oxford University Press.
Gould, G. and Sutcliffe-Braithwaite, F. (2019) 'Local government and the NHS: deliberative democracy and the devolution of power in Camden', *Renewal*, 27(4): 41–49.
Grant, M. (1978) 'Planning, politics and the judges', *Journal of Planning Law*, 512–523.

Grant, M. (1987) 'Devising new policy instruments: the lessons of history', *Journal of Planning and Environment Law*, Occasional Paper 13: 21–31.

Grant, M. (1992) 'Planning law and the British land use planning system', *Town Planning Review*, 63(1): 3–12.

Grant, W. (2018) *Lobbying*, Manchester: Manchester University Press.

Gray, M. and Barford, A. (2018) 'The depths of the cuts: the uneven geography of local government austerity', *Cambridge Journal of Regions, Economy and Society*, 11(3): 541–563.

Greed, C. (2000) *Introducing Planning*, London: Athlone.

Greed, C. and Johnson, D. (2014) *Planning in the UK: An Introduction*, Basingstoke: Palgrave Macmillan.

Griffiths, S. (2014) 'What was progressive in "progressive Conservatism"?', *Political Studies Review*, 12(1): 29–40.

Gunder, M. (2010) 'Planning as the ideology of (neoliberal) space', *Planning Theory*, 9(4): 298–314.

Gunn, S. (2019) 'Planning professionalism in the face of technocracy: ethics, values and practices', in M. Raco and F. Savini (eds) *Planning and Knowledge: How New Forms of Technocracy Are Shaping Contemporary Cities*, Bristol: Policy Press, pp 127–137.

Guttenberg, A. (2009) 'Planning and ideology', *Journal of Planning History*, 8(4): 287–294.

Guy, C. (2007) *Planning for Retail Development*, Abingdon: Routledge.

Habermas, J. (1996) *Between Facts and Norms*, Cambridge: Polity.

Hall, S. and Massey, D. (2015) 'Interpreting the crisis', in S. Davison and K. Harris (eds) *The Neoliberal Crisis*, London: Lawrence and Wishart, pp. 60–74.

Hall, S., Massey, D. and Rustin, M. (2015) *After Neoliberalism? The Kilburn Manifesto*, London: Lawrence and Wishart.

Hamer, M. (1987) *Wheels within Wheels*, London: Routledge and Kegan Paul.

Hanna, T. (2018) 'The return of public ownership', *Renewal*, 26(2): 17–32.

Harloe, M., Pickvance, C. and Urry, J. (1990) *Place, Policy and Politics: Do Localities Matter?* London: Unwin Hyman.

Harris, N., Webb, B. and Smith, R. (2018) 'The changing role of household projections: exploring policy conflict and ambiguity in planning for housing', *Town Planning Review*, 89(4): 403–424.

Harvey, D. (1978) 'On planning the ideology of planning', in R. Burchell and G. Sternlieb (eds) *Planning Theory in the 1980s*, New Brunswick: CUPR, pp 213–233.

Harvey, D. (1981) *The Limits to Capital*, Oxford: Blackwell.

Harvey, D. (2005) *A Brief History of Neoliberalism*, Oxford: Oxford University Press.

Hastings, A. and Matthews, P. (2015) 'Bourdieu and the Big Society: empowering the powerful in public service provision?' *Policy and Politics*, 43(4): 545–560.

Haughton, G. and Allmendinger, P. (2016) 'Think tanks and the pressure for planning reform in England', *Environment and Planning C*, 34(8): 1676–1692.

Hay, C. (2002) *Political Analysis*, Basingstoke: Palgrave Macmillan.

Hay, C. (2007) *Why We Hate Politics*, Cambridge: Polity Press.

Healey, P. (1974) 'The problem of ideology', *The Planner*, 60: 602–604.

Healey, P. (1985) 'The professionalisation of planning in Britain', *Town Planning Review*, 56(4): 492–507.

Healey, P. (1997) *Collaborative Planning*, Basingstoke: Palgrave Macmillan.

Healey, P. (2007) *Urban Complexity and Spatial Strategies: Towards a Relational Planning for our Times*, London: Routledge.

Hebbert, M. (2019) 'Planning, knowledge and technocracy in historical perspective', in M. Raco and F. Savini (eds) *Planning and Knowledge: How New Forms of Technocracy Are Shaping Contemporary Cities*, Bristol: Policy Press, pp 19–30.

Heppell, T. and Seawright, D. (eds) (2012) *Cameron and the Conservatives: The Transition to Coalition Government*, London: Palgrave Macmillan.

Heslop, J., Tomaney, J. and Morgan, K. (2019) 'Debating the foundational economy', *Renewal*, 27(2): 5–12.

Hewison, R. (1987) *The Heritage Industry: Britain in a Climate of Decline*, London: Methuen.

Hewison, R. (2014) *Cultural Capital: The Rise and Fall of Creative Britain*, London: Verso.

Heywood, A. (2012) *Political Ideologies: An Introduction*, Basingstoke: Palgrave Macmillan.

Hills, J. (2014) *Good Times, Bad Times: The Welfare Myth of Them and Us*, Bristol: Policy Press.

Holly, N. (2017) 'Accidental antagonism? Technical governance and local struggles over housing numbers in southern England', *Town Planning Review*, 88(6): 683–704.

Hopkins, D. (2010a) 'The emancipatory limits of participation in planning: equity and power in deliberative plan-making in Perth, Western Australia', *Town Planning Review*, 81(1): 55–81.

Hopkins, D. (2010b) 'Planning a city through "dialogue": deliberative policy-making in action in Western Australia', *Urban Policy and Research*, 28(3): 261–276.

Howells, R. (2015) 'Journey to the Centre of a News Black Hole: Examining the Democratic Deficit in a Town with No Newspaper', PhD thesis, Cardiff University.

Inch, A. (2015) 'Ordinary citizens and the political cultures of planning: in search of the subject of a new democratic ethos', *Planning Theory*, 14(4): 404–424.

Inch, A. and Shepherd, E. (2020) 'Thinking conjuncturally about ideology, housing and English planning', *Planning Theory*, 19(1): 58–79.

Innes, J. and Booher, D. (2004) 'Reframing public participation: strategies for the 21st century', *Planning Theory and Practice*, 5(4): 419–436.

IPPR Commission on Economic Justice (2018) *Prosperity and Justice. A Plan for the New Economy*, London: IPPR.

Jackson, B. (2012) 'The think-tank archipelago: Thatcherism and neoliberalism', in B. Jackson and R. Saunders (eds) *Making Thatcher's Britain*, Cambridge: Cambridge University Press, pp 43–61.

Jacobs, H. and Paulsen, K. (2009) 'Property rights. The neglected theme of 20th-century American planning', *Journal of the American Planning Association*, 75(2): 134–143.

Johal, S., Moran, M. and Williams, K. (2016) 'Breaking the constitutional silence: the public services industry and government', *The Political Quarterly*, 87(3): 389–397.

Jones, P. and Comfort, D. (2019) 'Commercialisation in local authority planning', *Town and Country Planning*, 88(1): 32–36.

Joyce, S. (2014) 'How Is Involvement in Neighbourhood Planning Changing Community Participants' Perceptions of Planning? Insights from Rural Oxfordshire', Masters in Spatial Planning dissertation, Oxford Brookes University.

Juppenlatz, L. (2016) 'What neighbourhood plans can do for democracy – a view from the north', *Town and Country Planning*, 85(7): 279–285.

Kanninen, V. (2018) 'Post-politics of (Scottish) planning: gatekeepers, gatechecks and gatecrashers? – commentary to Walton', *Fennia*, 196(1): 103–107.

Kemeny, J. (1992) *Housing and Social Theory*, London: Routledge.

Kingston Polytechnic (1973) *Ideologies in Planning*, London: Kingston Polytechnic.

Kitchen, T. (1997) *People, Politics, Policies and Plans*, London: Paul Chapman.

Kitchen, T. (2007) *Skills for Planning Practice*, Basingstoke: Palgrave Macmillan.

Krueckeberg, D. (1995) 'The difficult character of property: to whom do things belong?' *Journal of the American Planning Association*, 61(3): 301–309.

Lapavitsas, C. (2013) *Profiting without Producing: How Finance Exploits Us All*, London: Verso.

Layard, A. (2012) 'The Localism Act 2011: What is "local" and how do we (legally) construct it?', *Environonmental Law Review*, 14: 134–144.

Leach, R. (2015) *Political Ideology in Britain*, Basingstoke: Palgrave Macmillan.

Lee, S. and Beech, M. (eds) (2009) *The Conservatives under David Cameron: Built to Last?* London: Palgrave Macmillan.

Legacy, C. (2012) 'Achieving legitimacy through deliberative plan-making processes – lessons for metropolitan strategic planning', *Planning Theory and Practice*, 13(1): 71–87.

Lindblom, C. (1977) *Politics and Markets: The World's Political Economic Systems*, New York: Basic Books.

Lock, D. (2015) 'CMK business neighbourhood plan mega-ballots', *Town and Country Planning*, 84(2): 58–60.

Lord, A. and Tewdwr-Jones, M. (2013) 'Is planning under attack? Chronicling the deregulation of urban and environmental planning in England', *European Planning Studies*, 22(2): 345–361.

Lord, A. and Tewdwr-Jones, M. (2018) 'Getting the planners off our backs: questioning the post-political nature of English planning policy', *Planning Practice and Research*, 33(3): 229–243.

Lord, A., Mair, M., Sturzaker, J. and Jones, P. (2017) '"The planners' dream gone wrong?" Questioning citizen-centred planning', *Local Government Studies*, 43(3): 344–363.

Lowenthal, D. (1985) *The Past Is a Foreign Country*, Cambridge: Cambridge University Press.

Lowy, M. (2015) *Ecosocialism: A Radical Alternative to Capitalist Catastrophe*, Chicago: Haymarket Books.

Lucas, C. (2015) *Honourable Friends? Parliament and the Fight for Change*, London: Portobello Books.

Luke, S. (1974) *Power: A Radical View*, London: Macmillan.

Lund, B. (2015) 'The electoral politics of housing', *The Political Quarterly*, 86(4): 500–506.

Lund, B. (2016) *Housing Politics in the United Kingdom*, Bristol: Policy Press.

Macdonald, K. (1995) *The Sociology of the Professions*, London: Sage.

Maginn, P. (2007) 'Deliberative democracy or discursively biased? Perth's dialogue with the city initiative', *Space and Polity*, 11(3): 331–352.

Mansbridge, J. (1999) 'Everyday talk in the deliberative system', in S. Macedo (ed), *Deliberative Politics*, Oxford: Oxford University Press, pp 211–239.

Marsh, D. and Hall, M. (2016) 'The British political tradition and the material-ideational debate', *British Journal of Politics and International Relations*, 18(1): 125–142.

Marshall, T. (2009) 'Planning and New Labour in the UK', *Planning Practice and Research*, 24(1): 1–9.

Marshall, T. (2012) *Planning Major Infrastructure: A Critical Analysis*, Abingdon: Routledge.

Marshall, T. (2014) 'Infrastructure futures and spatial planning; lessons from France, the Netherlands, Spain and the UK', *Progress in Planning*, 89: 1–38.

Marshall, T. (2016) 'Learning from France: using public deliberation to tackle infrastructure planning issues', *International Planning Studies*, 21(4): 329–347.

Marshall, T. (2017a) 'How the UK deals with big infrastructure now', *Town and Country Planning*, 86(8): 289–295.

Marshall, T. (2017b) 'National policy statements: what sort of strange planning animal?', *Town and Country Planning*, 86(9): 337–342.

Marshall, T. (2018) 'What (national) infrastructure do we need?', *Town and Country Planning*, 87(10): 388–394.

Massey, D. (1991) 'The political place of locality studies', *Environment and Planning A*, 23(2): 267–281.

Massey, D. (2007) *World City*, Cambridge: Polity.

Matthews, P., Bramley, G. and Hastings, A. (2015) 'Homo economicus in a Big Society: understanding middle-class activism and NIMBYism towards new housing development', *Housing, Theory and Society*, 52(1): 54–72.

McAnnulla, S. (2012) 'Liberal conservatism: ideological coherence?', in T. Heppell and D. Seawright (eds), *Cameron and the Conservatives*, Basingstoke: Palgrave, pp 166–180.

McAuslan, P. (1971) 'The plan, the planners and the lawyers', *Public Law*, 247–275.

McAuslan, P. (1974) 'Planning law's contribution to the problems of an urban society', *Modern Law Review*, 37(2): 134–153.

McAuslan, P. (1975) *Land, Law and Planning*, London: Weidenfeld and Nicolson.

McAuslan, P. (1980) *The Ideologies of Planning Law*, Oxford: Pergamon.

McLellan, D. (1995) *Ideology*, Buckingham: Open University Press.

Media Reform Coalition (2015) *Who Owns the UK Media?* London: Media Reform Coalition.

Media Reform Coalition (2017) *Mapping Changes in Local News 2015–2017*, London: Media Reform Coalition.

Media Reform Coalition (2018) *Submission of Evidence to the Cairncross Review*, London: Media Reform Coalition.

Mediatique (2018) *Overview of Recent Dynamics in the UK Press Market*, Report for Department for Digital, Culture, Media and Sport, London: Mediatique.

Miller, D. (2015) 'Neoliberalism, politics and institutional corruption: against the "institutional malaise" hypothesis', in D. Whyte (ed) *How Corrupt is Britain?* London: Pluto Press, pp 59–69.

Miller, D. and Dinan, W. (2008) *A Century of Spin*, London: Pluto Press.

Ministry of Housing, Communities and Local Government (2019) *National Planning Policy Framework*, London: MHCLG.

Minton, A. (2009) *Ground Control*, London: Penguin.

Minton, A. (2013) *Scaring the Living Daylights out of People: The Local Lobby and the Future of Democracy*, London: Spinwatch.

Minton, A. (2017) *Big Capital*, London: Penguin.

Moore, J. (2017) 'The capitalocene Part 1: on the nature and origins of our ecological crisis', *The Journal of Peasant Studies,* 44(3): 594–630.

Moore, J. (2018) 'The capitalocene Part 2: accumulation by appropriation and the centrality of unpaid work/energy', *The Journal of Peasant Studies*, 45(2): 237–279.

Moore, M. (2018) 'Protecting democratic legitimacy in a digital age', in A. Gamble and T. Wright (eds) *Rethinking Democracy*, London: Wiley (special issue of *Political Quarterly*), pp 92–106.

Moran, M. (2011) *Politics and Governance in the UK*, Basingstoke: Palgrave Macmillan.

Morphet, J. (2017) *Beyond Brexit? How to Assess the UK's Future*, Bristol: Policy Press.

Morphet, J. and Clifford, B. (2018) 'Progress and current trends in local authority housing provision', *Journal of Urban Regeneration and Renewal*, 11(4): 324–334

Morton, A. (2010) *More Homes: Fewer Empty Buildings*, London: Policy Exchange.

Morton, A. (2011) *Cities for Growth: Solutions to Our Planning Problems*, London: Policy Exchange.

Moulaert, F. and Cabaret, K. (2006) 'Planning, networks and power relations: is democratic planning under capitalism possible?', *Planning Theory*, 5(1): 51–70.

Mudde, C. (2019) *The Far Right Today*, Cambridge: Polity.

Muller, J.W. (2016) *What Is Populism?* Philadelphia: University of Pennsylvania Press.

References

Murdoch, J. and Abram, S. (2002) *Rationalities of Planning*, Aldershot: Ashgate.

Natarajan, L., Rydin, Y., Lock, S. and Lee, M. (2018) 'Navigating the participatory processes of renewable energy infrastructure regulation: a "local participant perspective" on the NSIPs regime in England and Wales', *Energy Policy*, 114: 201–210.

National Infrastructure Commission (2016) *The National Infrastructure Commission's Interim Report into the Cambridge–Milton Keynes–Oxford Corridor*, London: NIC.

National Infrastructure Commission (2017) *Partnering for Prosperity. A New Deal for the Cambridge–Milton Keynes–Oxford Arc*, London: NIC.

Newman, I. (2014) *Reclaiming Local Democracy*, Bristol: Policy Press.

O'Sullivan, N. (2013) 'Conservatism', in M. Freeden and M. Stears (eds) *The Oxford Handbook of Political Ideologies*, Oxford: Oxford University Press, pp 293–311.

Owen, D. and Smith, G. (2015) 'Deliberation, democracy and the systemic turn', *The Journal of Political Philosophy*, 23(2): 213–234.

Page, R. (2014) '"Progressive" turns in post-1945 Conservative social policy', *Political Studies Review*, 12(1): 17–28.

Pahl, R. (1970) *Patterns of Urban Life*, London: Longman.

Papworth, T. (2015) *The Green Noose*, London: Adam Smith Institute.

Parker, G. (2008) 'Parish and community-led planning, local empowerment and local evidence bases', *Town Planning Review*, 79(1): 61–85.

Parker, G. and Salter, K. (2017) 'Taking stock of neighbourhood planning in England', *Planning Practice and Research*, 32(4): 478–490.

Parker, G. and Street, E. (2015) 'Planning at the neighbourhood scale: localism, dialogic politics, and the modulation of community action', *Environment and Planning C*, 33(4): 794–810.

Parker, G. and Street, E. (2019) 'Trust me … I'm a planner', *Town and Country Planning*, 88(2): 57–61.

Parker, G., Street, E. and Wargent, M. (2018) 'The rise of the private sector in fragmentary planning in England', *Planning Theory and Practice*, 19(5): 734–750.

Parker, G., Street, E. and Wargent, M. (2019) 'Advocates, advisors and scrutineers: the technocracies of private sector planning in England', in M. Raco and F. Savini (eds) *Planning and Knowledge. How New Forms of Technocracy Are Shaping Contemporary Cities*, Bristol:, Policy Press, pp 157–167.

Parkinson, J. (2006) *Deliberating in the Real World: Problems of Legitimacy in Deliberative Democracy*, Oxford: Oxford University Press.

Parkinson, J. and Mansbridge, J. (eds) (2012) *Deliberative Systems*, Cambridge: Cambridge University Press.

Parvin, P. (2008) 'Against localism: does decentralising power to communities fail minorities?', *The Political Quarterly*, 80(3): 351–360.

Pautz, H. (2013) 'The think tanks behind "Cameronism"', *Politics and International Relations*, 15(3): 362–377.

Pautz, H. (2014) 'British think-tanks and their collaborative and communicative networks', *Politics*, 34(4): 345–361.

Pendlebury, J. (2000) 'Conservation, Conservatives and consensus: the success of conservation under the Thatcher and Major governments 1979–1997', *Planning Theory and Practice*, 1(1): 31–52.

Pendlebury, J. and Veldpaus, L. (2018) 'Heritage and Brexit', *Planning Theory and Practice*, 19(3): 448–453.

Pennington, M. (2002) *Liberating the Land: The Case for Private Land Use Planning*, London: Institute of Economic Affairs.

Pepper, D. (1993) *Eco-socialism: From Deep Ecology to Social Justice*, London: Routledge.

Peters, B. and Pierre, J. (eds) (2012) *The SAGE Handbook of Public Administration*, London: Sage.

Phelps, N. (2012) *An Anatomy of Sprawl*, Abingdon: Routledge.

Picciotto, S. (1979) 'The theory of the state, class struggle and the rule of law', in B. Fine, R. Kinsey, J. Lea, S. Picciotto and J. Young (eds) *Capitalism and the Rule of Law: From Deviancy Theory to Marxism*, London: Hutchinson, pp 164–177.

Planning magazine (2015) 'Passing a business neighbourhood plan', *Planning*, 5 June, pp 24–25.

Planning magazine (2019a) 'How the local election results impact on planning and development', *Planning*, 10 May, pp 8–9.

Planning magazine (2019b) 'How locally-elected residents groups are affecting planning', *Planning*, 24 May pp 6–7.

Punter, J. and Carmona, M. (1997) *The Design Dimension of Planning*, London: E. & F.N. Spon.

Purcell, M. (2009) 'Resisting neoliberalization: communicative planning or counter-hegemonic movements?', *Planning Theory* 8(2): 140–165.

Raco, M. (2013) *State-Led Privatisation and the Demise of the Democratic State*, Farnham: Ashgate.

Raco, M. (2014) 'Delivering flagship projects in an era of regulatory capitalism: state-led privatisation and the London Olympics 2012', *International Journal of Urban and Regional Research*, 38(1): 176–197.

Raco, M. (2015a) 'Sustainable city-building and the new politics of the possible: reflections on the governance of the London Olympics 2012', *Area*, 47(2): 124–131.

Raco, M. (2015b) 'Conflict management, democratic demands and the post-politics of privatisation', in J. Metzger, P. Allmendinger and S. Oosterlynck (eds) *Planning against the Political*, Abingdon: Routledge, pp 153–169.

Raco, M. (2018) 'Private consultants, planning reform and the marketisation of local government finance', in J. Ferm and J. Tomaney (eds) (2018) *Planning Practice*, Abingdon: Routledge, pp 123–137.

Raco, M. and Savini, F. (eds) (2019) *Planning and Knowledge: How New Forms of Technocracy Are Shaping Contemporary Cities*, Bristol: Policy Press.

Ramsay, G. and Moore, M. (2016) *Monopolizing Local News: Is there an Emerging Local Democratic Deficit in the UK due to the Decline of Local Newspapers?* London: Centre for the Study of Media, Communication, and Power, King's College London.

Raynsford Review (2018a) *Planning 2020. Interim Report of the Raynsford Review of Planning in England*, London: TCPA.

Raynsford Review (2018b) *Planning 2020. Raynsford Review of Planning in England*, London: TCPA, https://www.tcpa.org.uk/Handlers/Download.ashx?IDMF=30864427-d8dc-4b0b-88ed-c6e0f08c0edd

Reade, E. (1987) *British Town and Country Planning*, Milton Keynes: Open University Press.

Ricketts, S. and Field, D. (2012) *Localism and Planning*, London: Bloomsbury Professional.

Roberts, M. and Greed, C. (eds) (2000) *Urban Design: A Primer*, Harlow: Pearson.

Rohr, J., Ehlert, H., Hörster, S., Oppold, D. and Nanz, P. (2019) *Bundesrepublik 3.0*, Dessau-Rosslau: Umweltbundesamt.

Rozema, J. (2015) 'The influence of institutional design on local environmental interest representation in the national polity', *Journal of Environmental Planning and Management*, 58(10): 1731–1748.

RTPI (2003) *The Gender Mainstreaming Toolkit*, London: RTPI.

Rustin, M. (2016) 'The neoliberal university and its alternatives', *Soundings*, 63: 147–170.

Rutter, J. (2012) *Opening up Policy Making*, London: Institute for Government.

Rydin, Y. (1993) *The British Planning System*, Basingstoke: Macmillan.

Rydin, Y. (1998) *Urban and Environmental Planning in the UK*, Basingstoke: Macmillan.

Rydin, Y. (1999) 'Public participation in planning', in B. Cullingworth (ed) *British Planning: 50 Years of Urban and Regional Policy*, London: Athlone Press, pp 184–197.

Rydin, Y. (2011) *The Purpose of Planning*, Bristol: Policy Press.

Rydin, Y. and Pennington, M. (2001) 'Discourses of the prisoners' dilemma: the role of the local press in environmental policy', *Environmental Politics*, 10(3): 48–71.

Sager, T. (2020) 'Populists and planners: "We are the people. Who are you?"' *Planning Theory*, 19(1): 80–103.

Salter, K. (2018) 'Caught in the middle? The response of local planning authorities to neighbourhood planning in England', *Town and Country Planning*, 87(9): 344–349.

Sampson, A. (1962) *An Anatomy of Britain*, London: Hodder and Stoughton.

Sampson, A. (2004) *Who Runs This Place?* London: John Murray.

Sanchez de Madariaga, I. and Roberts, M. (eds) (2013) *Fair Shared Cities: The Impact of Gender Planning in Europe*, Farnham: Ashgate.

Savini, F. and Raco, M. (2019) 'Conclusions: the technocratic logics of contemporary planning', in M. Raco and F. Savini (eds) *Planning and Knowledge: How New Forms of Technocracy Are Shaping Contemporary Cities*, Bristol: Policy Press, pp 255–267.

Saward, M. (1998) *The Terms of Democracy*, Cambridge: Polity.

Saward, M. (2003) *Democracy*, Cambridge: Polity.

Saward, M. (2010) *The Representative Claim*, Oxford: Oxford University Press.

Scruton, R. (2017) *Conservatism*, London: Profile Books.

Shepherd, E. (2017a) 'Liberty, Property and the State: The Ideology of the Institution of National English Town and Country Planning', PhD thesis, University of Cambridge.

Shepherd, E. (2017b) 'Continuity and change in the institution of town and country planning: modelling the role of ideology', *Planning Theory*, 17(4): 494–513.

Shepherd, E. (2020) 'Liberty, property and the state: the ideology of the institution of English town and country planning', *Progress in Planning*, 135.

Shepherd, E., Inch, A. and Marshall, T. (2020) 'Narratives of power: bringing ideology to the fore of planning analysis', *Planning Theory*, 19(1): 3–16.

Sheppard, A. and Ritchie, H. (2016) 'Planning decision-making: independence, subsidiarity, impartiality and the state', *Town Planning Review*, 87(1): 53–70.

Sheppard, A., Burgess, S. and Croft, N. (2015) 'Information is power: public disclosure of information in the planning decision-making process', *Planning Practice and Research*, 30(4): 443–456.

Sheppard, A., Peel, D., Ritchie, H. and Berry, S. (2017) *The Essential Guide to Planning Law*, Bristol: Policy Press.

Simmie, J. (1981) *Power, Property and Corporatism: The Political Sociology of Planning*, London: Macmillan.

Simms, A. (2007) *Tescopoly*, London: Constable.

Sinnett, D., Smith, N. and Burgess, S. (eds) (2016) *Handbook on Green Infrastructure*, Cheltenham: Edward Elgar.

Slade, D. (2018a) 'The Making of the National Planning Policy Framework', PhD thesis, University of Liverpool.

Slade, D. (2018b) 'Major infrastructure projects – the case for a Commission for Public Engagement', *Town and Country Planning*, 87(3): 111–116.

Smith, L. (2015a) *Planning for Onshore Wind*, House of Commons Library Briefing Paper, 04370, 19 May.

Smith, L. (2015b) *Permitted Development Rights*, House of Commons Library Briefing Paper, 00485, 20 May.

Spiers, S. (2018) *How to Build Houses and Save the Countryside*, Bristol: Policy Press.

Stahl, R.M. (2019) 'Ruling the interregnum: politics and ideology in nonhegemonic times', *Politics and Society*, 47(3): 333–360.

Stevens, J. (2019) *Greater Manchester Spatial Framework: Greater Manchester's Statutory Spatial Development Strategy for Homes, Jobs and the Environment*, Note prepared for the Highbury Group meeting, 25 May.

Stewart, J. (2003) *Modernising British Local Government*, Basingstoke: Palgrave Macmillan.

Sturzaker, J. (2010) 'The exercise of power to limit the development of new housing in the English countryside', *Environment and Planning A*, 42(4): 1001–1016.

Sturzaker, J. and Shucksmith, M. (2012) 'Planning for housing in rural England: discursive power and spatial exclusion', *Town Planning Review*, 82(2): 169–194.

Sturzaker, J. and Gordon, M. (2017) 'Democratic tensions in decentralised planning – rhetoric, legislation and reality in England', *Environment and Planning C*, 35(7): 1324–1339.

Sustainable Development Commission (2007) *Turning the Tide: Tidal Power in the UK*, London: Sustainable Development Commission.

Swain, C., Marshall, T. and Baden, T. (eds) (2012) *English Regional Planning 2000–2012: Lessons for the Future*, Abingdon: Routledge.

Swyngedouw, E. (2009) 'The antinomies of the postpolitical: in search of a democratic politics of environmental protection', *International Journal of Urban and Regional Research*, 33(3): 601–20.

Tait, M. (2012) 'Building trust in planning professionals: understanding the contested legitimacy of a planning decision', *Town Planning Review*, 83(5): 597–617.

Tait, M. and Inch, A. (2016) 'Putting localism in place: conservative images of the good community and the contradictions of planning reform in England', *Planning Practice and Research*, 31(2): 174–194.

Tewdwr-Jones, M. (2002) *The Planning Polity*, London: Routledge.

Tewdwr-Jones, M. (2012) *Spatial Planning and Governance*, Basingstoke: Palgrave Macmillan.

Thomas, H. (1994) 'The local press and urban renewal: a South Wales case study', *International Journal of Urban and Regional Research*, 18(2): 315–333.

Thomas, H. (1996) 'Public participation in planning', in M. Tewdwr-Jones (ed) *British Planning Policy in Transition: Planning in the 1990s*, London: UCL Press, pp 168–188.

Thomas, H. (1999) 'Social town planning and the planning profession', in C. Greed (ed) *Social Town Planning*, London: Routledge, pp 15–28.

Thomas, H. (2000) *Race and Planning. The UK Experience*, London: UCL Press.

Thomas, H. (2008) 'Race equality and planning: a changing agenda', *Planning Practice and Research*, 23(1): 1–17.

Thomas, H. (2017) 'Framing turbulence in the academy: UK planning academics in a period of change', *Town Planning Review*, 88(5): 557–577.

Thornley, A, (1991) *Urban Planning under Thatcherism*, London: Routledge.

Thornley, A, (1993) *Urban Planning under Thatcherism* (2nd edn), London: Routledge.

Thornley, A. (1999) 'Is Thatcherism dead? The impact of political ideology on British planning', *Journal of Planning Education and Research*, 19(2): 183–191.

Thurley, S. (2013) *Men from the Ministry: How Britain Saved Its Heritage*, London: Yale University Press.

Thurley, S. (2016) 'Tough choices: heritage or housing', lecture at Gresham College, http://www.gresham.ac.uk/lectures-and-events/tough-choices-heritage-or-housing

Thurley, S. (2017) 'The value of heritage and the heritage of value', lecture at Gresham College, http://www.gresham.ac.uk/lectures-and-events/the-value-of-heritage-and-the-heritage-of-value

Torrance, P. (2020) Doctoral work, unpublished, Oxford Brookes University, School of the Built Environment.

Toynbee, P. (2014) 'The war on windfarms is the Tories' latest sop to UKIP', *Guardian*, 28 October.

Toynbee, P. and Walker, D. (2015) *Cameron's Coup*, London: Faber.

Transparency International UK (2015) *Lifting the Lid on Lobbying: The Hidden Exercise of Power and Influence in the UK*, London: Transparency International UK.

Tuitt, P. (2019) 'Law, justice and the public inquiry into the Grenfell Tower fire', in D. Bulley, J. Edkins and N. El-Enany (eds) *After Grenfell: Violence, Resistance and Response*, London: Pluto, pp 119–129.

2070 Commission (2020) *Make No Little Plans. Acting at Scale for a Fairer and Stronger Future*, Final Report of the 2070 Commission.

Valler, D. and Phelps, N. (2018) 'Framing the future: on local planning cultures and legacies', *Planning Theory and Practice*, 19(5): 698–716.

Vigar, G. (2006) 'Deliberation, participation and learning in the development of regional strategies: transport policy making in North East England', *Planning Theory and Practice*, 7(3): 267–287.

Vigar, G. (2017) 'The four knowledges of transport planning: enacting a more communicative, trans-disciplinary policy and decision-making', *Transport Policy*, 58: 39–45.

Vigar, G., Gunn, S. and Brooks, E. (2017) 'Governing our neighbours: participation and conflict in neighbourhood planning', *Town Planning Review*, 88(4): 423–444.

Vincent, A. (1995) *Modern Political Ideologies*, Oxford: Blackwell.

Walton, W. (2018) 'Deregulated free-for-all planning, new settlements and the spectre of abandoned building sites in Scotland's crisis-hit oil economy', *Fennia*, 196(1): 58–76.

Ward, S. (2004) *Planning and Urban Change*, London: Sage.

Ward, S. (2012) 'Soviet communism and the British planning movement: rational learning or utopian imagining?', *Planning Perspectives*, 27(4): 499–524.

Wargent, M. and Parker, G. (2018) 'Re-imagining neighbourhood governance: the future of neighbourhood planning in England', *Town Planning Review*, 89(4): 379–402.

Welsh Government (2016) *Planning Policy Wales* (9th edn, November), Cardiff.

Weston, J. and Weston, M. (2013) 'Inclusion and transparency in planning decision-making: planning officer reports to the planning committee', *Planning Practice and Research*, 28(2): 186–203.

Whyte, D. (ed) (2015) *How Corrupt Is Britain?* London: Pluto Press.

Wilks-Heeg, S. (2015) 'Revolving door politics and corruption', in D. Whyte (ed) *How Corrupt Is Britain?* London: Pluto Press, pp 135–144.

Williams, R. (1976) *Keywords*, London: Fontana.

Zartaloudis, T. (ed) (2017) *Land Law and Urban Policy in Context*, London: Birkbeck Law Press.

Žižek, S. (ed) (1994) *Mapping Ideology*, London: Verso.

Index

Note: Page numbers for figures and tables appear in *italics*.

A

Abercrombie, Patrick 64
Abram, Simone 205
Adam Smith Institute 145, 147, 151
Adams, David 34, 195–197, 198, 222
Adonis, Lord Andrew 207
Allmendinger, Phil 4, 30, 31–33, 147
Apco Worldwide *143*
archaeology 185–186
architecture 132, 133–134, 135, 136
Areas of Outstanding Natural Beauty (AONBs) 106
Armitt, Sir John 136, 207, 236
astroturfing 151
Austria, women-friendly planning 57

B

Badiou, Alain 8
Barkan, Joshua 88
BBC television and radio 165
Beebeejaun, Yasminah 58, 176–177
Beetham, David 141, 143
Bell, Tim 142
Bell Pottinger 142, 150
Berry, Craig 19, 39
Berry, Sophie (Sheppard et al) 96–97
Beveridge, William 65
Blackburn, Dean 63
Blair, Tony 50, 51
Blomley, Nicholas 88, 90
Blowers, Andrew 27
Blunkett, David 103
Boles, Nick 73, 76, 147
Booth, Philip 94–95
Boughton, John 233
Bourdieu, Pierre 86–87, 97–98, 124, 184
Bowie, Duncan 82–83, 236
Bradley, Quintin 121–122, 124, 126–127
Brake, Rosie 203–204
Bramley, Glen 124
Brexit 44, 68–69, 185, 229
Brindley, Tim 27, 28
British Nuclear Fuels 150
British Retail Consortium (BRC) 138
Brown, Gordon 51
brownfield sites 201
Brownill, Sue 121–122, 124, 126–127
Buckinghamshire Local Plan 203–204
Bullock, Hugh 77
bureaucracy 106–109
Burgess, Sarah (Sheppard et al) 162
Burson-Marsteller 142, *143*
Buser, Michael 119–120
Business Neighbourhood Plans (BNPs) 156
Buxton, Richard 136

C

Cabaret, Katy 10
Cairncross Review 167–168, 170–171, 240
Cambridge–Oxford corridor 152, 190–191, 219–220
Cambridgeshire and Peterborough Strategic Plan 152–153
Cameron, David 42, 43, 77, 146, 155
Campaign to Protect Rural England (CPRE) 118–119, 134, 139, 189–190, 190–191, 202
Campbell, Tom 89
Capita 109, 110, 140
Carillion 34, 140
Cave, Tamasin 141, 147, 150, 151–152, 153–154, 155
central government
 communication 162
 impact of pressure politics 147–151
 power over planning 12–13
 structure 104–105
centralism 101–103
Chamberlain, Neville 65
Channel Tunnel 49
Cherry, Gordon 3
civil engineering 132, 133–134, 136
Clark, Greg 71, 73, 75
Clarke, Ken 42
Clifford, Ben 112, 164
Coalition government 2010-15 69–79
 austerity 70–71, 75–77
 balance of coalition 70
 deregulation 70–71, 73–74, 75–77
 green belts 72, 74, 77–78
 Gypsy and Traveller sites 69, 72, 74, 77
 interest group lobbying 148–150

limiting state action in
    planning 46–47
and localism 43, 72–75, 77, 78,
    79, 112
onshore wind farms 72, 74,
    77, 78–79
planning literature on 31–32, 37–38
tensions in 45, 49–50
see also Conservative Party; Liberal
    Democrats
Colenutt, Bob 155, 162
Colliers International 151
commercial development *183, 196,*
    206–209, 213–215
commercialisation 109–110
Commission for Architecture and the
    Built Environment (CABE) 191
Commission for Racial Equality 58
communication 159–172
    central government 162
    local government 160–162
    local media 164, 166–172, 204
    mass media 163
    non-governmental bodies 162–163
Confederation of British Industry
    (CBI) 137–138
Conservatism 36, 41–45, 64, 101–102
    and heritage, environment,
        design 186, 189, 191–192, 193
    Thatcherite Conservatism
        (Thatcherism) 3–4, 27–28, 42–43,
        47–48, 104, 199
Conservative Party
    before and after 1947 Act 65–67
    centralism 101–102, 103–104
    deregulation 45, 70–71, 73–74,
        75–77, 107
    and environmental policies 221–222
    and European Union 42, 43, 234
    and feminism 69
    future scenarios 4–5, 229
    heritage policy 184–185, 186–188
    housing policy 36–37, 47–48,
        198–201
    industrial and commercial
        development 209, 211
    lack of engagement with
        profession 236
    Left versus Right 41
    limiting state action in
        planning 46–47
    local government 27, 124, 204, 209,
        210–211
        Oxfordshire 115, 117–119,
            121, 170
        South Hampshire 119, 121
    localism 43, 102, 117, 122–123, 236

and nationalism 44–45, 59, 68–69
and neoliberalism 3–4, 41,
    42–43, 67–68
and participation 176, 178–179
and populism 44
and pressure politics 139, 142,
    145–147, 149–150
and property development 47, 77,
    199–200
transport policy 48–49, 218
and welfare state 43–44
Thatcher governments 45, 142,
    184–185, 211
    see also Thatcherism
Major premiership 27–28, 49, 55
Cameron leadership 42, 43
post-2010 governments 37, 162, 176,
    187, 201, 210, 221–222
Coalition government 2010-15 *see*
    main entry
May government 41, 217
Johnson government 41, 44, 45, 234
Cooperative Party 102
Corbyn, Jeremy 51–52
corruption 109, 142–144, 154–156,
    157–158
Cotter, Leanne-Marie McCarthy 242
council housing 47–48, 198–199,
    233
countryside *see* natural environment
COVID-19 pandemic 44
Cowie, Paul 123
Critical Race Theory (CRT) 58
Croft, Nick (Sheppard et al) 162
Crosland, Anthony 103
Crossman, Richard 103
Crossrail 186, 191
Crouch, Colin 8, 60
Cullingworth, Barry 2, 29
Curtin & Co (consultants) 142

D

Daily Telegraph 71, 154, 165
    'Hands off our Land' campaign
        149–150, 165, 166
Davies, Jonathan S. 120
Davis, Robert 154
Davoudi, Simin 123
De Vries, Michiel S. 107–108
Delaney, David 88–89
deliberation in planning 172–179
democratisation of planning 98–99,
    159–160, 234–235
    see also communication; public
        participation
Demos (think-tank) 145
design *183,* 191–194, 208

Index

development management (DM) 108, 112, *184*
Dinan, William 141–142, 145
Disraeli, Benjamin 64
Dommett, Katharine 148
Du Gay, Paul 107, 108

E

Eagleton, Terry 9
Eatwell, Roger 60
Edelman (consultants) *143*
Edinburgh, media in 168–169
Ehlert, Hannah (Rohr et al) 178
elitism 9–10
Ellis, Hugh 35
Engels, Friedrich 13
England, focus on 6–7, 68
English Heritage 186
Environment Agency 105, 188, 222
environmentalism 53–55, 68, 189, 200–201, 208
  literature on 36–37
  sustainable development 68, 77, 148–149, 240
  as 'thin' ideology 40, 41
  see also natural environment
Evening Standard 168
Exeter, retail development 210

F

Farthing, Stuart 119–120
Federation of Master Builders 138
Federation of Small Businesses 138
feminism 40, 55–56, 55–57, 69
Ferm, Jessica 230
Finlayson, Alan 15, 71, 160
Flew, Antony 13
Flinders, Matthew 242
Flyvbjerg, Bent 82
Foley, Donald L. 25, 26
Fox-Rogers, Linda 10–11
fracking 78, 150, 176
France 178, 237, 247
Freeden, Michael 9, 13, 14–15, 39, 40, 51, 52, 57, 60, 232
  influences in other literature 37, 38, 63
Friends of the Earth 139
Futures Network West Midlands 236

G

Gale, Richard 58, 69
Gamble, Andrew 234
Garnham, Nicholas 160
Geddes, Patrick 64
Generation Rent 139
Germany 178, 237, 241, 242, 247

Giddens, Anthony 50
Gilg, Andrew 30, 31
GK Strategy *143*
Goodwin, Matthew 60
Gordon, Michael 124–125
government structure 101–106
Gramsci, Antonio 5, 69–70
Grant, Malcolm 27, 93–94
Grant, Wyn 142, *143*, 150–151, 244
Grayling (consultants) *143*
Greater London Council (GLC) 54, 56, 236–237
Greed, Clara 6, 29, 30, 56
green belts 67, 74, 77–78, 150–151, 204
  see also natural environment
green ideology *see* environmentalism
Green Party 53, 68, 145
  in Oxfordshire local government 115, 117, 118, 212
Grenfell Tower fire 58–59, 89, 201
Griffiths, John 93
Griffiths, Simon 43
Grist, Berna 10–11
Group 4 34, 140
Guardian 154, 165, 166
Gunder, Michael 16–17
Gunn, Susannah 135
Guttenberg, Albert Z. 37
Gypsy and Traveller sites 69, 74, 77

H

H+K Strategies 142, *143*
Hall, Matthew 9–10
Hall, Peter 2, 65
Hall, Stuart 16
Hanover Communications *143*
Harris, Neil 83–84
Harvey, David 15, 17–18, 140
Hastings, Annette 124
Haughton, Graham 147
Hay, Colin 7, 12
Hayek, Friedrich 6, 42, 44, 145, 160
Healey, Patsy 2, 14, 25–26, 132–133
Heathrow Airport 165, 190, 244
Hebbert, Michael 135
Helm, Dieter 189
Henderson, Kate 35
heritage 182–188, 190, 193–194, 208
Heseltine, Michael 42, 67
Hewison, Robert 186
Heywood, Andrew 9, 13
High Wycombe, retail development 210–211
Highbury Group 236
Highways England 105, 192, 222
Hindmoor, Andrew 148

Hinkley Point 220–222
historic conservation 182–188, 190, 193–194, 208
Historic England 105, 186
history of planning 46–50, 63–69, 94
Holly, Neil 203
Home Builders Federation (HBF) 128, 138, 202, 203
Hopkins, Diane 172
Hörster, Sonja (Rohr et al) 178
housing 47–48, 77, *183*, 191, 195–206, 222–223
 council housing 47–48, 198–199, 233
 planning literature on 35–36, 36–37, 195–197
 politics and ideology 198–201, 201–205
 skills and expertise 205–206
Howard, Ebenezer 64
Howell, John 236
Howells, Rachel 167–168
HS2 rail project 111, 150, 190, 191

I

ideology
 analysis of 7–9, 13–17
 and planning
  approaches to 17–23
  proposed new amalgam 231–235
immigration 68, 201
Indigo Public Affairs 154
industrial development *183*, *196*, 206–209, 213–215
infrastructure planning 96, 136, 215–222
Institute for Government 145
Institute for Public Policy Research (IPPR) 145, 233, 241
Institute of Economic Affairs 145, 147
Institution of Civil Engineers (ICE) 136
Ireland 10–11, 178

J

Jacobs, Harvey M. 90–91
Johnson, Boris 41, 44, 59, 234
Johnson, David 6, 30, 56
Juppenlatz, Liz 121

K

Kelso, Alexandra (Flinders et al) 242
Keynes, John Maynard 65
Khan, Sadiq 233
Kitchen, Ted 26, 30, 31, 82, 108
Krueckeberg, Donald A. 90

L

Labour Party
 before and after 1947 Act 65–67

centralism 101–103, 101–104
ecosocialism 54
and feminism 69
future scenarios 5, 229
housing policy 47–48, 198, 200–201
industrial and commercial development 209
integrated planning 49–50
lack of engagement with profession 236
Left versus Right 41
local government 27, 54, 102, 209
 Oxfordshire 115, 117, 118, 170
 South Hampshire 119
and localism 102, 122–123
and nationalisation 52
and neoliberalism 41
and regionalism 103
think-tanks 145
transport policy 48–49
 1920s-1970s 102–103
 New Labour years 50–51
  and centralism 103
  consultation 162
  deregulation 107
  design 193
  environmental issues 55, 220–221
  heritage policy 185, 186
  and land 47
  and lobbying 138, 150
  local government 104, 119–120, 242
  and localism 72
  and neoliberalism 41, 67–68
  in planning literature 27, 31–34, 37
  Private Finance Initiative 33–34
  and public relations 142
  Third Way 31, 50
  transport policy 49, 217–218
  zero carbon housing 200–201
 Corbyn leadership 51–52
Labourism 45–50, 101–103
 see also socialism
land 47, *183*
Lavery, Scott 19
law, planning and 85, 96–99
law literature
 law and geography 88–89
 law and politics 89
 law and property 89–91
 law and sociology 86–87
 planning and law 26–27, 91–95
lawyers, planning 95–96, 136
Left versus Right 40, 41
Letwin, Oliver 71, *73*, 75, 76, 77, 236
Lewis, Brandon 71, *74*
Liberal Democrats 41, 145

local government 115, 117–118, 204
see also Coalition government
    2010-15
Liberal Party 64, 65, 70–71, 102, 198
liberalism 41, 64, 186–187, 189, 193
Lindblom, Charles 9
literature *see* law literature; planning
    literature
Livingstone, Ken 60, 233
lobbying 132, 137–142, *143*, 148–151,
    153–154, 244
Local Enterprise Partnerships
    (LEPs) 105
local government
  communication 160–162
  impact of pressure politics 148,
    151–156
  and large infrastructure projects 215
  planning function 102, 103–104,
    111–112
  politics of housing 202–205
  proposals for change 239–240, 242,
    245–247
  structure 105–106
local planning 111–121, 202–205
  see also Local Plans; neighbourhood
    planning; plan making;
    strategic plans
Local Plans 76, 202, 203–205
  and neighbourhood planning 78,
    122, 123–129
  proposals for change 239–240, 246
  Wales 83–84
  see also local planning; plan making
localism
  Coalition government 2010-15 43,
    72–75, 77, 78, 79, 112
  Conservative Party 43, 102, 117,
    122–123, 236
  Labour Party 102, 122–123
London
  2012 Olympics 33, 110, 140
  Greater London Council (GLC) 54,
    56, 236–237
  local government 53, 104, 105–106
  local media 168
  London Plans 20, 82–83, 203, 237,
    243–244
  planning system 243–244
Lord, Alex 31, 38
Lowenthal, David 186
Lukes, Steven 11–12
Lund, Brian 34, 198

M

Manchester Combined Authority
    Strategic Plan 152, 203
Mannheim, Karl 13
Mansbridge, Jane 174–175
Maragall, Pasqual 60
Marsh, David 9–10
Marx, Karl 13
Marxist approaches 8, 10–11,
    17, 89–90
Massey, Doreen 16
Matthews, Peter 124
McAnulla, Stuart 43
McAuslan, Patrick 18, 26–27,
    91–94, 95, 98
McLellan, David 14
Meakin, Alexandra (Flinders et al) 242
media *see* communication
Miliband, Ed 51, 236
Miller, David 141–142, 144, 145
Milton Keynes Neighbourhood
    Plan 123, 156
Minton, Anna 35–36, 153–154, 155
Moran, Michael 42
Morphet, Janice 30–31
Morris, William 187
Morrison, Herbert 103
Morton, Alex *73*, 146
Mouffe, Chantal 126
Moulaert, Frank 10
Mudde, Cas 44
multiculturalism 57–62
Murdoch, Jonathan 205
Murphy, Enda 10–11

N

Nadin, Vincent 29
Nanz, Patrizia (Rohr et al) 178
national government *see* central
    government
National Infrastructure Commission
    (NIC) 104, 136, 152, 178, 191,
    217, 219–220, 222, *240*, 241
National Infrastructure Projects
    Association (NIPA), 96
National Parks 105, 106, 189
National Planning Policy Framework
    (NPPF) 56, 75–76, 77, 78, 155,
    187, 188, 207, 210
  drafting of 72, 148–150
National Trust 148–149, 186, 188, 189
nationalism 40, 57–62, 68–69
Nationally Significant Infrastructure
    Projects (NSIPs) 162, 246
Natural Capital Committee
    (NCC) 189
Natural England 105, 188
natural environment *183*, 188–191,
    193–194
  see also environmentalism; green belts

neighbourhood planning 78, 106, 121–128, 134–135, 156, 202
  democratic deficit 122, 234
  see also local planning; plan making
Neill, Bob 75
neoliberalism 6, 8, 15–17, 32, 140–142
  and Conservative Party 3–4, 41, 42, 67–68
  and Labour Party 41, 67–68
  and Liberal Democrats 41
  and universities 99, 235–236
Netherlands 57, 237
Network Rail 105, 222
New Economics Foundation 145
New Labour see Labour Party: New Labour years
Newington Communications 142, *143*
Newman, Ines 10, 177, 235
newpapers
  local 164, 166–169, 204
  UK national 164–166
Northern Ireland
  decision making 21
  nationalism 68
  Planning Appeals Commission (PAC) 110–111
Nozick, Robert 122–123
nuclear power stations 220–222

O

Olympic Games 2012 33, 110, 140
onshore wind farms *74*, 77, 78–79, 136, 220–221, 222
Oppold, Daniel (Rohr et al) 178
Osborne, George 76, 77
Ostrom, Elinor 188
O'Sullivan, Noël 43, 44
Overman, Henry 146
Owen, David 175
Oxford, retail development 211
Oxford Times 169–170, *171*
Oxford University 212
Oxford–Cambridge corridor 152, 190–191, 219–220
Oxfordshire
  media in 169–172
  planning in 112–119, 121, 152, 191

P

Parker, Gavin 82, 85, 121, 124, 125, 127, 135
Parkinson, John 174–175
Parvin, Phil 122–123
Patten, Chris 67, 102
Paulsen, Kurt 90–91
Pautz, Hartwig 43
Peel, Deborah (Sheppard et al) 96–97

Peel, Robert 64
Pendlebury, John 184–185
Pennington, Mark 146, 164
Peters, B. Guy 106, 108
Phelps, Nicholas A. 111–112, 120
Picciotto, Sol 89–90
Pickles, Eric 71, *73*, 161
Pierre, Jon 106, 108
PINS see Planning Inspectorate
plan making 84–85, 109–110, *184*
  see also local planning; Local Plans; neighbourhood planning; strategic plans
Planning Act 1947 46, 66, 165
Planning Act 2008 78, 96, 159–160, 213, 222
Planning and Environment Bar Association (PEBA) 96
planning and law 85, 96–99
  literature 26–27, 86–95
  planning lawyers 95–96, 136
planning consultancies 106–107, 133–136
planning education 99, 192
planning history 46–50, 63–69, 94
Planning Inspectorate (PINS) 104, 106, 162, 230, 235
  roles 105, 110, 202, 204–205, 215, 245–246
planning lawyers 95–96
planning literature 25–38
  academic articles 37–38, 226
  classics 25–28
  general books 30–33
  opinion and advocacy 35–37
  participation and deliberation 172–173
  planning and law 26–27, 91–95
  planning education 99
  property sector and housing 33–35, 36–37, 195–197
  skills and expertise 82–83
  textbooks 29–30, 96–97
Planning magazine 78, 95–96, 134, 154, 163, 204, 230
planning profession 132–137, 202
planning skills and expertise 82–85, 205–206
planning system
  complexity of 98–99
  current state in England 229–231
  future scenarios 4–5, 229
  introduction and overview 1–7
  new ideas and values 235–237
  politics and ideology 237–238
  approaches to 17–23

Index

suggestions for further
 work 237–238
proposals for change
 new ideological amalgam 231–235
 to politics and institutions 238–245
 to public planning
  processes 245–247
Planning Theory journal 226
pluralism 9
Policy Exchange 72, 75, 145, 146, 147, 191
political consultants *143*
politics
 analysis of 7–9, 9–13
 and planning
  approaches to 17–23
  introduction and overview 1–6
  proposals for change 238–245
populism 4, 44, 59–60
post-politics 8
power 9–12
Prescott, John 51, 103
pressure politics 131–158
 corruption 109, 142–144, 154–156, 157–158
 impacts on government 147–156
 lobbying 132, 137–142, *143*, 148–151, 153–154, 244
 planning consultancies 106–107, 133–136
 planning profession 132–137
 and power 9–10, *20*, 21
 pressure groups 131–132, 137–139, 202
 proposals for change 244
 think-tanks 144–147
Private Finance Initiative (PFI) 33–34
Property Week magazine 149
public administration 106–111
public participation 172–179
public relations (PR) 141–142
Purcell, Mark 16–17

R

Raab, Dominic 201
racialisation 58, 60, 69
racism 57–62, 69, 201
Raco, Mike 33, 110, 134, 135–136, 140, 244
Ramblers Association 189
Rancière, Jacques 8
Raynsford Review 98–99, 159, 225, 227, 229–230, 235, 237, 244, 248
 recommendations 239–240, 241
Reade, Eric 26, 82
regional government 103, 105
Remarkable (consultants) *143*

Renewable UK 138
retail development *183*, *196*, 206–213
Ritchie, Heather (also Sheppard et al) 96–97, 110–111
Rohr, Jascha 178
Rowell, Andrew 141, 147, 150, 151–152, 153–154
Royal Institute of British Architects 136
Royal Institute of Chartered Surveyors (RICS) 136, 208
Royal Town Planning Institute (RTPI) 58, 83, 133, 136, 148, 155
 activities 139, 230, 235
Rozema, Jaap, G. 111
Rustin, Michael 16, 99
Rydin, Yvonne 6, 27, 28, 29–30, 36, 164, 176, 177–178

S

Saatchi & Saatchi 142
Sager, Tore 60
Salter, Kat 124, 125–126
Sampson, Anthony 11
Sargent, Lyman Tower 39
Savini, Federico 134
Saward, Michael 173–174, 176, 247–248
Scotland
 legislature and voting 53, 242
 nationalism 59, 68
 renewable energy 220–221
Scottish National Party 68
Scruton, Roger 186
Self, Will 165
Serco 34, 140
Severn Barrage scheme 221
Shelter 139
Shepherd, Edward 37, 65, 148–149
Sheppard, Adam 96–97, 110–111, 162
Shucksmith, Mark 124
Silkin, John 103
Simms, Andrew 153
Skeffington Report 26, 92, 172
skills and expertise in planning 82–85, 205–206
Slade, Daniel 75, 148–149, 162
Smith, Graham 175
Smith, Robert 83–84
Smith Institute 145
socialism 45–52, 186–187, 189
 see also Labourism
South Hampshire, planning in 119–121
South Wales Echo 164
Spiers, Shaun 36–37, 146
Stahl, Rune 5
Starmer, Sir Keir 52

Stears, Marc 39
Stephenson, Tom 189
Stevens, James 203
Stewart, John 10, 242
Stoker, Gerry 27, 28
Stonehenge 186
strategic and regional planning
    (to 2010) 50, 67, 128
strategic plans 126, 152–153,
    202–203, 246
    see also local planning; plan making
Strategic Rail Freight Interchanges
    (SRFIs) 213–215
Straw, Jack 103
Street, Emma 82, 85, 125, 135
Sturzaker, John 124–125
Sunday Times 155
surveying 132, 133–134, 135, 136
sustainable development 68, 77,
    148–149, 240
Swansea Bay tidal barrage 221

T

Tait, Malcolm 108–109
Tesco 153
Tewdwr-Jones, Mark 30, 31, 33, 38
Thatcher, Margaret 49, 54, 55
Thatcherism 3–4, 27–28, 42–43,
    47–48, 104, 199
'thick' and 'thin' ideologies 39–40
think-tanks 144–147
Thomas, Huw 58, 60, 69, 99, 133, 176
Thornley, Andy 4, 27–28
3 Monkeys (communications firm) 151
Thurley, Simon 188
Times, The 165
Tomaney, John 230
Torrance, Paul 210–211
Town and Country Planning
    Association (TCPA) 139, 235
    see also Raynsford Review
Town and Country Planning in the UK 29
trade unions 27, 102–103, 137, 235
Transparency International
    UK 140–141
transport infrastructure *197*, 213–222
transport policy 48–49, *183*

Traveller and Gypsy sites 69, 74, 77
Tuitt, Patricia 89

U

UK Independence Party (UKIP) 44,
    59–60, 68, 71, 78, 79
    and environmentalism 44, 204, 222
universities, neoliberalisation of 99,
    235–236
Unwin, Raymond 64

V

Valler, Dave 111–112
Veldpaus, Loes 185
Vigar, Geoff 173, 243
Vincent, Andrew 14

W

Wales
    Local Plans 83–84
    nationalism 59, 68
    proportional representation 53
    renewable energy 220–221
Ward, Stephen V. 63
warehousing developments 213–215
Wargent, Matthew 85, 121, 127, 135
Watkins, Craig 34, 195–197, 198, 222
Webb, Brian 83–84
Weber Shandwick *143*, 150
Weberian tradition 8, 107–108
West of England Strategic Plan 152
Westbourne Communications 142, 150
Weston, Joe 161
Weston, Michael 161
Whyte, David 144
Wigan, retail development 210–211
Wildlife Trusts 189–190
Wilks-Heeg, Stuart 141
Williams, Raymond 19
wind farms, onshore 74, 77, 78–79,
    136, 220–221, 222
Wood, Matthew 148
Wright, Tony 234

Z

Zartaloudis, Thanos 26, 92
Žižek, Slavoj 8, 9

www.ingramcontent.com/pod-product-compliance
Lightning Source LLC
Chambersburg PA
CBHW070914030426
42336CB00014BA/2411